Behind Our Eyes

When adversity
strikes courage
is your journey

[illegible]

Behind Our Eyes

Stories, Poems and Essays by Writers with Disabilities

Edited by Marilyn Brandt Smith

Sanford Rosenthal
Executive Director
Behind Our Eyes, Inc.

iUniverse, Inc.
New York Lincoln Shanghai

Behind Our Eyes
Stories, Poems and Essays by Writers with Disabilities

Copyright © 2007 by Behind Our Eyes, Inc.

All rights reserved. No part of this book may be used or reproduced by any means, graphic, electronic, or mechanical, including photocopying, recording, taping or by any information storage retrieval system without the written permission of the publisher except in the case of brief quotations embodied in critical articles and reviews.

iUniverse books may be ordered through booksellers or by contacting:

iUniverse
2021 Pine Lake Road, Suite 100
Lincoln, NE 68512
www.iuniverse.com
1-800-Authors (1-800-288-4677)

Because of the dynamic nature of the Internet, any Web addresses or links contained in this book may have changed since publication and may no longer be valid.

The views expressed in this work are solely those of the authors and do not necessarily reflect the views of the publisher, and the publisher hereby disclaims any responsibility for them.

ISBN: 978-0-595-46493-7 (pbk)
ISBN: 978-0-595-70303-6 (cloth)
ISBN: 978-0-595-90791-5 (ebk)

Printed in the United States of America

Contents

Preface

The idea of writing about disability has tugged at me for many years. Social work training and experience expanded my awareness of the challenges for many minority groups. Advocacy became part of my perspective when I was first refused access to facilities with my dog guide.

I often considered encouraging other disabled people to help me convince our able-bodied friends and associates that we are more like them than they realize. In 2005 I joined the National Writers Union and petitioned them for support for a workshop open to disabled writers. As a result, we have formed a group that meets every Sunday night by teleconference. By the time Ernie and Nicole finish the teleconference on the United States west coast, it is time for dinner. For Michael in Ireland and Tanja in Germany, it's the middle of the night.

Guest speakers and teachers critique some of our work. We share resources and inspiration pertaining to our craft. Writing exercises focus our attention on a variety of techniques that can be applied to an assigned subject. We also have an active mailing list.

With the generous support and encouragement from iUniverse, we're offering this anthology as an outgrowth of our first year's experiences. We use prose and poetry to take diversity to new heights. Our stories and articles don't represent a group with a cause. We write as individuals, sharing life experiences or stretching our imaginations beyond them.

I would like to thank our primary editor, Marilyn Brandt Smith, who assembled a team of qualified individuals to assist her with critiques, corrections, and proofreading the manuscript. She guided our writing quality and book organization to form a product we can offer with pride.

Never before have we possessed the technology to fully realize our dreams. Behind the keyboard, many disabilities disappear. We hope some of our introspection and sharing will come alive on the following pages—and will enhance understanding outside and within the disability community.

Our futures and the futures of disabled children in school today will be well served if we can broaden communication and acceptance. Let this book help you see behind our eyes.

Consider subscribing to our list or visiting our Sunday-night conferences to blend your thoughts and experiences with ours. To join the list, send a blank message to: writtenwordpartyline-subscribe@yahoogroups.com.

Sanford Rosenthal, Disabilities Chairman
National Writers Union, At-Large Chapter

Acknowledgments

Many professionals help us keep our group list and teleconferences filled with fresh ideas. Over three dozen guests offered their expertise during the first eighteen months. Several have made return visits.

The National Writers Union and Seth Eisenberg helped us define our purpose and audience. Susan Driscoll and her staff from iUniverse gave us the incentive to move forward with this anthology. They assisted us with the details involved in publication and marketing.

Arnold S. Goldstein provided the legal assistance necessary to form our corporation.

Michael Koretzky, media advisor at Florida Atlantic University and managing editor for Jazziz Magazine, offered to be our copyeditor for this project. He helped us rethink and rewrite, dotting our I's and crossing our T's when we forgot. Michael also assisted with formatting issues and content evaluation. This book would have been much longer in the making without his guidance and weekly attention to our submissions.

Our primary poetry critics include: Margo LaGattuta, Anastasia Clark, and Alice Rogoff. These poets teach workshops, edit anthologies, and publish collections of their own work. Brittney Wallman, a journalist with the South Florida Sun-Sentinel, assisted with essay and prose evaluations.

Kayla Rigney, an original editor, who left us due to health concerns, helped with technical issues and a plan for the initial collection of our written submissions. Don Rosenthal and Jayson Smith provided technical assistance.

We asked recognized leaders concerned with the disability advancement cause to review our work for use in announcements and releases. Their validation of our written work will help substantiate our conviction that we and the able-bodied are more alike than different.

We are grateful for all of this support as we launch our first effort for a better understanding among all members of the human race.

MBS-ED

Introduction

When twenty-seven people with disabilities put their minds, hearts, and perspectives together to present an anthology reflecting their experiences and abilities, diversity is the welcome result. We reach back for memories of coping techniques and forward to present some fiction and fantasy about the world we imagine.

Sometimes disability, primarily blindness and low vision, is the focus of our work. But often, our lives and our writing are more about situations confronting all humans: family, love, discord, appreciation of nature, and the desire to see the world beyond our doorstep.

Travel with us to Hawaii, contemplate sending a personal package into space, cry with misunderstood children, and laugh with adults who found themselves in the wrong places at the wrong times.

Watch us practice our craft as we share the results of writing exercises, poetry critiques, and our journals. We'll show you scary moments, thrill you with our successes, and make you think about advocacy and discrimination issues. Because accommodating for disability is an experience that varies from person to person, you'll note we don't all accomplish our accommodations in the same way.

During the preparation of this anthology, one of us published a novel, another a poetry chapbook and several have sold or optioned articles to magazines or collections such as the *Chicken Soup* series. One of us hosts a radio show about reading and writing books.

Where subject content allowed, we placed two or more pieces of prose and/or poetry by the same author in sequence. Look for a storyline connection in some of these poetry and nonfiction sequences. This special showcasing will allow readers to identify favorite authors whose other published work might be of interest. Learn more about your favorite authors in the Contributors section of this book.

It has been my privilege to be the primary editor during the collection of prose and poetry for *Behind Our Eyes*. Almost every group participant has contributed in some way to the mechanics of this workshop. In addition to those named on the Acknowledgments page, I would like to recognize my editorial team: Janet Schmidt and Heather Kirk for editing, formatting, and proofing, Gertie Poole and DeAnna Quietwater Noriega for critiques and corrections, and Nancy Scott for poetry expertise and crunch-time conspiracies. Jayson Smith provided technical and Internet research assistance.

Thanks are also due to Sanford Rosenthal, without whose determination and dependability, our workshop—and this anthology—would not exist.

Marilyn Brandt Smith, Editor

PART ONE
Celebrating Survival

A Preview

When we lose control—a spouse betrays our trust, a villain invades our space, the healthcare system fails us—we must take charge today so tomorrow will be better.

Beyond the Call of Duty

Bobbi LaChance

It was a hot summer night in Portland, Maine—well over 100 degrees. We left the windows open when we went to bed, hoping for a breeze. Half awake and half asleep, I heard footsteps in the kitchen. One of the children must be sneaking a cookie. I thought I heard the familiar clink of the glass lid on the jar, but I didn't want to wake up.

On the edge of drifting into a deeper sleep I heard footsteps tiptoe into my bedroom, then tiptoe out—squeaky floorboards. From the kitchen, I heard a strange noise, then all was quiet. With sudden awareness, I bolted upright in bed listening. I heard another movement in the kitchen. "Oh My God," I thought, "there's someone in the house. Are my children all right?" Ever so slowly, as my feet touched the floor, reaching down, I unhooked my guide dog, Wicket, and crept softly toward the bedroom door. Wicket stayed right at my side. Just as I reached the threshold of the doorway, I slipped my hand around the door molding and flicked the kitchen light on.

Suddenly, I heard a scream as my five-year-old daughter, Lisa, barreled into me yelling, "There is a man in the kitchen!" I felt Wickets fur go by my leg, and then all hell broke loose.

My seven-year-old son, Christopher, appeared to the left of me in the hallway. "Mama, I've got my baseball bat, I'll get him."

I heard a menacing growl, and teeth clicking as if to bite. For an instant, the room seemed still, then a voice screeched, "Call off that dog! Call off that dog!"

Christopher started toward the intruder. I grabbed him by the collar of his pajamas and pulled him close to me. Sure that the bat was our defense, he was not letting go of it. "Where is he?" I cried. There was a roaring in my ears, and I could hear my heart beating.

"Wicket has him pinned between the refrigerator and the cabinet," Christopher told me. "Every time he tries to move, Wicket acts like he's going to bite him."

Once again, Christopher stepped forward with his bat raised. I pulled him in again.

"Call off that damn dog!" squealed the man.

I held my two children tight against me. The roar in my ears wouldn't stop. I could neither think nor react. I felt my daughter quivering against my left side, and noticed warm liquid on my toes as my daughter lost control of her bladder. As I reached behind me and dialed zero on the phone, the growling and cursing continued.

"Operator," said a voice.

"Police!" I yelled into the phone.

In a matter of seconds, a male voice responded, "Portland Police Department."

In one breath I said, "There is a man in my kitchen—my guide dog won't stop growling—my daughter just peed on the floor because she is scared."

"Where do you live, ma'am?" asked the officer.

"I don't know," I hysterically answered.

Again the shrill voice of the man cut through our conversation, "Get rid of this dog! Get rid of this dog!"

"He's in the kitchen," I stammered, "the children and I are here alone—I am blind."

"Ma'am," said the officer very patiently, "can you tell me your address?"

"Address," I repeated. "Let me think—what's my address?" Today they could find me instantly, but our trouble that night preceded 911.

"I need your address, ma'am," the officer said again very patiently.

"I don't know," I repeated, agitated by these questions. I stood holding the phone away from me as if it were some strange object. Nothing made sense.

Christopher grabbed the phone out of my hand and began talking to the officer, telling him, "Her name is Mommy, but her real name is Jenny Gilmore, and we live at 12 Myrtle Street, second floor, in Portland. I have a baseball bat, and he is not going to hurt my mom or my sister."

Relieved that Christopher had answered the officer's questions, I took back the telephone. "There is a man in my kitchen and my dog is holding him at bay and I have two very frightened children," I told the officer with a great deal more composure. The dog's growls seemed to get deeper, and I could hear the snapping of his teeth.

"Don't you try to move," threatened Christopher holding up the bat.

Tightening my arms around him, "Down, hero," I said.

"Mrs. Gilmore, someone is on the way," the police officer said in a reassuring voice, "I will keep this line open until the officers arrive. Can you tell me—does the intruder have a weapon or is he armed with anything?"

"Christopher," I pleaded, "Can you see from here? Does he have any type of weapon?"

Christopher responded, "No, Mama, I don't think so. He's standing between the cabinet and the refrigerator. He's sweating like crazy, and he's got his hands over his ears. Mama, he looks scared Wicket is going to bite him." I repeated what Christopher told me.

"I will continue to keep this line open," repeated the officer.

We felt a moment of relief, knowing the police were on their way. "Mama," Christopher whispered, "He's starting to move. I bet he wants to get away."

Wicket, seeing this movement, suddenly lunged forward, giving three ferocious barks. I could hear the sound of his snapping teeth. "Get him away! Get him away! He's gonna kill me!" he screamed.

Suddenly, whether from anticipation or fear, silence prevailed. I could hear the ticking of my kitchen clock, as well as traffic in the street below. The refrigerator motor kicked on. Every muscle in Christopher's back tightened. I hugged him closer to me as he raised the bat in his hand, whispering, "I'll protect you and Lisa, Mama."

In the distance, I could hear sirens wailing, then I heard the sound of car doors, slamming, heavy footsteps in the stairwell, and a loud banging at my front door. Christopher bolted out of my arms and ran to answer it. Doing as he had been taught, he asked, "Who is it?"

"Portland Police Department," boomed a voice from the other side.

Christopher opened the door wide to let the officers in. There seemed to be mass confusion as two police officers entered the kitchen.

My daughter Lisa, squeezing my waist tight, burying her face in my nightgown, in a muffled voice asked, "Mama, They've got guns. Are they going to shoot us?"

I couldn't find my voice, but I patted her shoulder reassuringly. Finally, I leaned down and whispered, "No, sweetheart. They're here to help us."

The roar in my ears became louder. My legs felt like rubber.

One of the police officers sized up the situation very quickly. "Ma'am, take a seat there at the kitchen table." Gently, he placed his hand on my shoulder, guiding me to the chair. My daughter dragged her feet as I pulled her along with me.

Christopher came to stand at my side, bat still held tightly in hand. Evidently the man tried to move from his position, teeth snapped and the growls sounded like they came from a wolf instead of my gentle guide dog. The officer pulled out a chair.

"Check out the rest of the apartment." He ordered his junior partner.

"Call off this dog," pleaded the intruder. The senior officer didn't respond. Leaving the situation alone, he began filling out his paperwork. The intruder begged again, "Please get this dog away from me!"

The officer replied, "Your troubles have just started, pal, never mind the dog." When his partner returned, explaining that the rest of the apartment was secure, the senior officer told him, "Cuff him."

His partner asked, "What about the dog?"

The senior officer very quietly said to me, "Ma'am, call off your dog."

"Wicket," I said, "come." Wicket obediently came around the corner of the table, sat down, and put his head in my lap. I rubbed his shoulders and ruffled his ears to let him know that everything was all right. "Good boy," I whispered.

After the man was removed from the apartment, the senior officer shut and locked the window through which the intruder had entered. "Better have your landlord check this window tomorrow," he suggested. "If you need further assistance, just call."

As soon as the police left, Christopher, Lisa and I pushed the refrigerator in front of the window. I bathed Lisa, and found her a clean nightgown. We decided to leave the kitchen light on for the rest of the night. Crawling into bed, I began to shake from head to toe. If this was a nightmare, I just wanted to wake up.

"Mama, can I sleep with you?" came a small voice from the bedroom door.

"Sure," I said, lifting the cover, "Come on in."

"Christopher's coming, too."

I heard small bare feet on the kitchen floor, then Christopher came through the doorway. "Can I sleep here, too?" he asked, "That way I could protect you."

Feeling warm tears in my eyes, I threw back the other side of the covers. He crawled in, baseball bat and all! The three of us snuggled together.

All of a sudden I felt the weight of two paws on the foot of the bed. I reached down, "Just this once," I said. As a smile crossed my face, I felt the dog's weight settle across my feet. "You deserve this, Wicket. You went way beyond the call of duty."

My Healthcare Nightmare

Sanford Rosenthal

"Mr. Rosenthal, look at all that fluid you've been carrying!"

"Mr. Rosenthal, open your eyes. Turn this way now!"

I hurt too much to remind them I couldn't see. The pulmonologist and the X-ray tech screamed their way through my drug-induced sleep during weeks of hospitalization. How had it come to this? The memories from that day still make me shiver. Healthcare personnel had been my friends for decades. I counted on their competence. Blindness from Retinitis Pigmentosa was my biggest challenge, wasn't it? I was a reasonably healthy middle-aged man until the summer of 2006. Where else could I turn now for support and solutions?

In September of 2005 my primary care physician prescribed Naproxen for arthritis-like symptoms. It's a generic equivalent for Aleve, and it's dangerous for heart attack survivors. He knew that I had a heart attack ten years ago. If the doctor had his reasons for prescribing Naproxen anyway, he never shared them with me. I should have been at least warned to watch for fluid retention. A bit skeptical of his arthritis diagnosis, I changed physicians during the year—but the new doctor continued the Naproxen prescription—even though I complained about swollen ankles.

By July 28, 2006, I was having trouble breathing. Fluid buildup hid my ankles. My legs were so stiff and heavy that I could barely walk. The doctor prescribed Lasix, a diuretic, and recommended bed rest. My appetite had vanished over the past two months, but my weight was increasing because of the retention. Gallons of fluid held me hostage. Over the next three weeks, I lost twenty-six pounds. I spent many hours lying down every day because I had no energy. When I struggled to breathe even in bed, I knew it was time for some serious intervention.

I called my brother for his opinion. He could hardly understand me between my coughs and gasps. He came over, took one look and one listen, then calmly convinced me that I needed emergency care. I barely dragged myself to his car.

The hospital admitted me immediately and determined through blood tests that I was suffering from Naproxen poisoning. I was malnourished and my kidneys were in renal failure. That's when I met the pulmonologist.

With no sedation, he placed a needle between my ribs and into my lung cavity to remove the fluid. "Look in that tank behind you! Two liters!" he bellowed. "That's two or three times as much as I remove from most people in your condition." I tried to help by coughing. My lungs were shriveled and tried to collapse. I was crying, screaming, and threatening to faint from the unbearable pain. I was leaning over a table during this procedure and was beyond dizzy with clammy skin and very little control. "Hold him up! Hold him up!" he yelled to the nurse. After that fluid was gone, I had some relief in breathing.

He whisked me off to the next room for a chest X-ray that would confirm my lungs hadn't been perforated during this procedure. These professionals never noticed the information on my chart acknowledging my blindness. They continued to gesture and commanded me to open my eyes. Finally the tech told me to get out of my wheelchair and hold on to the bar. I was in too much pain to carry on a conversation with her. "Turn this way." What did that mean? The guessing game began. Left was wrong, so she must have meant right.

When they assigned me to a room, they put up a sign that read, "Blind Patient." Still I had to explain that I couldn't reach and take something from them unless they told me it was there. I was getting the message that getting well might not be very easy, and that healthcare workers needed some in-service training in dealing with disabled patients. Based on past experience, I had advocacy skills, but I was too sick to be in "active mode" today.

The doctors couldn't justify to me why Naproxen was prescribed to a heart patient or why kidney function wasn't monitored in view of Naproxen's possible side effects. They gave me a lot of medicine, but I was too sick to know or care what it was.

In six days, I was released and chose to go to my mother's apartment because I wasn't strong enough to care for myself. After four days, my breathing and coughing got worse and I wasn't gaining any strength. We called an ambulance to take me to a different hospital. Maybe, in the hands of different professionals, I could get well.

The song-and-dance was similar: remove another liter of fluid from my chest cavity (this time with an anesthetic), assign me to a bed, pump me full of pills, and wait to see what happens. After nine days, my doctor recommended a move to a rehab center. I agreed that I needed their support to finish my treatment. The social worker on my case tried to change his order—she even called my mother trying to sell the idea that I needed to go home. That hadn't worked last time. This time I had Bronchitis and Pleurisy. I needed more careful monitoring and some assistance with the medications, so moving to a rehab center made sense.

On the last day, the insensitive social worker marched into my room accompanied by, well, let's call her "Hard-Hearted Hannah," the nurse who always resisted giving me my cough medicine prescription because she didn't hear me coughing. Along for the ride was "Mean Janine," who never had time to empty a urinal when I needed it. Finally, she was forced to provide me with a second one so that I could maintain my dignity and have some peace of mind, not to mention that it saved her a trip down the hall. Didn't she understand that I was taking medication to get rid of all that fluid so my kidneys could handle their normal workload?

It wasn't my place to justify prescriptions or physicians' recommendations, but it seemed to be my job to convince the social worker that she didn't have the last word. "Mean Janine" didn't want to give me the Darvocet that had been prescribed for pain relief. She said she was concerned about my becoming addicted. That wasn't her decision and I knew it. She pulled me by my arms out of bed and onto the floor and "Crazy Horse social worker" was right behind her to help. Nobody told me there were orders or policies requiring me to go anywhere. I kept asking, "Where are we going?"

"You're going for a walk," they announced.

"A walk?" I questioned with disbelief. I hadn't been able to do anything but creep for weeks.

Shouldn't this have been done in a supervised therapy session and on a gradual basis? They told me we needed to prove that I could walk on my own and that I didn't need a rehab center. I was in the middle of a drama that I couldn't anticipate and in which I had very limited control. In the end, I resisted and wouldn't step away from my bed. I begged for my Darvocet and after throwing the "talk to my doctor" threat around a few times, I got it. With reluctance, they told me they were preparing my paperwork for the rehab center. I felt good, winning a few battles, until I realized that I never signed up for a war.

The rehab staff made me feel welcome. They actually told me I was a good patient! This was not "your mama's cooking," but no institution's is. Finally, my appetite was coming back. I quickly learned which restaurants delivered. Prescriptions were administered as ordered, but I couldn't seem to shake the respiratory infection completely. About once a day, an aide asked me if I wanted to have my diaper changed. Many of the patients continually calling for help probably needed that service, so I tried to be tolerant of the repeated request. The Darvocet eased my pain and I was getting stronger.

When I was released, I went home for a few days. My coughing was a continuing problem and I had trouble breathing again. The idea of another fluid buildup frightened me, so with reluctance, I went back to the hospital, where they finally successfully treated my respiratory complications with stronger antibiotics. My trio of troublemakers was back in full force, reminding me what a terrible patient I was and shaking a proverbial finger at me because I couldn't "see" my bed, my food, etc. When I reminded them I was blind (they didn't remember?), they told me I was rude. They never offered to help me with meals, and sometimes I needed help. I wanted a different part in this movie. I was tired of being the villain when I was supposed to be a good guy who happened to need healthcare services and wanted a little respect.

I was finally almost walking and breathing normally and was ready to go home. As a free man, and a healthier man, my life could get back to normal.

Reconciling billing from four institutional stays took several months and much patience. I talked with two phone reps on separate days and got two different figures that I might or might not owe. Also, my primary care physician recently told me he has discovered a prostate infection that may have been caused by the respiratory infection some time ago. Did somebody fail me again, or am I expecting too much from healthcare professionals?

Though blind, my eyes are open now and I see very clearly the importance of being one's own healthcare advocate. I cringe when I consider the plight of the uninformed and the mentally challenged, those with language barriers, and the disabled or sensory impaired like myself who need some accommodation. The shy or obedient souls who place complete trust in their caretakers could be at great risk. Although I was assertive enough to protect myself, I'll move mountains to stay out of the healthcare circus as much as possible in the future.

We hear stories about the problems of others, but too often, we don't understand their significance unless they involve us directly or others we know well. We become dangerously vulnerable when we're ill. When negligent or rude caretakers complicate our efforts to get well, we react depending on our personalities. Sometimes staff shortages cause hospitals to hire people who shouldn't be in the medical field at all. That could change with better training, better pay for good performance, and careful reviews of patient evaluations.

Some issues cannot be resolved with a simple phone call or letter. We all have to do our part. Doctors should be able to X-ray in their offices when they have the equipment instead of being forced, because of insurance company guidelines, to send patients to emergency rooms for those procedures. They should be held accountable when they fail to address side effects or contraindications. Hospitals and insurance companies should make sure that patients aren't going to require immediate readmission before releasing them. Healthcare professionals and paraprofessionals should take their jobs—and their patients—seriously and should be monitored. Insurance companies and HMOs should make sure their representatives know their policies so patients don't get misinformation.

I certainly voiced my recommendations to Patient Relations Coordinator Bethann Bor when I met with her during my final release from the hospital. Perhaps former patients could be appointed to advisory boards that help govern healthcare facilities. At the cost of more than $1,000 a day, with no surgery involved, I should have felt like I was in caring hands. Instead, I often felt like a thorn in the side of the system—a bad day in the lives of people who didn't care whether I got well or not.

I applaud those who treated me with dignity and explained or understood what help I needed. They need to join us in warning their peers that punishing patients with patronizing authority or negligence is simply not acceptable. Ms. Bor listened to my concerns with an open mind and assured me that problems encountered are really opportunities for change. Let's make sure she's right.

Battered Soul

Nicole Bissett

I'd sooner feel free to bear my breast
To a thousand pairs of critical eyes
Then bare my battered soul to even one,
For flesh provides a camouflage
To hide the damage that's been done.

Prison

Nicole Bissett

The silence in this house is loud,
Like the words no longer spoken between us,
But muttered under your breath now and then
In hopes I will hear and hurt.

Your words are the bars that keep me in this place,
Keep me in disgrace,
For past crimes committed.
The sentence never ends.

And when do you pay for yours?
The words, the rage, the actions?
The lives you've left behind?
The destruction you've brought to mine?

Will the acid from your anger
Ever stop eating away
At the tenuous thread from love remembered
That tries to hold us together?

Could I make it outside?
Has the mix of love and hate
Cost me the vision of freedom,
And the confidence I need to reach it?

Perhaps a lawyer can free me from you,
But who will free me from me?
Defend me from myself
When I cry alone at night?

Who will remind me I'm worth the fight?
My life is worth living?
Freedom tempts me
For I have never known life outside these bars,
Only imagined the wonder of it,
The way I only imagine the wonder
Of color I can scarcely see.

Freedom has its price,
And I can only hope
I will be strong enough
To pay my way out of here.

Ice

Nicole Bissett

I'm used to ice.
I walk on it,
Even in sunshine,
Always fearing it will crack beneath me.
No one sees or guesses.

But now I'm getting older,
This walk is getting colder,
And I know I can't do this forever.

Tentatively I try a new path,
Away from the cracks and bumps,
For I know where I have been.

Soon the sunshine will warm me.
I'll sit in a lounge chair
And drink from a tall glass of lemonade,
Freshly squeezed and filled to the brim with ice.

Make Lemonade

Kate Chamberlin

I wiped the fog from the bathroom mirror and touched the place where my face should have been. The nape of my neck prickled. As a silent scream slammed through me, I could not see my own face.

I was only 40 years old, and would never see my eleven- and nine-year-old sons star on their high school volleyball teams; never see my four-year-old daughter in her first prom dress; never see my handsome husband's hairline recede.

I called upon my religious faith for answers, but the silent scream continued.

I went through a million-dollar checkup, but it didn't determine a specific reason why the feeder blood vessels to my retinas engorged and burst, so the doctors labeled it Eales' Disease, a rare eye disease of unknown etymology.

They told me not to bend over, pick up heavy items or jar my head. They wanted me to basically sit and stay.

As the floating gobs and strings of debris became more prevalent, I had to stop driving my Chevy Astro van and ask a colleague for a ride to the school where I taught.

I'd look at the papers of my Teddy Bear Trail Nursery School children and not know which were pencil marks, photocopy specks or my own floaters. When I knocked things over and bumped into children, it seemed that my being among the youngsters put them at risk, so I resigned my teaching position. It nearly destroyed me to give up the passion of my life.

One fall afternoon, my husband came home early. He'd lost his job in a general workforce reduction. My eyes had hemorrhaged so much I could see only shadows.

Were these shadows ominous foretellings of what lay ahead? I was the first blind person I'd ever talked to, and I had more questions than answers.

As it turned out, my husband's being unemployed was a mixed blessing. The first several months, we helped each other cope. The next several months, he concentrated on a job search. By the time he began a new position, I had mastered enough daily living blind skills to be on my own. There were still things in life to be grateful for.

In the spring, it saddened me to hear that my nursery school children thought I'd died. It shocked me into action. I took my talking watch and long, white, collapsible cane in to show them, and brought along a large coffee can with a sock top on it so they could feel what was inside. I put a peppermint candy inside a salt shaker for them to sniff. After I demonstrated how I use the long, white cane and explained the reflective white tape on each section, one child asked why the bottom section was red.

Before I could answer, a boy who lived on my street said, "Mrs. Chamberlin, I know why the tip of your cane is red. It's so when you fall into a snowdrift, you can poke it up and we can find you."

While I've never needed to try it out, it's my favorite reason why the long, white cane tip is red. Hearing the children's excitement, answering their questions and accepting their hugs made me feel happier than I'd felt in a long time. For me, it was the beginning of the way back to life itself.

I had no choice about being blind, but I could choose how I would handle it. I had to believe there would be some method in this madness. With faith in the Lord, I'd get through it.

My thoughts turned to my garden, and how it used to be my pride and joy—not to mention a source of food for our family. The weeds seemed to mock me as they took over during the time the doctors said to "sit, stay." I was totally blind by then. What more could happen? So I'm blind, but that doesn't mean I must also be an invalid.

I felt around the various stems with my bare hands, hoping not to touch any bugs, snakes or slugs. I checked for the familiar feel of a dandelion taproot, the tenacious sticky vine with small round burrs on it, and knife-sharp quack grass blades. With each extraction, I began to feel better and to regain control of my garden and my life. I placed planks between the rows of flowers and vegetables, so I could sit on my skateboard and roll along the planks to weed the garden and harvest nature's bounty. My gardening days are far from over.

The tall, proud, apricot iris now reaches up to share its heady fragrance with me as the wind jostles the peonies' cinnamon scent up to me, and the shy lemon thyme patiently lets me rub its tiny, stiff leaves to marvel in its citrus fragrance.

I found there were many things I'd done so often as a sighted person that I could do them with my eyes closed. My family of three young children and a husband could generate a lot of dirty laundry each week, and now I was glad I'd insisted our washer and dryer be upstairs near the bedrooms. Early on, I'd taught each of the children how to do their own laundry, but I was the one with lots of time to actually do it. I learned how to measure from the gallon jug with a pump top sitting on our laundry room counter. One stroke up and down provided the correct measure of liquid detergent. I kept liquid fabric softener in a smaller pump bottle. Bleach was in a third bottle with a Braille label on it. Each person had an assigned day for laundry. I did the washing and drying of their clothes, but they each did their own folding (or not) and putting away (or not). I still use those techniques today.

Machine sewing and mending by hand are things I've done so often they're almost automatic. It takes me longer to thread a needle, but I've discovered a sure way of getting the job done with a wire-loop needle-threader and improved finger sensitivity. My friend transferred my favorite tissue-paper patterns onto poster board. I can easily cut out my own patterns again, but switched to safety pins instead of straight pins, so I won't get stuck. It is satisfying to know that I can still look good, even if I can't see.

Learning Braille allowed me to mark my patterns, cassettes, CDs, office files and many of my home appliances and clothing. I do as much for myself as possible.

My family did several sensitivity activities. Each in his turn came to realize how important it is to leave chairs pushed in, flatware in the traditional location, dishwasher door in the closed position, kitchen drawers and cupboard doors closed, and boots on the boot board. They realized the importance of accurate verbal directions such as left or right (not "over here") and understood why dials need Braille or tactile high-marks.

Mobility became a problem, but I didn't want my handicap to also handicap my family, so we discussed what it would mean to have a "working dog," rather than a "pet dog" in the family. With their encouragement, I swallowed the butterflies in my throat and trained with my first guide dog, Future Grace, an eighteen-month-old golden retriever.

I found it hard to trust my life to a dog. After all, I'd just become used to trusting my life to my husband. The turning point for me came during a training walk in White Plains, New York, as we stood on the corner waiting for the traffic light to change. The rear wheels of a delivery truck turning right jumped over the sidewalk. If Future hadn't pulled me back, I would have been part of the pavement. She'd earned my trust. As I learned to relax, being part of a guide dog team became less awkward. After I brought her home, she quickly bonded with my husband and three children as littermates—with me as the alpha dog in her new family.

My husband has emerged as quite the chef. One year, he fixed a fabulous holiday dinner with all the trimmings. Later, we sat on the couch as he watched football and I knitted. "That training I've given you over the past twenty-some years has really paid off," I teased.

"Training? I just had the good sense to stay out of your kitchen," he quipped. "And I hope you'll do the same."

I fought back tears of hurt and humiliation as the blood pounded in my head. Then, I realized it was his way of freeing me from my nagging guilt because I couldn't continue to be the perfect super-sighted "housewife" I used to be. I silently vowed that for the next twenty-some years I would be a super "Dave's wife." Then, we'll renegotiate the kitchen duties.

Perhaps the most rewarding thing I do now grew out of visiting the nursery school children. I couldn't quite give up teaching altogether. My "Feely Can" and "Sniffy Jar" program now includes talking calculators, my published twin-vision children's book, Braille demonstrations, various gadgets, high-technology equipment and catalogues, and video and audio tapes. I travel with my guide dog from schools to scout troops and from Lions Clubs to Garden Clubs sharing the motto I've adopted: "When life rolls you a lemon, make lemonade." My passion for teaching is as strong as ever.

When it came time to train with a new guide dog, someone asked me what the guide dog could do for me that I couldn't do with the long white cane. Where should I have begun? How could I explain that it isn't just a matter of increased independent mobility to go for the mail or even to the bathroom, to be able to safely return to being a volunteer tutor and mentor in the elementary school, as well as go for long, healing walks?

A guide dog can break the downward spiral of depression, isolation and obesity, and can be a constant, uncritical companion. She supplies a person's need to be needed, and to demonstrate a sense of responsibility. At times, being totally blind is overwhelming and quite intimidating. It requires a push to reopen doors, restore confidence, and bring new love into a person's life.

Life is very different now, but not impossible. Each time I hug my grown children, I know how beautiful and loving my daughter is, and that my sons are men of confidence, compassion and integrity. When I hear "Hey, Mimi!" and feel my guide dog wiggle and waggle all over, I brace myself as I know one of my six grandchildren is about to jump into my arms for hugs and kisses.

I can feel my husband's hairline has gone all the way when I pat his bald pate, but we'll be celebrating our thirty-seventh wedding anniversary on August 15, 2007, and he still feels great to me.

There is definitely fun, faith and fellowship after trauma—when you make lemonade.

Manna

Janet Schmidt

Liberation of a sort hovered close by. The distance to the attainment of this end was quickly shrinking. Jim, who was my witness, and I left his home early to be at the Cambridge courthouse on time for my divorce hearing. His friendship as well as his assistance would bolster me through this perilous part of my journey.

The trolley we boarded lurched to a start. My hand jerked loose from the pole I was grasping. All of my size-ten, miniskirt-clad body landed in the lap of a male passenger. He maintained the expressionless, glazed look of most transit riders during rush hour. Flailing my bare legs in the air, I tried to extricate myself from his lap with no assistance from him. Do you suppose he was dead? Manna from heaven in the guise of a tall, willowy, blond had fallen into his lap. What a perfect time to arrange an assignation.

"Are you alright?" Jim inquired as I regained my footing.

"Yes," I situated myself on my three-inch, spike heels in a rather unladylike stance, no more inadvertent throwing of myself at another rider.

Jim and I met my lawyer at the courthouse. He took us to a large, crowded room.

"People, may I have your attention," shouted a court officer over the noise of the crowd. "Uncontested cases take the elevator on the left, outside of this room, to the courtroom on the third floor."

In my imagination the scene resembled the epitome of a Dickensian courtroom. The dark wood wainscoting was dull and scarred. The wooden floor creaked and groaned as we moved over it, amplifying the clatter of the women's shoes. The judge was seated high above us. Before our case was called, we sat on long, hard, splintery benches bearing the marks, dents and scratches of age.

The large almost-floor-to-ceiling windows of the courtroom were open. Noises from the street and trolley station bounced off the walls. The judge was deaf. Clients and lawyers shouted at each other, and at him. Eleven women before me each took their turn standing beside the high bench on which he was seated.

I nearly became hysterical at this scene of people yelling their cases to a deaf judge above the din from the street. Being true to the tradition of the Murphy women, I told Jim, "I am going to find the ladies room."

"Do you want help?"

"No, I'll be okay."

Sitting in the ladies room, I contemplated the surreal situation. The feeling of looking through a dirty, cobweb-filled window at another me persisted.

I returned to the courtroom. "I was afraid you weren't coming back," Jim whispered. He was more correct then he knew. There was a dark, lonely spot deep inside my mind where I was hiding, a place of emotional death with no mourners present, not even myself.

My case was called. With the pretense of confidence, I visually groped my way to the stand and faced the indistinct judge. My lawyer stated my case.

"Did he hit you?" the judge bellowed.

"No."

"What did she say?" he yelled at my lawyer.

"No, your honor, we are claiming emotional abuse," he shouted at the deaf judge.

Madness

Janet Schmidt

Insanity possessed me. Janet was winning the war of destroying me.

Shock and denial were replaced by depression and the absolute conviction I was completely mad. There is a Hell and I was in it. The choices were: check out or check in. I chose to check in to Saint Vincent's psychiatric unit. Someone else had to monitor my daily living. Someone else was going to protect me from the inner voice of the personal demon telling me to kill myself. The choice of the psychiatric ward, at Saint Vincent's, was less crazy than suicide.

It seemed incredibly important my parents be protected from the truth of my insanity. Dealing with my divorce was difficult enough for them.

If I had made better choices this horrendous condition would not have occurred. How could I be so inept? I've never been able to meet their, or our, religion's expectations of how I was supposed to develop as an adult. No doubt I was always on the fringe of lunacy. Nonetheless, I could play it so Mom and Dad wouldn't have so much to explain about me.

"Mom, I can't take your offer of a trip to Oregon. I'm so tired and I don't feel well. I can't handle it."

"Alright, Janet, if you're sure. Your dad and I just thought a visit with Carole and a change of scenery would do you a lot of good."

"Mom I'm going to Saint Vincent's to rest."

"Okay. You do what you think is best."

"Mom, my doctor thinks I need to." The word psychiatrist wasn't mentioned. Doctor was okay. It implied physical healing. Their daughter would get better.

I was safe from Mrs. Janet Murphy Marshall, formerly Mrs. David Marshall, yesterday's rubbish. Whichever one wanted to get rid of me didn't stand a chance here.

There were four of us to a room on the psychiatric unit at Saint Vincent's. During the day the beds were made up like sofas. The routine was simple and mandatory. We got up in the morning, showered, dressed, went to breakfast, and took our medication. We ate lunch and took our medication. We ate supper and took our medication. All the medication kept my assassin too drugged to strike. Janet was safe from Janet. She may have lurked in the shadows of my days and nights, but I couldn't see or hear her.

There must have been some kind of recreation room to keep us busy. It was of no consequence to me. Sleeping was on my agenda. I did so with the aid of some pretty, little pills. I roused myself from sleep only when I was expected to eat and swallow cups full of those wonderful, multi-colored, magic, numbness inducers. They provided blessed relief from the voices dictating, "Kill yourself, Janet. Don't be a coward."

Though I slept long and often, I knew immediately when someone entered my space. More often than not, if an individual didn't announce the invasion of my space, especially in the dark of night, it elicited terrified screams. After all, the invader might be Janet. Perhaps she had escaped the bondage of medication to torment me into killing us. People developed the routine of awakening me from a distance.

The rooms were over air-conditioned. At night my roommates would spread magazines across the top of the unit to keep out some of the cold air. "Gotta keep the nuts cool so they won't crack," I thought to myself.

During the day the magazines were piled on the windowsill. I suppose they were intended to entertain us during idle moments. I don't recall looking out of the window. Why would I? It was dangerous out there. Looking inward or outward was to be carefully avoided.

Eating was almost as important as sleeping. I never lost my appetite. I was always hungry. I was "queen of the clean plate club." Seconds, thirds, and desserts were devoured with great momentary pleasure. Little did I know voracious eating was a symptom of my depression.

All of the patients in the psychiatric wing had to eat together in the dining room. One of the patients kept asking me my name when we were seated at the same table. "I get shock therapy," she explained, "and it causes short term memory loss."

None of us, as I recall, discussed with each other why we were there. Someone did mention the nun in the group had passed out from too much alcohol and scalded her arm under the hot water faucet in her bathtub.

I don't remember anyone asking me to tell my story. I guess we all knew this was a temporary oasis. We were only strangers momentarily sharing the same place.

The psychiatrist assigned to my case was a quiet man—probably in his late fifties. He was very kind. He seemed not to be put off by my taciturn demeanor. He didn't probe or try to push me into self-revelations. Then again he was probably only there to monitor my medications and my mood to determine whether or not I was out of my mind. Undoubtedly, he was going to decide if I should return to the land of the living. He came to the room one day when I was lying half-asleep on my sofa. I decided if he cared whether or not I lived or died, he would awaken me. He didn't. He just left the room. Who was going to care enough to help me live? He returned again to say he had visited me before and thought he should let me sleep.

"Janet, I called your father," my friend, Myra, informed me one evening when she came to visit during my first week as a mental patient. "He should see this place and find out you are not locked behind bars like a raving maniac."

"Yeah."

"Janet, I tried to explain to him you had to work this through in your own way and you were getting good help. But he should come to see you and the special conditions here."

"I suppose so."

The most difficult time of day was the evening visiting hours. If my roommates had visitors I couldn't go to bed and sleep until they left. I longed for the escape into drugged sleep. I had to sit in the ward lounge in the glare of florescent lighting. My body language clearly stated, No Trespassing. I didn't want to visit with anyone. The minute hand plodded around the clock face slowly wiping away the time used up in waiting for the visitors to leave.

One evening, Myra asked, "Janet, do you want visitors or would you rather just be left alone?"

"I guess I would just rather be alone and sleep, but I can go out on Saturday if the doctor says it's okay."

"Why don't we go someplace then? Where do you think you might like to go?"

"Maybe we could go shopping for some things for my apartment."

"Alright. Call me if you get permission and we'll go to Shoppers World in Framingham."

The psychiatrist gave me permission to spend Saturday afternoon shopping with Myra. She left me alone to think my own thoughts during the ride to Framingham. If being dead felt this way then I was dead. I waded through the atmosphere around me with leaden feet unengaged with my surroundings, my friend, and myself. Myra suggested we go to Sears. I followed.

"Janet, what do you want to buy?"

"Some wastebaskets and a lamp for my apartment, I guess."

"Do you have any money with you?"

"I have David's credit card. It's good until the divorce is final I think."

Myra helped me pick out some stuff.

On Sunday Dad came to see me. After lunch I was sitting on the edge of a patio lounge, beginning a conversation with the guy using the other half, when a nurse informed me, "Janet, your father is here."

Annoyed at the bad timing, I entered the building to greet him. "How are you doing, Babe?" he inquired uncomfortably as he kissed me on the cheek. There was no hug.

"I'm doing alright." Dad wouldn't be able to deal with any self-revelation on my part. His philosophy demanded nothing more than the answer I gave him. We went to my room and sat on my sofa.

"Is this your room?"

"Yes."

"It's nice. How are you feeling?"

"Alright. I'm sleeping a lot."

We conversed like casual acquaintances talking a little about nothing. We parted—glad to have it over.

When Dad said goodbye, he gave me a quick kiss on the cheek. As I watched him walk away, he seemed cloaked in sadness. Gone was the jaunty, business-like stride he usually exhibited and the tuneless whistling or humming he did under his breath. He appeared hunched over, drawn in upon himself as he vanished from my sight into the murkiness of the hallway. A profound melancholy washed over me.

I longed to run after him and comfort him but I had nothing to give. My inner resources were depleted. I couldn't comfort myself; how could I comfort anyone else?

Oh, Dad, why couldn't I throw myself into your arms, crying and tell you how I feel. Why couldn't you embrace me and ask about my pain? Why couldn't two people who obviously love each other be able to communicate? Why couldn't I say, "Dad, I'm so lost, so weak, please hold me and let me cry and still love me?" Why couldn't I?

It wasn't in the plan for me to end up in a psychiatric ward being cared for by strangers. I was broken. Was I ever going to get fixed?

What horrible sin had I committed? What was my crime? Am I so despicable a human being I am condemned to this hell? Is this my punishment because I can't believe in the God presented to me in my childhood? What is going to become of me?

Lee, a Worcester Poly Tech student, with whom I had a rather disappointing one-night stand, visited me. "Janet, I brought a book of poetry. Let's go out on the lawn and I'll read some to you."

Lee was always trying to stage life. If I went to his place to listen to music we were both supposed to wear headsets and lie on the floor becoming immersed in the music. His personality was a bit unusual.

"What I would really like to do is look at the babies."

"Let's go."

We took the elevator to the maternity floor. "What are you doing up here?" demanded an irate nurse. We left in a hurry.

The next stop was the lawn of the hospital. Lee proceeded to carry through on his poetry reading scenario. He staged the way we sat, like the cover on a Victorian romance novel. I felt like an observer—not a participant—in this little scene until an angry voice quickly returned me to reality. "You are to come into this building, right now," commanded an irate nurse.

"I had better go in. I guess I've been bad." Getting up I wandered toward the voice I could not see.

"Someone called me saying one of my patients was roaming the halls and was out on the lawn. You are not to do that again." I went meekly back to my room. Lee didn't make a return visit.

During the course of my second week on the psychiatric ward one roommate left. An older woman replaced her. Every night, we three veterans were awakened by her incredibly loud snoring. This cacophony was accompanied by the noisy sound of gas being expelled. We would giggle uncontrollably, shushing each other so as not to wake our sleep-disrupting roommate. We soon discovered she would probably be able to sleep through the upheaval of World War III. We used this opportunity to engage in some humorous conversation concerning our new roommate's discordant serenade.

One morning, a roommate entered our room crying because the bitchy head nurse (the same one who reprimanded me for being on the lawn with Lee) had said her skirt was way too short. "All of my clothes are this length. This is the style. I don't have anything else to wear." I was actually able to muster the energy to comfort her and agree this was no way to treat people in our condition. Did this mean I was getting better?

I was the bitchy nurse's next victim. "That dress is way too short. It's inappropriate on this ward." I just walked away angry. Was she afraid we were going to get the male patients all hot and bothered and engage in some type of assignation? Where? We couldn't leave the ward without permission. We certainly couldn't sneak out at night. We were locked in and checked on periodically. Perhaps she was just jealous of our youth.

She probably mourned the demise of prefrontal lobotomies and ice baths. At least at Saint Vincent's, therapeutic treatment was humane. I wondered later whether or not her job was to see if we were alive enough to get angry.

The inner voice continued to torment, "Watch it. Janet seems to be exhibiting normal behavior," it warned. "We mustn't let it continue. She hasn't paid her debt yet. She may decide to live. We can't have that. She has got to pay for her sins." But the voice didn't seem as loud any more.

The psychiatrist came to see me shortly before my dismissal. He told me I had an appointment to see the referring psychiatrist, who was the chief administrator, at Worcester State Hospital the following Monday. My two weeks were up on Friday. Did I have some place to go?

"Yes."

Myra picked me up. I returned to her sofa at night. This time, however, I had a plethora of pretty, little pills to make me sleep and to elevate my mood during the day.

I kept my appointment with the psychiatrist at the state hospital.

"Janet, we have a new, young psychiatrist who's just out of the service and joined our out-patient clinic staff. Your insurance would cover his fee. Would you like to have me arrange an appointment for you?"

"Yes."

A Widow in Winter

Marilyn Brandt Smith

Dawn on the porch steps; salt on the sidewalk;
Car at the curb, chains ready;
Planter box covered; geraniums in—
Maybe this time I'm ready—
Extra bread and milk, batteries, candles.

Double lock the door. My scarf meets carpet,
It's playtime for my Persian—
My cure for alone—the radio plays
But it's a dirge I can leave.
Tune it to weather. Radar says it's here.

They tell us, "Stay home; this wind is vicious,
Threatens power lines and trees."
TV shows pileups on the interstate;
Roads and bridges in trouble;
Reminds us, no school; no games; no garbage.

We see street people crowd into shelters.
They need winter coats, warm clothes.
And I wonder about four-legged strays,
It's below freezing out there.
Who will hear their cries; feed them; keep them warm?

The mailman zooms by, dressed for the arctic.
In my recliner I doze
Till the wind wakes me, rattles the downspouts.
Oh God! The lights just flickered.
Ice beats at the door; peppers the windows.

I dash to the porch, drip that faucet good.
How could I have forgotten?
My hands are so cold I can't turn the knob.
"Leave that door open next time,
You should know better, Push hard and twist, now!"

God bless french roast and the power to brew.
Grandma must wear her button,
If she fell today I couldn't help her.
I should call to remind her.
She's so proud; she hates it when I worry.

Faint whines startle me; a siren speeds past;
Outside something bumps around;
Strong gusts bend branches, howl around corners;
Chasing our autumn away.
It gives me goose bumps, I cover my ears.

Time to do something, maybe some music?
Cue up that new disk with the
Dixieland marches. Shut out that north wind
On this shortest and longest
Of days to get through and nighttimes to dread.

Those presents can stay asleep in their bags.
I can't find the faith to do
Red gold and green. Grey fur beside me,
Kitty needs a good rubbing,
She won't tell secrets—she purrs unashamed.

Am I hearing things? Sounds like my doorbell.
UPS with a package?
Mom said it would get here; I sign their form.
He says this storm's a booger;
Our street's a glacier; says it's turned to snow.

He's in a hurry, route almost finished.
This present doesn't shake much.
It's the biggest one underneath my tree
And the prettiest bow, too.
I grab a sandwich, take cardboard out back.

Love that wood smoke from my neighbor's fireplace.
Snowflakes look soft and harmless
But I know better, sirens of winter.
I shiver, hurry inside
And check the weather. Cleanup has started.

Meow demands milk since I'm making fudge,
Not so good for the body
But good for the soul. Grandma says that's right;
She hopes it clears by Christmas.
I wish she were already here with me.

Cocooned in velour, quilts smell like cedar;
The furnace is still humming;
The wind has moved on. Kitty at my feet
I watch the moon reflect white
And drift into another place and time.

Measure the coffee, turn on the weather,
Reporters show us the worst.
I freeze in place when they show a semi;
It's the same bridge, the same ice …
He left the road, left me, left everything.

Two years ago I lived through this nightmare,
But this man still clings to life.
My heart says a prayer, no, I won't watch this!
Show me the mayor shoveling;
Show me that snowman with the silly hat.

Dawn on the porch steps, thick ice on the walk;
I'll call that boy who shovels.
This snow is deep but if the sunshine holds
And the temperature rises,
I'll wrap those presents and store all my salt.

PART TWO
Going Places

A Preview

Companions, vans, pups, or canes; busses, subways, boats, or planes; we don't all travel from point A to point B in the same manner. We're ready for varying degrees of comfort or confusion, but by golly, we get there!

Special Dedication

During the final six weeks of editing this anthology, two of our dog partners had to be euthanized, and another died of natural causes. We respectfully dedicate this section about travel to Griffin, Mamie-Moo, and Melita, who served DeAnna, Roger, and Ernie faithfully for years. "Meet you at the bridge."

MBS-ED

A Fork in the Trail

DeAnna Quietwater Noriega

From the very beginning of our walk together,
I knew the day would come.
Your steps would slow, your eyes would ask for rest.
We would both know that our time together
Had come to an end.
Like the sands in an hourglass, our time slips away.

Soon, we will come to that fork in the trail,
You will go west, and I will turn east.
I dread that day of parting.
My head knows it must come,
But my soul cries out, "Not yet!"
My hand will long to touch the velvet of your ears.
I'll listen in vain, for the sound of your tread.

When you go your way, and I mine,
For awhile I will walk alone,
Until another joins me
On my journey through this life.

When that day comes,
I'll say, "Fare thee well, dear friend,
Take with you my thanks,
And know that a part of me goes with you,
As a part of you stays with me.
You will leave paw prints on my heart."

Dog Gone

DeAnna Quietwater Noriega

Almost every guide dog handler will face a time when one guide dog is retired from service and there's no successor waiting in the wings. In the interval while longing for a class date, that ill-mannered and obstinate cane must be located in the back of the coat closet.

Perhaps because it has been ignored for so long, your cane is likely to be sulky. It will stand silently in corners refusing to come when you need it. It will maliciously seek out other pedestrians' ankles and bruise them and your pride as it clobbers furniture, poles, dumpsters and anything else in its path. Even when you give it a cute name like Candy, Sugar or something more adventurous like Hurricane, it will continue to misbehave at all opportunities.

If you opt for one of the stiff-backed fiberglass varieties, it will sprawl across floors in search of an unsuspecting foot to send skidding or tripping. The jointed limber ones like to lose internal control and leave you grasping a handle while the various sections of its length go rolling off in all directions. The telescoping types like to get loose-jointed and imply there's a drop-off where none exists.

Forget being told about overhead obstacles. Barriers above waist height don't impress canes at all. However, a crack or slight elevation in a sidewalk or grating will inevitably snag a cane's attention. It will halt your forward momentum so suddenly that you will find you are being launched into an unexpected pole vault or skewered on the cane handle. Worst of all, no matter how often you verbally correct such failures to perform the task of keeping you safe, or even snap the wrist loop at its top, it will refuse to learn not to do such things in the future.

If you go into settings where other visually impaired people are present and place your companion in a corner with others, it will allow you to leave without it or refuse to let you know which of several like creatures is theoretically yours. I find it useful to mark mine with some distinctive key chain or other emblem to circumvent this lack of loyalty.

There are some advantages to having one of these difficult creatures in your life. They don't shed, need to be fed, groomed, and taken out to perform bodily functions. Their good health is maintained by replacing parts at a lower cost than visits to a veterinarian. No one of my acquaintance ever claimed to be allergic to a cane. The funny thing is, no one ever comments on their beauty and good manners, or expresses pleasure that your cane is present.

Somehow though, they just aren't as good company. They don't display any initiative in problem solving. They don't offer emotional support when things go wrong and aren't very cuddly.

My cane is as bad at judging traffic as I am. It seems to have a reckless disregard for danger. Several canes of mine have met with an untimely demise through unfriendly encounters with elevator doors, automobiles, and even stationary hazards like storm drains. German Shepherds can be noisy, labs can be food-oriented and golden retrievers too friendly to the public, but they all are much better at self-preservation.

There is one good use for a cane: It's wonderful at locating stuff that has rolled under furniture. But keeping company with one of these cane critters always reminds me why I choose to be a guide dog handler.

Starting Over

DeAnna Quietwater Noriega

Got my E-ticket today.
I am actually going!
What should I pack? Who will I meet? What dog will I get?
Will it be a lab? A golden? A shepherd, a cross?
Will it be large? Small? A male or female?
Will it like me? What if it doesn't?
When I pick up that harness handle, will it feel right?
Will I be able to trust and just go?
Will I know the right things to do?

I long to put this cane in the back of the closet,
But can I start over with a young silly pup?
It won't be my old dog,
It won't know how I like things to be,
Or where I like to go.
Will it like my family and friends?
Will it hate my cat? Will it scavenge and distract? Chew up my shoes?
So many questions that circle my head.
Sometimes the best we can do,
Is take it in stride.
Step out in faith and have fun finding out.

Hawaii Five-O

Brenda Dillon

"I know what we could do to make it better," Dan said. We were grilling steaks and soaking up the welcome winter sun on the deck in our cozy subdivision outside Nashville. My husband was referring to my insecurity about turning fifty. Should I celebrate or vegetate, I wondered. I loved my four grandchildren. That part of middle-age suited me fine. Early retirement allowed us to throw our hearts and souls, time and telephones, into community and church activities, and administrative responsibilities with the local and state chapters of the American Council of the Blind.

Was it time now to join AARP, collect those early senior discounts, and make appointments for regular physical exams?

"Anything to make it better sounds good to me. You know bold bouncy Brenda isn't ready to go down without a fight," I laughed.

"What about your dream?" Dan proposed.

"Which one?" I giggled. My wish list of things to do, clothes and dishes to buy, projects to support for our families and for various organizations, was endless.

He left the grill to sit beside me on the swing. "Let's play Password backwards. If I said 'Five-O', what would you say came before it?"

It didn't take me long. "Hawaii?" I whispered hopefully. He didn't say anything. I reached for a hug. "Hawaii!" I squealed.

I anticipated the smile in his voice. "How about for your birthday next July?" he chuckled. "You think it would be too hot over there? I've got to see about those steaks."

We enjoyed our steaks with all the trimmings, but it took a long time to get through dinner. With every bite I had another question, another thought, another something or other over there we wanted to: try, taste, touch, hear, or learn.

Dan and I knew the thrill of being able to go anywhere, any time we wanted to. With a little research ahead of time, and lots of planning, I knew I could make Hawaii come alive for us. After all, hadn't we put independent travel to the test in Cancun? Our sombreros were definitely off to the hotel staff who treated us like royalty. I knew courtesy, a little extra tip money, and patience could work wonders. In Cancun, a staff person took us to the open market for local bargains. Sure, there were some language barriers, but nothing could detract from the enthusiasm we shared with our guide on the speedboat excursion. We did the swim-up bar and lounge, experienced casino night at the resort, and oh, the beach! Dan and I are nautical enthusiasts. We even planned our wedding with a backdrop of water. Planning Hawaii Five-O would be a welcome challenge, not a chore.

I made some contacts with blind friends of friends who lived in Hawaii, hoping to learn a little about their education and rehabilitation programs. Maybe because they were frequently contacted by American tourists, or maybe because their schedules were full, we were not able to make our way into the blind community, so we could visit facilities or private homes. Since we were only there for a week, we were probably expecting too much.

The Hilton Hawaiian Village was our final choice. It is a large resort, but I related well with the booking staff, and they promised us a good room and plenty of guide service. With almost a hundred boutiques, restaurants, and places to play on the property, I believed we would have an entertaining stay.

I have minimal vision beyond light perception, and my husband Dan is totally blind. Our first adventure on our own took us to Myrtle Beach. We enjoyed access to the beach, the pool, the lazy river, and restaurants and shops just outside our door. We vacationed with very little help from others.

I took my first serious plunge into travel research when we decided to visit Washington, D.C. for four days. Guides and docents were available for monuments and museums, but it was necessary to schedule ahead of time. We decided to make travel arrangements a part of the vacation, and booked a deluxe sleeper car on the train. There were movies and music in our efficiently organized, compact quarters, and the food was excellent.

Our congressman and senator welcomed us, naturally with a photo opportunity. We had a private hands-on and ears-on guide to the Capitol, with a visit to congress in session. I carefully examined the tactile map featuring streets and attractions. It helped me understand where we traveled when we moved from one monument to another, out to Arlington Cemetery, and to the Vietnam and Korean War memorials.

At the Smithsonian we gained valuable information from a docent who happened to be a pilot herself. Dan particularly enjoyed the wood-turning exhibit in another gallery, as he is a skilled wood craftsman.

There weren't many hands-on opportunities at Mount Vernon, but the glimpse into George Washington's life made the trip down the river well worth taking. Our guide there was a former secretary at the White House. Our questions and her comments about her experience there helped ease our disappointment about not being able to schedule a tour. The White House was still closed to visitors for security concerns after 9/11.

At the Kennedy center, personal narration was available for the comedy performance. Knowing what's taking place on stage makes a production come alive. Since then we have opted for descriptive narration any time it is available.

At the Franklin Delano Roosevelt Memorial, the Braille signage, replicas, and, in particular, the thin statues representing the starving men and women in the breadlines during the depression, made lasting impressions. This unusually tactile exhibit gave new meaning to the word "accessible."

As the date for Hawaii drew near our anticipation mounted. Could two blind people really do this alone? "Don't miss the …" and "Could you bring me back a …?" were familiar refrains from our friends who coached us with envy.

Would the Hilton care as much about our comfort level as the staff on the Grand Princess had? On our Caribbean cruise we took advantage of a self-contained floating holiday. The cabin steward assigned to us read our daily choices of activities, and helped us find guides when we needed to go to unfamiliar parts of the ship. On the Grand Princess, we participated in trivia games, Bingo with our Braille cards, Karaoke and talent show fun. Early scheduling of shore excursions guaranteed adequate assistance. And oh, the food. The variety, the quality, and the frequency defy explanation.

On all of our trips we have taken small tape recorders to keep track of directions or information people gave us. We knew how to plead our case if something didn't go right—lost luggage, a guide who failed to show. In general, we have always found the tourism industry very accommodating.

The flight to Hawaii was long. We managed to move around every few hours, and to be prepared for our biological clocks to be a little out of sync after changing time zones. When we got to the Hilton, we unpacked in our delightful corner room with two balconies facing the ocean. We were oriented to the part of the property near our room, and were able to get to some destinations independently. We both carried folding canes which we used carefully in crowds, for the safety of other guests. When we traveled in open hallways or on the grounds, they served us well. Assistance was only a phone call away, and carts provided mobility for all guests to the various shops, restaurants and activities. After all, we would return with our arms full of packages, wouldn't we?

We kept an audible locator in our beach bag. When we were ready for a dip or a chase with the waves, someone from the hotel took us to a spot where we could leave the bag and easily walk into the water. With assistance from our locator we could find our blanket again. Someone from the hotel returned in a couple of hours to help us make our way through the other sunbathers back to our room. We offered generous tips for this extra service.

Experiences on the island included: a luau, a speed sailing trip, and a visit to Paradise Cove where we sampled native cuisine and cocktails. Fresh seafood and pineapple were high on our list of favorites. Dan, an accomplished guitarist, tuned into the lectures and hands-on demonstrations with the ukulele.

He insisted on a visit to the USS Missouri. We touched guns, shells and bunks. How did they crowd so many men into such a small space? The Pearl Harbor story put us in touch with American history in a way books can't equal.

We took in the Don Ho show, and tried our hand at lei-making. Fragrant garlands, steel guitars and rippling water are the traditional drawing cards taking tourists away from their scheduled lives on the continent, to this sensual paradise of the Pacific. We tried to soak up every second of cultural awareness available to us. What would it be like to have the wonderful scent of the plumeria wafting through my backyard in Tennessee?

Of course, we ate too much, spent too much, and brought home more than we could carry. Turning fifty didn't bother me at all. I was having the time of my life!

Blind people can tackle almost any travel project if they set their minds to it. Book everything ahead that you know you want to do, take credit cards or travelers' checks and cash in small denominations, keep your expectations reasonable, and keep free time open for the things you can't anticipate now. "Please" and "Thank you" still win friends and influence people. And remember, a smile is the same in any language.

Tell That Blind Man to Move his Truck!

Roger Smith

"I'm sorry, officer," I explained, "I didn't realize we were blocking the drive. My driver just ran inside for a minute. You really don't want me behind the wheel. Here, I have a set of keys, if there's a better space empty now, you could move it."

Owning a vehicle is a bit of a challenge for blind people. I needed to deliver pianos when I had a business in Lubbock, Texas, tuning, repairing, and selling old uprights. Movers were too expensive, and I didn't have enough friends with pickups who shared the same hours free. My wife loves to learn towns and plan trips on Braille maps, but they won't let her behind the wheel either.

The inability to read print and drive are the two limitations most complained about by blind people. Scanners with speech, even handhelds, have made reading available. But technology has not yet given us complete freedom in mobility. When using a taxi, public transportation, or special services for the disabled, there are catches: scheduling, time in travel, cost, and/or inconvenience. Even when you can "hoof it" with a cane, dog, or sighted guide, truly independent travel is still a dream. Most of us would love to get behind the wheel when we choose, drive where we want to go, and return after stopping for dinner or to shop.

To this end, many blind folk have played at driving, sometimes just to know how it would feel to have so much power at their fingertips, and sometimes to entertain themselves and their friends.

Your coach shows you the pedals and the sensitivity of the steering wheel. The beginner's snail's pace may speed up if you're not in a small parking lot (vacant of course). "Hands-on" is the unspoken option, and "feet ready" is the default backup. I've tried it. It can be scary and exhilarating. For laughs, read Ronnie Milsap's account of driving his bus.

Our first vehicle was a banged-up seven-year-old half-ton Chevy. The price was right. We put a cheap sign over some of the dents. The hydraulic lift cost more than the truck itself. We had a driver with a good record, so our insurance policy carried his name as the primary operator.

Four years after we sold the piano business I was in college, we had two kids and a guide dog. We found ourselves making six-hundred-mile trips in Texas, and cross-country trips to Kentucky. We needed elbow room. Molly looked like a milk truck. She was a high-cube Chevy. We air conditioned the back, put in carpet, paneling, couches, and a stereo system. We enjoyed her for the next four years.

Our hired drivers, who averaged about six thousand miles a year, always had good records so insurance costs were reasonable.

We had a multilevel marketing business with deliveries all over Lubbock. Once, a driver called us in a panic from a convenience store. "I can't stop! I've lost control! I slid to the curb by this store, but I'm afraid to go any further. What do you want me to do?"

Thank God for towing insurance. The master cylinder cost more than three-hundred dollars. We had to use the driver's car for a few days, but we were soon back in business.

You might wonder why we don't always use the driver's car. It's not always available, and not always dependable. Careful mileage records have to be kept. The owner makes decisions about smoking, seatbelts, gas stops, and speed choices. We like to have that control. We only pay tickets if we authorize speeding or if there is something wrong with our vehicle. Several fuzz busters helped but we don't use them anymore. Helicopter surveillance and ticketing in Florida taught us to be leery.

My dad taught me to fill a gas tank when I was a kid. I thought I was the expert on mileage. Since I couldn't do much about operating the vehicle, I tried to squeeze every drop out of a tank, hoping for a lower price down the road. Late one night in Benjamin, Texas, my little game caught up with me. Someone had to wake the owner of a gas station. We paid triple the price for him to fill our tank. My driver didn't say, "I told you so," but the take-home message was clear.

When I served seven school districts for a special education co-op in Texas, and my wife worked seventeen counties with the Texas Commission for the Blind, we each had a vehicle. Our drivers were paid by our employers. She put three thousand miles a month on her Olds. I hit two thousand in our Econoline. We both rolled over the hundred-thousand mark on the odometers. Talk about saddle sore.

When we added a travel trailer I learned about hooking up, dumping, and propane. I can talk truck and house batteries with the best of the road warriors. We enjoy the camaraderie at the parks where we stop. Our destinations may be the mountains of northern New Mexico or the beach sand in Texas and Florida.

Our drivers were as green as we were at this new hobby.

Of course, Mom wanted it warmer, Dad wanted it cooler, the driver wanted the window open for smoking, teens wanted the radio at night, little brother wanted to wait for McDonald's, Cracker Barrel's line was too long, the dog threw up, and the shower overflowed, soaking the carpet. We lived through it all, and loved it.

We bought a mini Winnebago, and found it easier, if less flexible, than a car or van with a trailer attached. Once, we pulled a small van behind the motor home so we could detach and get closer to the nightlife in Austin and New Orleans.

We had two thirty-five-footers. They were luxurious for sleeping and eating, but one of them was the "home from hell." We blew tires, and almost set ourselves on fire with a glitch in the exhaust which caused damage to our plumbing. We bought gallons of water, and filled up jugs along the way when we could, for cleaning and drinking. The headlights went out. The manifold gasket blew giving us an extra day at the beach. We sold the sucker as soon as we got home. We are tolerant of breakdowns, and try not to take anybody with us who isn't. Stress in a small space is miserable.

These days we use our twenty-five-foot Coachman for in-town driving as well as road trips. It means we have to hire drivers with some skill, which is not a bad idea anyway.

I have a dump station at home feeding into the sewer. We have her waxed and maintained, and keep records about oil and other fluids.

It's hard to find drivers with enough free time from family and other jobs to travel as much as we'd like. Our pattern has been a ten to fifteen day trip every other year with a shorter one in the alternate year.

Tracey, our driver for the past seven years, says we travel by restaurants, amusement parks, beaches, and friends. She and our adult son live for the next wild roller coaster, and the biggest, saltiest waves.

When the next dump hose breaks in mid-stream, the steps don't fold in as usual, the dash shows a light we can't explain, or the backup camera goes out, we'll be looking up the nearest service center, and watching the clock till we're "on the road again."

That's better than sitting in the mud at a sixty-degree angle off an access road in south Texas on a soggy September Sunday afternoon, waiting for a tow truck, and shifting weight so we won't tip. Now that was something else again!

Bud and Me Around the World

Sanford Rosenthal

Within a month after giving up driving, I found myself partnered with a most observant pal. He was Bud, a seventy-five-pound golden retriever, my dog guide for the blind. Sometimes he was a little too good at figuring out solutions for himself, like when we entered the men's room at the Lighthouse for The Blind in New York City for the first time.

He observed me standing up about twenty feet from where I told him to "stay." I had enough partial vision to determine that we were the only ones in the room. All of a sudden, I heard a faucet sound that shouldn't have been there. It came from Bud's direction.

I wasn't sure what to do. I wanted to go investigate, but it was a most inopportune time. Let's just say it took longer than it needed to for me to get my act together. I voted in favor of stopping what I was doing.

I looked behind me and saw Bud standing in a concentrated pose. As I approached, it became obvious that what I feared was true.

"Stop, Bud!" I begged for the second time. He didn't move as he usually did when I was returning to him. The gushing sound stopped, but I could tell he was confused. I could just hear him say that if it was good for the goose, then it should be good for the gander.

I thought it was prudent to grab some paper towels for the mop-up before we headed for the door. Then we hurried outside for the curb. He finished his business out there while I informed him of his misunderstanding. He never made a mistake like that again.

Misunderstandings weren't usually Bud's fault. Shortly thereafter, one subway transit worker decided Bud should be in a carrier. She wouldn't sell me the token needed for entry onto the platform. She wouldn't listen to me when I tried asking, "If he's in the carrier, how can he guide me?" I have to credit New York's inhabitants. A helpful passerby placed a token in my hand. I remember trying to give him the money, but he refused. I never looked back.

Many blind people with dogs don't know it if a cab whizzes past while they are frantically signaling. I had enough vision to know I was being ignored. On one occasion, a passerby helped me get the license plate number. The newspapers loved the story when it ended up in the Court system. They were going to take his license away for an extended time. I actually interceded on the driver's behalf to reduce his sentence, because I wanted this to be a learning experience for all taxi drivers, and not a power play which would only create more resistance.

I lived in California for a short time. There were many places where we were refused accommodations. Apartments suddenly became occupied when we arrived. Sometimes they blatantly stated the obvious: One of us was a dog. It didn't matter to them that the law was on my side.

When we moved to Hawaii, neither Bud nor I liked the hoops we had to jump through. We "did time" in the animal quarantine station located in Mauna Loa Valley, Honolulu, but were allowed to escape from the assemblage during daytime hours until the clock struck 5:00 P.M. The thousands of less-fortunate dogs and cats residing at the quarantine station were forever howling at odd hours, day and night. I really didn't blame them. It's not much fun to find yourself separated from your loved ones in a small caged-in area.

Bud and I stayed in a cottage alongside the other inmates. We approached the newspapers, TV, radio, and legislators. It took about twenty one years for our plea to change the law.

Bud and I could leave the premises if we had an escort. I convinced one companion to accompany us to visit the lieutenant governor on a "brown-bag lunch day," when the public was invited to lodge complaints. Bud was quietly tucked away under the table. No one knew he was there. We arrived before the others.

When I introduced us, there were some mixed responses. Some thought they were sitting too close to a possibly rabid dog. Others thought if I had papers proving Bud already had his shots that would be good enough. Some moved away while others moved closer.

One night, when the outer gate of the quarantine station was locked, a strange guest showed up. Over the intermittent cacophony of barks and meows, I heard a knocking at my door. Was someone checking to make sure we were where we were supposed to be? Was it more media coverage for our plight?

No, this slender and innocent looking woman claimed to be an angel. She wore a white uniform and seemed to be on a mission. I got the picture—this had nothing to do with Bud. She begged me to let her put her hands on my head to make me see again. "Oh brother," I pondered to myself. "How do I get out of this?"

She was attractive and assertive. She embarrassed me when she wanted to become a little more familiar than I expected. Her mission was to visit people like me to bring them closer to The Lord. I couldn't make her believe I already was close to The Lord. I was supposed to believe in her version of it all. I never heard of angels doing what she intended and refused her two offers. Thank goodness she gave up on me. The only miracle I was after was freedom for Bud and me.

In Israel, the rules would have kept me from entering a kibbutz. A vote was taken and the rules were overturned. There was a memorable night in Jerusalem:

The guards protecting the Western Wall of King Solomon's Temple thought Bud and I didn't belong there. At gunpoint, we had to make a decision. We left, as I was pushed away with a rifle barrel at the small of my back. It seemed prudent not to push the envelope at that moment.

When I came back to the States, I joined my family in Florida. Bud was with me in Miami but had been retired from working. Age and medical problems took their toll, and I made the difficult decision to wish him well on his journey beyond our sphere. I tried three other dogs with varying degrees of success, but none lasted as long, or endured as many trials with me, as Bud did. He is truly one of those "golden" memories.

The Wandering Butterfly

(Gaelic: an féileacán fanach)

Michael Coleman

During my childhood, I had two very serious accidents which resulted in the loss of my eyesight. Despite this, I retained a distinctly visual mind.

Over two decades ago, when I lived in Switzerland, I planned a trip to Ireland.

At the time, I was going out with a girl named Claudine. She had a friend named Brigide. Claudine spoke to Brigide about me, and spoke to me about her—so we only knew one another indirectly. We were both going to be traveling to Ireland at the same time, and decided to travel together. Renting a Toyota, we set out from Dublin in the east, across the Emerald Isle.

Brigide was extremely visual and profoundly uncommunicative. In this island of forty shades of green, she must have taken forty thousand photographs—and we stopped countless times. The trouble was, when we stopped the car, it died and wouldn't start again, so she told me to get out and push, so we could get going. We repeated this drama over and over and over.

When traveling with this lady, at times, when I attempted to speak, I was brutally cut short. She growled, "Shut up! I'm trying to concentrate." And when I found myself frozen in a stunned silence, she imperiously commanded me to keep her company and talk to her. I couldn't win for losing.

Finally, we arrived in the northwestern county of Donegal, spending the night in a breakfast house (a bed and breakfast).

The hostess served us scrumptious pieces of apple pie. There was a wonderful, crackling fire. Even the hostess glowed with life. The whole atmosphere of the breakfast house nourished my spirit.

My traveling companion, on the other hand, was like an astronomical black hole that devoured all life, light—and hope. Though physically personable, she seemed utterly impersonal. There was a heavy, angry, corrosive silence that joylessly engulfed any desire to communicate.

The life-giving glow of the hostess made one feel light-hearted, but this heavy, empty, hateful presence eradicated the slightest vestige of mirth.

We set out the next day along the west coast, weaving in and out of one enchanting inlet after another.

It was raining cats and dogs. This life-draining female threatened to put me out in the cold, drizzling rain. I wouldn't be intimidated. I maintained, "Brigide, I think we should separate."

Twenty miles further up the road, she retracted her threat, urging, "I really don't mind our traveling together, Michael."

Finally, we stopped at a charming little village called Killala in County Mayo. We spent the night in a lovely breakfast house. I found myself once again by a warm, crackling fire, with another life-giving, personal presence.

Brigide, silent like death, went to her room and read her book about transcendental meditation, and I stayed and chatted with the host for about two hours, after which I decided I wouldn't travel with her any longer.

The next morning, at the breakfast table, out of the blue, Brigide pleaded apologetically, "I really don't mind our traveling together, Michael."

After a brief, almost ominous silence, I replied, "But Brigide, I do mind. You're one of the most unbearable women I have ever met." At this, she erupted like Mount Vesuvius.

Despite the fact that we were still at the breakfast table, the host, apparently startled by the uproar and sensing the tension, opened the door. This Swiss female volcano, attempting to conceal her true feelings, sputtered nervously, with a heavy, French accent, "It is a wonderful breakfast and it is a beautiful country."

We set out again, stopping in front of a little grocery store in another village. In the shivering rain, she removed my suitcase from the trunk, opened it, dropped it in the grimy, wet gravel and piled about five books on the open suitcase. She slammed the door furiously and, as she sped away, the car seemed to spit gravel back at me with contempt—and I have never seen her since.

I stuffed the books in the suitcase, sat on it and closed it, and then made my way to another breakfast house in the village of Oughterard ("high cream" in Gaelic). There my spirit thawed out amidst a warm, loving environment.

It was the owner of this breakfast house who sold me the land where I had a house built more than twenty years later. The house is located less than a mile from the sea.

Rebel with a Cane

Valerie Moreno

I remember the first time I walked home from school by myself. It was May of 1968. I was a thirteen-year-old, blind-teen. Recently I had taken lessons in mobility (cane travel skills). My teacher was excellent. I was thrilled about learning how to travel independently.

Unfortunately, my excitement was ruined by fierce opposition from my parents. Though they let me take the training, they wouldn't allow me to do anything with my cane, except hide it in the back of a closet.

"Why can't I walk home from school?" I argued, "All the other kids do, and I know how to do it with my cane."

"You don't need that thing," my mom or dad would holler, "We'll give you a ride home."

I was frustrated and heartsick. Often I prayed one day I'd be able to prove it to them.

The day came, a dreary, rainy Wednesday. We had our farewell class luncheon as prospective eighth-graders. I'd forgotten to tell my mom we'd be getting out early, but I'd brought my cane with me in case of a mobility lesson. It was canceled because of the pouring rain. This was my chance to prove myself.

Walking up the block toward my first street crossing, I was exhilarated and a little frightened. "Listen to the traffic," the instructor's voice said in my mind, "When the traffic at your side is moving, and the cars in front of you are idling then cross."

I waited through a couple of lights to make sure I was ready, and then stepped off the curb. Perfect! I reached the other side with a grin on my face stretching from ear to ear. "I did it!" I cried out loud skipping up the sidewalk. I was soaked to the skin, and freezing by now, but it didn't matter. "Singing in the rain, I'm singing in the rain," I crooned as I walked and danced up the next block.

Another successful crossing completed, then another, and another. Suddenly, I felt a flash of apprehension upon reaching the corner of our street. This was the hardest part, a four-way intersection with a short light. A truck sped past tossing a wave of cold water over me as I stood there through a half-dozen lights, summoning the courage to go ahead. Finally, I stepped off the curb. My body was shaking with terror, and from the dripping water. My excitement bubbled up with each step. Reaching the other side, I literally jumped up and down, racing for the house. "Whee!"

As I put my key in the back door lock a car pulled to a stop. My mother's angry voice cut through my joy. "I'm going to kill you!" she yelled.

Swallowing hard I entered the house, tears burning my eyes. Wasn't she proud, I'd done so well? She wasn't, and neither was my dad. They punished me for a week, including no television. Still, no one could take away the fact I could travel alone. Punish me, fine, but I still believed in me. I did it, no regrets.

White Water Rafting? Me?

Mary-Jo Lord

"We're going white water rafting," Denise announced.

"Oh." I set a plate of food and a Diet Coke on my desk.

"Is that all you can say is, 'Oh?'"

"Well, it sounds like fun. When are you going?" As the coordinator of the disabilities services office at a community college, my mind was usually on hundreds of things, and I was preoccupied with my own thoughts. I hadn't really paid attention to her conversation, but I thought Denise said she and someone were going white water rafting.

"We," Holly laughed. "You're going, too."

"I am? I mean, I am." What was I saying? There was no way …

"What's the matter?" Denise asked breaking my train of thought. "Don't you want to go with us?"

"It's not that, it's just …" my voice trailed off, as thoughts of plummeting hundreds of feet over waterfalls into a bed of rocks, or hitting a mass of waves and being thrown from the raft filled my head.

"Come on," Sally said. "I'm going."

"It's going to be fun," Holly said. "We can take my van, and we'll hook the camper to the back. It's in Pennsylvania, near the Virginia border. The camper sleeps six, and we can take sleeping bags. I have four. Does anyone else have sleeping bags?" It wasn't really a question, since she never stopped to take a breath. "We can camp in the camp grounds right outside of town. We can go the last three days of finals week, since most of the students will be finished. Jo can't go, so she said she would run the office. We can take all of our food, and we'll have to wear wetsuits."

"Someone needs to call Pam," Denise broke in. "Sally, why don't you call her?"

"Can we count you in?" Holly asked. "It's a lot of fun."

"I don't know," I said hesitantly. "Do you get thrown from the raft or mangled by rocks?"

"Oh no," Holly assured me. "We went before, and we'll ask for a guide in our raft. I don't think we will have a problem since we are going off season."

"We need a sixth person," Denise said.

"Well, if I'm going," I laughed, "then I think we should ask Tammy."

"Hey! Good idea!" Holly was out of her chair and half way to the phone before the words were out of her mouth. "I'll call her. Does this mean you're going?"

"Well, okay." What had I gotten myself into? But then again, if Sally was going and they could talk Pam into it, why not?

So it was settled. Tammy agreed readily, and Pam reluctantly said, "Yes." So we made our reservations and made plans over several dinners.

The day before we left, Jo held a going-away meeting. She gave us survival packs with bags of sugar, gum, and soda crackers to use if we were thrown from the raft and lost for days in the woods. She also gave us a large comb she called a "bear comb." As if that wasn't enough, she asked us all to write up our wills and turn them in before our departure. "Just in case," she laughed.

"I've never been camping," Tammy said. "Are there really bears?"

"Oh, yeah," Holly said. "We saw one go right up to the tent next to ours."

"What kind of bear?" I didn't think she was telling the truth, but what if she was?

"Well, I don't know. It was black. He wasn't very big, but boy could he empty a picnic basket."

"No really, Holly," Denise sounded nervous. "There aren't actually bears, because if there are, I'm not going."

"Don't worry," Jo laughed. "They're more afraid of us than we are of them. But you better be careful Denise, because I heard they think people from England are a delicacy."

"You're not funny!" Denise's English accent was always more pronounced when she was caught off guard. Then the phone rang, and Sally stifled a laugh as she answered.

We all met at Holly's house, and left by 9:30. Our destination, Ohiopile, Pennsylvania, was "just six hours away from Detroit," according to the brochures.

Nine hours, two games of Trivial Pursuit, one meal, and five rest stops later, we arrived at the campground. The van, with camper attached, almost didn't make it up a few of the hills in town.

"I think I can, I think I can, I think I can," Sally and I chanted.

"If we stop," Pam laughed. "We're going to roll backward."

We didn't, and after several attempts at getting the camper backed into the campsite, it was time to get set up. We managed to get everything in order and had a fire going before dark.

After dinner, Tammy and I learned our way around the campsite and attempted to find the bathroom. Both of us were used to traveling with our leader dogs, who we wisely decided to leave home.

After dinner, we heard movement in the woods near the camper.

"What is it?" I asked.

"I can't see anything," Denise replied, peering between two trees. For a second, I panicked. Holly said she only saw one other group in the whole campground.

"I see it," Sally exclaimed. "It's some kind of an animal."

"It's a skunk," Pam said.

"No," Holly said, seeming unsure. "It looks too big to be a skunk."

"I don't smell anything," I said, as if that settled it.

"It's a skunk," Pam laughed.

"If it's a skunk, then I'm going in the camper." Sally picked up her glass and headed in that direction.

"Hey, wait for me!" Tammy didn't want to be left to fend off an unknown animal.

"Oh, look at him," Holly giggled.

"We can look at him from inside the camper." Denise's voice had that take-charge tone.

"He sounds cute. Hear kitty kitty kitty kitty!"

"Would you stop!"

Pam and I snickered as we headed for the camper.

None of us slept much that night. We each lay there, believing everyone else was sleeping soundly. I tried to imagine what it would be like riding over rapids in a rubber raft. What if it tips, or we get thrown? How fast is the current? Then I reminded myself that hundreds of people go rafting every year and never get thrown. Besides, we were going to have a guide with us. I hated being awake with nothing to do, and I must have drifted off at some point.

The next morning, I woke up to the smell of bacon and coffee. Denise, the culinary expert, and Holly, the camping expert, had breakfast on the table before some of us were out of bed. We ate, and packed the cooler. Although the price of our ticket included lunch, we were advised to bring our own food. We all felt excited and a little nervous as we climbed into the van.

When we reached the Laurel Highlands office in downtown Ohiopile, we rented wetsuits and met our guides. They looked at our bakery bread, delicatessen lunchmeat, and snacks and decided they didn't need to provide lunch. We climbed into the Laurel Highlands van with one of the guides and the other two women, sisters from Ohio, who would be joining us.

Five minutes later, we were at the Youghigheny River. Dave, our guide, went over some instructions. He demonstrated correct paddling motions and showed Tammy and me what to do. He put his hands over ours on the paddle and showed us how to move it in a backward circular motion so we would be pushing it against the current. He pushed the raft into the river, jumped in, and steered us into the deep water.

With our life jackets on and buckled tightly, we were ready for our trip down the "Upper Yough." It was an unusually hot day for the end of April, and I was beginning to regret wearing a wetsuit.

We paddled for a few minutes, and then we approached Cucumber, the first rapid. It sounded like the Niagara Falls, and I couldn't help thinking about all of the people who had died at the bottom.

"Oh, my God!" Sally and Denise exclaimed.

"Don't scream, 'Oh my God' and not tell us what you're Oh-my-Godding about," Tammy said.

"Hey, maybe we should make them face backward so they can't see, either," I suggested.

"Paddle hard," Dave commanded. "Remember, paddling will keep you in the raft."

I felt the raft move faster, as if going downhill. A heavy mist of ice-cold water hit my face, and I was instantly glad we had rented wetsuits and spray jackets.

"Paddle harder," Dave commanded again.

I felt the raft drop, and was doused with a heavy spray of water. We all shrieked.

"Oh shit!"

"Pam, you never swear."

"Harder, harder!" Dave shouted above our laughter and screams.

I tried to keep paddling, and wedged my feet as firmly under the rubber tube in front of me as I could. Finally, we were through the rapid.

"Okay," Dave laughed, "now you can relax."

We went through three more rapids, each more difficult than the previous one. Tammy and I found ourselves in the center of the raft in the middle of one set of rapids. We grabbed onto each other to avoid getting thrown. Our sneakers were water-logged. The bumpier the rapid, the louder we screamed! How exhilarating to be scared to death and delighted with the next surprise. It was better than Six Flags!

Finally, we made it through Dimple and stopped and went on land for lunch. Dave and the other guide had most of the food unpacked and set out on rocks and tree stumps before we all made it out of the raft. The women from Ohio had brought cookies, brownies, and snack mix, so we had a sort of a potluck lunch. We inhaled the sandwiches and snacks. After lunch and a few pictures, we climbed eagerly back into the raft, all anxiety gone.

We made it through two more rapids and then we stopped to go swimming. Holly, Tammy, and I slid into the water. It was ice cold, and we screamed and jumped back in the raft quickly. It felt good, though—the sun had been out for the entire day, and it was eighty five degrees.

The trip went too fast. We tackled several more rapids, and all found ourselves in the center of the raft at one time or another. Once, Denise landed in Sally's lap.

The four-hour, nine-mile trip took us two-and-a-half hours, because we only used two rafts. We wanted to go again and hated to get out of the raft.

When we arrived back in town, we did some shopping and headed back to the campground. We planned to get some beer for the evening. Pam went into a store and came back quickly.

"Hey," she said with a disappointed laugh. "This is a dry county."

That evening at dinner, a deer paid us a visit. He stood watching us from the edge of the woods. Of course, after dark, the skunk or whatever it was came back to visit.

We all slept soundly that night, and the next morning we packed up disappointed that the trip was almost over. On the way home, we toured the Falling Waters House, a mansion designed by Frank Lloyd Wright. From the description in the brochure, we expected the waterfall to run through the house. Instead, we learned that although the mansion sat right by the falls, there wasn't even a good view of it from the house. The mansion was beautiful however, and well worth the visit.

After our tour, we went back to the van and ate lunch. As we backed out of the parking lot, it started to rain.

It seemed to take longer to drive home than it took to get there. We played Twenty Questions and Trivial Pursuit, and made plans to go again.

Exhausted, we finally arrived home. As I fell asleep that night, I could still hear the rushing sound of the rapids, and felt the sliding, bouncing motion of the raft.

The Ride Home

Elizabeth Fiorite

At 4:23 my 4:00 pick-up rolls to the curb and stops. The van door opens slowly. I stand, my white cane at attention, identifying me as the disabled person that the driver is looking for, though I'm the only person outside now, in this ninety degree weather.

"You Elizabeth?" the driver hollers out his door.

"You my driver?" I holler back as I pick up my bag and start walking toward the van.

"Three steps up," the driver says, as he guides me to the door.

I ask, "Are there any wheelchairs on board?" so I will be prepared to maneuver my way to one of the seats in the back.

"One now, one more to pick up." I sidestep around the wheelchair to my place, pay my fare, and buckle up.

"Gracie?" I ask, thinking this may be one of my regular co-riders.

"This Alma," the driver volunteers, but Alma must be dozing.

Music from the radio blares loudly as we pull away. The dispatch radio starts to squawk too, as other drivers report unlocated passengers, ask directions, or receive berating from a beleaguered dispatcher, all in the specialized jargon used by the military, police, and cab drivers.

"What's your twenty, 14-10?"

"What's your ETA for 16-30?"

"I'll 21 and get back to you."

"10-4."

I settle in. The AC must not be working—the hot air blowing from the driver's window barely makes its way to the rear of the van. One strand of hair sticks to my brow. I don't bother brushing it back. If this ride were to take me directly from work to home, it would only be a matter of fifteen minutes. I rarely get a "direct flight" however, and my ride easily takes an hour or more. I envy Alma's ability to sleep.

The qualifications for drivers astound me. Potential drivers must be willing to incur severe hearing loss. The dispatch radio must be set to the highest possible volume so the driver will always be aware of other drivers' whereabouts, and also to discourage conversation with passengers, who may ask questions like, "Where are we?" or "How much longer?"

We arrive at one of the dialysis centers where the driver learns his patient has already been picked up. I'm not sure I'm happy because this person will be home sooner than she's supposed to be, sooner than I will be. We wasted the time coming to pick her up. On the other hand, we would've spent at least ten minutes while the driver lowered the platform, secured the patient, raised the platform, unstrapped the wheelchair to roll it into the van, secured patient in wheelchair, wheelchair to van floor, slinging straps and buckles as easily as tying shoe laces. Then, what if she were taken home before me?

The dispatcher is asking if there's a driver who can help with an ambulatory. I think the location may be close by, but the driver either isn't listening or chooses not to respond.

"Good," I uncharitably think to myself. "Maybe I'll get home before 5:30."

We must've turned onto a highway. I can't see the outline of trees, and we pick up speed. My mind drifts. I wonder if Alma has died in her wheelchair and worries no more about rides or dialysis or pain. When we get to the nursing home, will the attendants even notice that, slumped in her chair, she's stopped breathing? Will they wheel her to the dining room, where the meal is already over, and the aides begin to look for her tray and put the cold food in front of her? Then will they notice Alma has died? How would events unfold? Would I ever know about it?

The van comes to a sudden stop, almost missing the right turn, four blocks and another right turn, one more right turn, and a lurching stop at my mailbox—I've learned to recognize the lurches. My talking watch tells me it's 5:47. I sidestep around Alma's chair, failing to perceive signs of life.

The driver asks me, "You okay?" as I descend the three steps and exit.

"I'm fine," I reply. "Thanks."

The door closes behind me. I remove the mail from the mailbox and reposition my shoulder bag. I can walk the familiar driveway without my cane. In the fifty eight paces to my front door, I have time to reflect that I'm happy to be coming home hot and weary and hungry again.

An Unforgettable Amtrak Ride

Ernest A. Jones

This was a crazy idea, I thought as I sat in the empty train car, wondering if I had been forgotten. From Pasco, Washington, to Chicago, a helpful hostess frequently checked on me. After she showed me how to find the restroom, I managed on my own.

"Someone will be here soon to help you to the station and your train connection," the friendly hostess told me as she exited the car. Now I was alone.

Minutes passed, and no one came to help me. Finally gathering up my things, I found my way off the train. Stepping down into the milling crowd, I was slowly pushed backwards by the pressure of the people.

"Ernie, don't move back any more."

"What?" I asked in alarm.

"There is a drop-off going down about five feet to another track. Better move away," a female voice advised. "You're only about one foot from the edge."

I swung my white cane, checking for the pavement, and was startled to find only empty space in front of me. A little shaken, I thanked the lady who had warned me. She had been a passenger in the same train car with me. About fifteen minutes later, a man loudly stated, "There's some blind man on the train someone must go get."

"Here I am," I called out, holding up my cane.

The man grabbed my arm, hustling me to a heavily loaded cart. He ordered, "Hold on to the back of this cart."

We took off at a run. With a jolt my left shinbone found a trailer hitch extending out behind the cart. I did not dare let go of the cart to investigate the damage to my leg.

The man assisted me into a waiting train car for the next part of the ride. My round-trip ticket was from Pasco, Washington, to Cleburne, Texas, a small town, about one hour beyond Dallas. But I was put off at Dallas. Someone told me there was a mistake when my ticket was printed. My family was waiting for me in Cleburne. It took them two hours to find out where I was and come for me.

My son assisted me in boarding the train in Dallas for my trip home, since Amtrak didn't seem to care about offering that service. The ride to Chicago was uneventful but slow. We arrived two and one-half hours late to find the train I needed had left fifteen minutes earlier. Around fifty unhappy people demanding help were assisted while I sat in the chair where I had been told to wait.

About an hour later, a voice called, "There's still that blind man over there."

A friendly lady took a seat next to me, saying, "You'll have to wait until tomorrow for your train. We'll pay for your taxi fare, hotel room and meals." She helped me call my wife, Dorothy, to let her know what had happened.

The lady ushered me into a taxi for the ride to the hotel. "You alone?" the cabby asked.

"Yes, the train left me. I have to wait until tomorrow."

"I see. Do you need some company tonight? Just let me know and I'm sure I can find you someone to help you pass the night with," he said in a tone I didn't like.

After helping me into the hotel lobby, to my relief, he immediately left. In a few minutes, someone took me to my room. Stranded thousands of miles from home in the large metropolis of Chicago, I made sure my room door was locked securely. The cabby's offer bothered me—well, maybe it scared me.

The hotel workers were very friendly and helpful. The next morning, I caught a taxi (fortunately not with the same cabby) to the train station. I asked a porter where the ticket desk was. "Over there," he pointed, ignoring my white cane. My very limited vision showed me a hand movement, but I couldn't get any direction from it. To keep this story short, I'll say I was thankful I arrived at the station four hours early. It took two hours just to be directed to the ticket desk.

"I can help you," the lady said. After changing my ticket, she pointed saying, "Go over there and wait." Again, I saw her hand move, but it gave me no information I could use.

"Where?"

"Right over there where those people are," she said carelessly.

"Where? I don't see the people." I held up my white cane for her to see.

"What? You can't see them?" In a fretful voice, she called for a porter who hurried me to a chair.

By this time, I was quite upset and worried. Was I ever going to get home?

"Hi," a man said as he sat next to me. "I understand you cannot see well. Can I help you?" His voice was warm and friendly with no sign of pity, or of one who placed me in a lesser class than himself.

"I need to get on the train heading for Portland, Oregon."

"That's the train I am going on. I'll make sure you get on it, too." For the next hour we chatted, making the time pass quickly.

This wasn't the last of my troubles. An elderly lady traveling alone in our car for the handicapped became confused. She was angry, but her sentences didn't make any sense. I wasn't sure she even knew where she was. As a former nurse, I know this can happen to the elderly when they're in a strange place.

"I bet she needs the toilet," I suggested to another lady.

"I'm sure you're right. Maybe I can help her." She assisted the old lady to the restroom.

This didn't clear up the problem. The lady kept saying, "They can't treat me this way! I'm just going to walk out of here!"

Afraid she might get hurt when the train stopped, I explained the problem to the porter.

He spoke a few words to her. Returning to me, he said, "I'm going up above. If you need help, come and get me."

"Is that all the help we get?" the nice lady asked.

"I guess so," I replied. It *was* all the help we got. That night, I stayed awake. Two ladies took turns checking on the elderly woman.

The next morning, we arrived at the Pasco depot. No one came to help the poor old lady. With the coming of daylight, she seemed to be a little calmer.

I don't plan to ever again ride Amtrak alone. When I complained to Amtrak about my trip, no one seemed very concerned. I refused a free ticket, and finally, one-half of my original ticket cost was refunded.

Gotta Catch That Bus

Diane Fenton

I was in a hurry to get home from school. The first bus I rode took me to the transfer point, and the second bus was there waiting. Everyone was running for it. Since I knew the transfer point well, I crossed the street quickly. "Hop up, hop up," I told my guide dog.

As I stepped up on the curb, she went a little faster, but that wasn't quick enough for me. "Hop hop, Cloe," I begged, urging her on. She got the message and really started moving.

All of a sudden, I found myself tripping on a brick ledge and falling into a flower bed. Cloe was trying to be cautious, but I just got too close to the edge because I didn't want to miss that bus. I was embarrassed because I knew everyone saw me fall. But I jumped up laughing, in spite of skinned hands and knees.

Back on the sidewalk, I coaxed her again, "Hop hop!" I felt like I was in a race. I wanted to get home. I didn't want to wait for the next bus.

When I finally made it, hands reached out to me. "Are you okay? Are you okay?" they all wanted to know. I laughed and assured them I was fine.

A few years later, when I used a cane instead of a guide dog, I was waiting on the bench at a bus stop. Once again, I wanted to get home. The bus pulled in, "Gotta catch that bus," I thought.

I asked the people around me, "What number is this? Please, what number is this?" I couldn't afford to get on the wrong one. Everyone was in a hurry. They didn't answer.

There was only one way to find out. I would have to ask the driver myself. I could hear the engine, but because people were getting on and off the bus, I couldn't figure out which door I was near. I stuck my cane out, and found the door. Apparently the driver didn't see me, and he closed what turned out to be the back door on my cane.

The bus was leaving. I had to think fast! People were still around. "Can someone please stop the bus?" I begged, "My cane's in the door. I have to have it."

Someone managed to get the driver's attention and stop the bus. My cane was handed to me, no worse for wear, and I sat down on the bench to wait for the next bus. I hated to have to ask them to chase the bus, so I offered a big smile and lots of thanks. What else could I do? I was certainly more careful where I stuck my cane in the future.

Sometimes, even after you catch that bus, everything isn't perfect. In an effort to get out of the way one day, I stepped on a lady's toe, and you would have thought I killed her. Finally she settled down, but it embarrassed me that she made such a public scene. I've been thrown into laps when the bus lurched, thought I found an empty seat when I didn't, and missed my stop a few times, but when you want to get there from here, you "gotta catch that bus."

Dancers

DeAnna Quietwater Noriega

We are cloud dancers.
You lead and I follow,
Our steps synchronized,
Our bodies swaying to the same rhythm.

We are swept along in the current of the jet stream,
Floating lightly on the swell of an updraft,
Swooping into a glide down the slope of a down draft,
Side slipping around a gaggle of migrating geese,
Pausing a few beats to let a thunderhead rumble past.

Through fog and mist, through falling snow we whirl,
Our movements in perfect unison.
Where your paws lead,
My feet follow.
What does it matter,
If only we two hear the music?
We move together as one being.
We are cloud dancers, you and I.

Part Three
Writing to be Read

A Preview

What's the best way to choose a good nugget from your journal? Do readers like your humor, your drama, or your attention to detail? You beg, borrow, or buy the equipment and programs you need, and fine-tune until your work is marketable. When you find the right editor who can put your gem in the hands of your chosen audience, you've earned the pride you savor. That's what our workshop is all about.

Behind Our Eyes (Acrostic)

Sanford Rosenthal

Burning desire to write,
Enlightening the world, one word at a time,
Hailing each other by phone and E-mail,
Intensive effort sifting and compiling,
Need to evaluate each other's work,
Does it make the cut? Yay or nay.

Overwhelmed momentarily by critiques,
Use creative thinking,
Revise, review, re-edit.

Electronically challenged at times,
Young and old share experiences,
Effective exchanges through keyboards and synthetic speech,
Screen readers and magnifiers declare our independence.

On Organization

Marilyn Brandt Smith

I can't miss the deadline. The editor said mine
Looks a bit stale, needs current detail.
That's easy to tweak, I read more last week.
Was it in a book? Oh, where should I look?

Big bulky Braille books block my bookshelves.
Cassettes cascade from my cabinets in quantities.
Disks defeat my darndest efforts to direct them to a definite home.
Print pages pile up aplenty pleading to be perused or pitched.
A myriad of magazines and mailings mingle with my medical mysteries.
Tiny trinkets tumble when touched unless tethered together.
Souvenirs surround me, scavenged on a sweet Summer Sunday from some
unsuspecting shop.

Oh, the woes that we chose when we accumulated those
Hard to file and compile with a smile, but meanwhile,
If we try, by and by, like that pie in the sky,
We will find what we crave, for we know that we saved it,
The question is, "Where?"

Telling the Truth

Heather J. Kirk

I have a terrible habit of telling the truth, which often gets me into trouble. Each time, unsuccessfully, I vow never to succumb to its power over me again. The affliction only worsened with my late-onset Attention Deficit Disorder.

As a child, I was a model student. Now I'm incapable of sitting through a TV commercial. Okay, bad example, especially since I haven't owned a television for more than ten years. I could run a racket of selling televisions donated to me by people who think I must be impoverished. They can't believe someone would make a conscious choice not to own an object so culturally pervasive as a TV set.

What was my point? Oh yes—the ADD seems to have short-circuited the portion of my brain that provides verbal impulse control, intercepting and evaluating thoughts before they leave my mouth. I'm not mean necessarily, just not tactful. I routinely warn people about my condition, especially when prompted with, "Can I ask you a question?"

I warn, "If you don't really want the answer, it's best not to ask."

Some people forge ahead, in spite of my preparatory honesty.

"Do I look like I've gained weight?"

"Well, kind of. I mean you have, haven't you?"

Then there are dangerous phone conversations: "What are you wearing right now?"

"A bra and underwear."

"You weren't actually supposed to tell me!" he explained.

"Oh" (Note to myself: If your goal is to cool a relationship, never tell a man you are only wearing undergarments—even if it's the truth!)

At times, I feel transmuted into Jim Carey's "Liar! Liar!" character, who physically loses the ability to lie. Picture this: I exit the Post Office, after hours, with vending machine-bought stamps in hand. A beggar asks, "Do you have any change?"

I freeze and look him straight in the eye, uncharacteristically quiet as I run through the range of a "normal" person's possible excuses. He becomes nervous, and backs away slowly, still caught in my gaze. Suddenly my uniquely insensitive answer blurts forth, "Yes! But I'm gonna keep it!"

The man, in shock, begins a mantra, "Thank you, thank you, thank you …," bowing like an old Japanese caricature. "It's good to have a little change in your pocket, isn't it?" he exclaims, ecstatic at my response. I feel good too, almost ecstatic myself. Telling the truth rarely has such a positive effect.

Although my writing style can be spontaneous, the revision phase allows me to collect my thoughts, delete any uncalled for honesty, and create a desired result. Still, writing has its drawbacks. Since friends and family are familiar with my lack of experience in telling lies, my poems, essays, and even fiction often create unintended problems. I get in trouble when I write in the second or third person, because people see themselves in every "he," "she" or "you"—and I get in trouble when I write in the first person, because everyone thinks the "I" is me.

Sometimes I keep editors guessing. When they ask me for a short bio, I sit back and ask, "Are you sure you want to know?"

Beyond My Dreams

Bonnie Blose

"Bonnie, I'm so glad you're here. We have a problem, and I don't know what to do," Nancy said.

What could possibly have gone wrong, I asked myself. Books and Beyond, my show on American Council of the Blind Radio, was too new for anything really terrible to have happened. John (the editor of Books and Beyond) and Nancy (the producer) and I were in constant contact.

"What's the matter?" I asked. "What's wrong?"

Nancy said, "While John and I were talking on the phone with John Foppe, our scheduled guest for tonight, Eric showed up. I know Eric was the original guest, but when he didn't show up for the mid-week prep meeting, we thought he'd lost interest, so we scheduled another guest. Now they're both here, so what are we going to do? We can't have them both."

After thinking for just a moment, I said, "The answer is simple. I will ask Eric if we can schedule him for another date. John was willing to come in at the last minute and save us. I'm not about to disrespect his commitment."

Although I knew Eric heard what I said to Nancy, I felt the need to address him directly. "Eric, we scheduled another guest when you failed to show up for the prep meeting and didn't respond to our e-mail. I'm sorry. Could we schedule another date for you to do the show?"

I hoped I was reaching out with the proper degree of understanding, tact, and consideration for his feelings. This was certainly an embarrassingly awkward moment. I needed to keep Eric on the schedule. He was one of my first mainstream authors.

Eric said, "Don't worry. It's my fault. After all, I didn't show up after giving my word. I still want to do the show." We quickly scheduled another date.

I've been in love with words and the music of language all my life. As a very young girl, I remember finding print books irresistible, although I couldn't see them. I held them, touched them, paged through them, enjoying their texture and smell.

Do you remember the first book you read? At the age of six, I received my first books from the National Library Special Service branch in Philadelphia, eighty miles from my home. My father walked in loaded down with boxes of books just for me, some in Braille, and some on record. Christmas can come more than once a year.

A lifetime of love, discovery, and devotion began that day. It started with New Eyes for Stevie, a book about a little blind boy, and it continues today with Where the Heart Is, a romance set in Idaho Territory during the 1880s.

Books have always been my best friends. On a bad day, when I feel misunderstood, they comfort and console me filling my life with hope and leading me to laughter. In short, they entertain and explain the world to me.

During my high school years, my mother listened patiently as I told her about books she had no time to read. She was my first audience. As I sat at the kitchen table telling her about my books, neither of us had any idea how important these conversations would prove to be.

Throughout the years, I've kept book lists and talked about books with friends and strangers.

On a bitterly cold January night in 2001, I called a weekend talk show hosted by Jordan Rich on WBZ radio in Boston. Although his show covered the gamut of subjects from celebrities to psychics to car repairs, Jordan did a show twice a year all about books. People from around the country talked to him about books they loved or were looking forward to reading. I wanted to be a part of this. "Jordan, you can fulfill a dream for me."

"Oh, I can? What is it?"

"Well, you host a talk show on books, and I would like to co-host that show with you."

"Give your number to my producer. I will call you sometime this week. We'll talk about it and see what we can arrange."

True to his word, Jordan called. He asked me to be ready to discuss briefly 15 books. This was the beginning of a dream come true. It was the most exciting and intensely rewarding night of my life.

Some people dream of Hawaii or a trip to a far off exotic locale. If we're lucky, we realize our dreams. Twice a year, I relive this incredible dream with Jordan. Together, we talk to callers and answer questions. I remember the night he asked me to contribute questions and comments during an interview with an author. It was the mountaintop, the apex of all my dreams. I had traversed the heights and found my niche, but it was just the beginning of what life held in store for me.

Five years later, my best friend Nancy suggested I might want to be a guest on Marlaina Lieberg's American Council of The Blind radio show. Absolutely certain she'd be interested in having me as her guest, Nancy wrote telling Marlaina about my WBZ talk show and how deeply I loved books. Marlaina called. On a Sunday night shortly after our conversation, I was interviewed about my life, hopes, dreams, background, and my love of books. Who among us would not want to talk about ourselves? Exhilarating as the experience was, I would have been quite content to go back to life as I knew it.

Marlaina had other plans. "Have you ever thought of doing a show on ACB radio?" she asked.

"No. Do you have something in mind?"

A few weeks later, she told me what she wanted for me was my own show. She explained the chat room, the way Internet radio worked, and asked me to prepare plans for four shows.

"What am I expected to do?"

Marlaina said, "You have the show. Come up with a name. You have carte blanche to do whatever you want."

Although half of me wanted to do it, the other half of me was convinced I was crazy for entertaining such a ludicrous idea. The logical half of my nature said, "You don't have a degree in English or creative writing or communication."

"I know, but I want to do it," said the other half.

That is how Books and Beyond began.

Each week, I tape an hour show. I interview novelists, essayists, poets, Internet columnists, motivational speakers, and unique people who have had incredible life-changing experiences. These are people I would never in my wildest dreams have ever imagined meeting.

Books and Beyond could not be done without the help of my team. Nancy and I would be lost without John, our editor and friend, who does his utmost to make us look and sound our best.

This show is the culmination of a lifelong love of books. It's about a team of people who believe in and are committed to its nurture and growth. Dreams are best when they're lived and shared. Most of all, it's about the opportunity people have to share their thoughts with an audience eager to listen and to hear. Things don't always run smoothly. A microcosm of life, it's filled with moments of embarrassment, wonder, and tears.

One night, we soldiered on completing a show with Anne Varnum, in which the recording quality was poor due to a bad phone line. I had to ask her to do the show over. After waiting on tenterhooks while she checked her busy schedule, we worked out a new date. Sometimes Internet service is lost, making alternate arrangements necessary. I discovered this could happen quite suddenly, when on the very first show, my Internet connection vanished right before we began recording. Thinking quickly, I called Marlaina Lieberg, who was taping and editing the show, and told her I needed to be patched in by phone. When the show was over, Marlaina said, "You have had your initiation, your trial by fire."

On one show, I told the audience our guest the following week was a Christian author. Nancy said, "You will have to do the ending over. Do you know what you said when you introduced Nancy Swartz?"

"Oh no!" I responded. "What did I say?"

"You said Nancy was a Christian. I know you didn't mean to, but you'll have to fix it. She's Jewish."

We were able to re-record it to correct the error. This is one of the advantages of not hosting a live show. Live productions are on the drawing board, but it would be naive to think the idea doesn't make us a bit nervous.

Roger Kiser, one of the guests on the show, told us heartbreaking stories of growing up in an orphanage. At a Christmas party, a woman from the orphanage took away the present he'd been given by Santa with no explanation. Santa Claus got down on his knees to talk to him. Roger's tearful question was, "Am I a children?" He certainly was, and Santa got the gift back for him, and Santa became a hero to one little boy. There were tears in many eyes that night.

People from all over the United States and some other countries visit my show and participate by asking questions. They become part of the interview.

I try to ask authors provocative questions: "Who are your heroes?" "What's your favorite book that taught you something, and how did you use it?"

Some questions don't relate to books, but to life in general: "What do you think is the worst invention that Man has developed?"

"What could we do, or encourage society to do, to make the world a better place in which to live?"

A few authors decline to answer, because of a reluctance to offer a spontaneous response. Most do answer, however, and what they say gives us a "freeze-frame" glimpse into the heart and soul of that author. That's a prize not available in a press release or rehearsed publicity clip.

The show is an exercise in creative imperfection. It's about a group of people who believe in survival, accomplishment, achievement, and building memories to cherish.

For me, it's about the love of words, books, ideas, and my commitment to all of them. Imagine reading a book one afternoon and being able to ask its author the same evening why he had a character do what he did, or how he decided on the ending.

Why does it work so well? I've asked myself countless times. The simple answer is, I really don't know. Looking back, I had the love, commitment, and desire, and I was given a tremendous opportunity. I believed in a dream and the possibilities inherent in it.

Come join our experience Wednesday nights at 8:00 P.M. Eastern in the Politics room at www.acbradio.org.

You Can't Skip the Scary Stuff

Marilyn Brandt Smith and Bonnie Blose

"What is something you did which, given the chance to repeat, you would not do again?" That was one of the questions in a voicemail phone group to which Bonnie and I belonged. We had become friends in a writers' group on the Philmore system a few months earlier. One December morning with the 3:00 AM courage of a wide-awake night, Bonnie answered that question.

"I never tell this story to strangers," she began. "This came from a Bonnie you don't know. I was ignored, almost undermined, by the people I moved to Ohio to share my life with. Being blind, and being interested in cultural and educational things like books and informative radio and TV shows, I didn't fit into their world. They didn't talk to me on the phone, and they didn't listen when I asked for simple courtesies like not blocking my path with their cars always parked in front of our house.

"I suppose I had been subconsciously waiting for a defining moment, and it came one Sunday morning when I was home alone. I found another one of those cars blocking my way. It was just a little thing, we weren't expecting company who would need to park in that spot, but I guess you could say the dam broke. I started out by kicking the car. Then I beat on it and scratched it. The adrenalin was pumping, the rage had to go somewhere. I went into the house and found the toolbox. What I couldn't do with my hands, I did with a hammer. Did I care about watchers? No! Did I care what happened later? Not at all. Scratches became scars and dents became valleys. Finally satisfied, I went inside, and waited for the other shoe to drop.

Bonnie almost whispered, "It never did. Did I win? Did they finally get the message that I was a voice to be dealt with? I felt better, of course, later I felt guilty or at least amazed, that I let my anger and frustration lead me to a violent solution.

"Nothing was ever said at the time, but years later, I learned it was a vintage collectable from the 60's, being restored by a close family member. It cost thousands to repair. My sister-in-law told me much later that she admired and respected me. I suspect that my little temper tantrum might have had something to do with that. Although I didn't make any drastic changes at that time, I think I understood that there was an unmeasured strength somewhere inside me. If push came to shove, as it did later, I subconsciously knew that there was a Bonnie who could cope. I just had to find her."

A few months later, I was reminiscing with Bonnie about that story. "It's hard to picture this young blind woman taking a hammer to some jock's prize auto like that, especially knowing you as a mature, problem-solving, sensible woman of today. You've had quite a life."

"By the way," she laughed, "did you get those essays I E-mailed you?"

What she really wanted to know was whether I had read them. I needed that nudge, and when I read them, I couldn't wait to get back to her with my comments.

"Your essays are thought-provoking," I commented, "You realize what you're doing is journaling? Of course, you don't have dates and times, and everything isn't exactly sequential, but I might feel an autobiography brewing here."

"Jordan has hinted at that," Bonnie told me, "when we're just chatting before or after the talk show we do together about books. But talk to me some more about journaling. Should I be doing that?"

"Not if essays work better for you," I told her. "Just save everything. You never know when it's all going to gel, and you want to be ready. You can get editorial help so you don't have to worry about every little punctuation mark or simple word choice."

"But who would want to read it, and who would publish an autobiography about someone they've never heard of?"

"You never know," I told her. "You have a following from Jordan's show on WBZ, and from your own listeners on ACB Radio. You have an unusual perspective from growing up in Pennsylvania Dutch country."

"Oh, those V's and W's," she laughed, "I worked at getting rid of that accent. My brother still has a lot of it."

"You had the hard-working parents, the large extended family, and the small town that didn't know much about blindness. You wrote about being fascinated by the phone and the radio. That essay about animals was good, but we need specific references to the kitty or puppy or farm animals you knew as a child, and how you came full circle, and have two adorable cats today. We don't feel your love if you don't talk about rubbing them, feeding them, and worrying about them. I loved the way you talked about sneaking extra phone calls with a little help from your mother. Anything that let you reach beyond your close-knit world grabbed your attention."

"I think that's why I was so captivated by my aunt," Bonnie explained. "In her own frivolous way she expanded my horizons beyond our world. She was flamboyant, daring, and paid special attention to me. I almost lost sight of how valuable my mother was in my life. Aunt Gloria was my heroine for quite a while."

"When you write it, you need to show us things your aunt did that your parents never would have done. Show us what drew you to her: movies, clothes, travel, humor. You said your mother didn't act jealous, and didn't protest your attachment to her?"

"She waited it out. I think she knew I needed to see another view of the world to appreciate my own world better. When the new wore off, I could see that stability mattered. Unfortunately, I lost my mother when I was twenty-one, so I never got a chance to show her, as an adult, how much I appreciated her letting me learn that lesson. If she had lectured, I would have misunderstood her motives. And speaking of misunderstandings, did I ever tell you about the money on the back porch?"

"I'm all ears," I answered.

"My twin brother found a bag of money on our back porch. It was over a thousand dollars, way too much to have been there. We couldn't figure out where it came from. Finally, my mother had to explain. She and George, a friend who was like an uncle, and who was losing his vision, were saving money secretly for the operation they believed would one day be available to restore my sight. There were many material things our family could have used, and it was a sacrifice based on the truest, deepest, and most unselfish kind of love. But I was a teenager without any confidence or self-esteem, and I misread it. I thought it meant they didn't love me the way I was, and were willing to spend money so I could meet their standards. It hurt my feelings, and of course, it hurt them that I had to find out about it at the wrong time."

"Bonnie, you are so good at looking back and seeing the little things that made big impressions on your life. That will help you write with depth. You write about a classmate who received all the attention and did everything right."

"I never thought I could equal her. Everyone held me up to her. The comparison frightened me and made me feel inadequate. Sure, we were both blind, but we didn't have the same abilities and skills. Books gave me a broader world to explore for fun or for escape."

"Did you stay friends, or was it a constant cat fight? You could show us some dialog. We'd get a better picture of the teen-aged Bonnie. Also, we need to see more of you as a young adult if you decide to write an autobiography. Did you continue to read?"

"Other endeavors slowed me down a little, and Braille and books on record were hard to wag around, but yes, I read. I guess I'd have to think back to the jobs I tried to get, my days in college, and the young men I corresponded with or dated."

"You'd also have to share experiences from your long-term relationship, and about being a blind mom with a sighted son. You've made them a part of your recent essays. You've told us about the seizure that almost killed you, the fire when you lost everything you had ..."

"What made that so devastating," Bonnie sighed, "was that I had been sitting in the room with all my music and books the afternoon before, thinking how lucky I was to have it all. My next vivid memory is the tug in the middle of my sleep, 'Bonnie, we have to get out, we're on fire, it's bad!' he said. I just froze. I was paralyzed. Half asleep, he helped me get out of there. If Bill hadn't been there, I wouldn't be here. An electrical short, who could have known? We stayed busy figuring out where to live, how to get clothing and food, and help Kevin deal with this traumatic change in our lives."

"I'm not sure you ever completely recover or forget the sirens, the shivering cold, going back to the empty lot and smelling the smoke where the house used to be," Bonnie continued. "Music haunted me for years. I didn't want to let myself love it again. Finally my best friend helped me get past my repression, and music is a big part of my life now. The reason you don't see anything in my essays about some of the earlier years is that everything was lost in the fire. I didn't have the courage or the energy to put all my memories and conclusions together again."

"When you write your book, you'll have a chance to explain things in greater detail than you can in an essay. You did a good job with the smoke and the need to make peace with the fact that your house was gone, but we could use a little more. It would help us feel your loss if you mentioned specifics on the day before the fire—your Dan Fogelberg collection, the Braille magazines you were looking forward to reading, specific books you loved. Most of us have never been through anything like that. The morbid curiosity in us all makes us want to know the details. How long did you stay around and watch, were you able to save anything at all, did you have any animals?"

Bonnie was silent. I knew I had touched a nerve, so I moved on to another topic. "I read what you wrote about losing your partner, and your son losing his father."

"I couldn't help but compare my son's loss with that of Will Reeve after he lost both his parents. My son was devastated, but no matter how many apparent advantages Christopher and Dana Reeve's son had over mine, the pain is the same. Money won't buy relief from loss. Will received national attention. Kevin had family and community sympathy. But maybe the Reeve boy would have preferred not to be the focus of public attention."

"Do you think you're a stronger woman after what you've been through?" I asked.

"I know that I am. I had stayed at the shallow end during most of my adult years, reasonably comfortable with my life. Suddenly, I was forced to face debts with no salary to pay them. I was angry with God. I had a son to finish rearing, and no one to help me make decisions."

"Books preserved my sanity. I took an interest in preparing talks for the congregation at church, and became a lay speaker. That focus has taken me visiting to many churches outside my area. I had something to contribute to the world."

"Then the opportunity to co-host a show on books came along?" I asked.

"Yes, I still love doing that show. When I interview an author, I like to try to find out what they like to read, and what made them make a career of writing."

"You have some funny thoughts about spam, voicemail systems, and technology. You'll have to let that humor come through."

"Yes," she laughed. "People thought I was crazy when I complained about not getting any spam. That was when I was new to computers."

"Do you embrace the new ways of doing things?"

"I have to," she stated. "Blind people have at least six format choices for reading material, and we read newspapers by phone through the National Federation of the Blind News Line. If you're going to contribute or produce something you want to share with the world today, it has to be in a format they are likely to access. I still read Braille books to friends on the phone, and I moderate an 'Author a Day' group on the Philmore voicemail system to increase readers' knowledge and curiosity about books and authors."

"You wrote about your best friend's health issues."

"I haven't written much about it, because I think that's really Nancy's story. I was there when she needed me through chemotherapy and beyond."

"Yes, I remember talking to you around Thanksgiving when it was 'touch and go.' You may very well have saved her life."

"No one knew," she said, "her resistance was so low. I only knew she had to get help. I did what any best friend would have done."

"You can make Nancy's story come alive from your perspective without looking like you're a glory seeker. Show us your efforts to find Nancy's dad, and to notify her friend in town who cared for her guide dog and visited her in the hospital every day. Let us feel your frustration when Nancy couldn't talk, and you couldn't get information from the nurses. We need to be able to touch your compassion."

"I was so scared of losing her," Bonnie acknowledged. "Doing my show without her just wouldn't be the same."

"You write about your dreams too, I assume you have some new ones?"

"I believe dreams are often our expectations for ourselves. They show us the potential, the light, and the magic. Reality tests our dreams at times, and we have to push the envelope. Risk is valuable. I want to take my interviewing, speaking, and love of books as far as I can."

"Just be sure you write it all down," I reminded. "Share your story, it might plant a seed or move somebody's mountain. You just never know."

Paper Trained

Nancy Scott

I've had my nose rubbed
in clichés I've left
on the carpet
been punished for puddles
of prepositions even
when I sneaked them in corners
where lines meet.

The masters praise meaning,
music and mystery centered
on paper, not smelling
too much of first person,
offered for strokes and being
called by name.

I'm famous in my neighborhood
till the next mad-dash failure
when I am banished again
from the library and sent
to the cellar with an old
bone to chew on.

Keeping an Artist's Journal

Nancy Scott

Do you want to know yourself better as an artist? Do you understand your unique motivations? Do you know which alternative techniques work for you? Try an artist's journal.

I am a writer. Much of what I say here, though, can be applied to any artistic form.

By 1993, I wanted to write five hours per week. Not tracking my creative time allowed me to lie to myself. I also wondered what inspired and encouraged my art.

From the beginning, my journal had rules. I used a 5 x 8-inch notebook, so no long entries. (I kept a larger journal for life ramblings.) Entries were weekly (Sunday through Saturday). I noted where ideas came from, what I was doing when I became inspired, how much time I worked and on what specific projects.

June 26 to July 3, 1993: Rough drafted Vignettes of Dying Mother 2 hours. Idea from possible market Poets and Writers©. 5 hours presentation for Lions. Can the speech also be an article?

I listed books I liked, what times of day were most energized for work, the environments I preferred, what experiments I tried, and landmark acceptances or rejections.

After six months, I read it back and found working patterns. Journals show what you've completed, what you've started, and what you've ignored. And you can't lie to yourself.

October 6 to 12, 1996: Class didn't like my poem May Mittens. Go deeper. Revise half hour. Chased manuscripts by letter that have been out for more than six months 1 hour. Two hundred copies of my first chapbook delivered Friday. Scary. David and I celebrated with Irish coffee at Pearly Baker's. The book is real.

August 30 to September 5, 1998: Sandy's birthday card modified published in the Express Times. My first local newspaper column. Good advocacy about a wheelchair-user and a blind person. Comments from friends, people on the bus and even a cashier at Weis'. Shift of Weather 2 hours. Will submit for second newspaper essay? I am not invisible. I am not just a wacky blind person. People here now know I am a writer. The headshot they published must look like me.

March 21 to 28, 1999: This feels like writer's block. Half hour looking through rough draft poetry for ideas at 6 A.M.

In 2001, I began keeping the artist's journal in my Braille 'n Speak. Now, I can find things with key words. I still reread the journal at least once a year.

July 22 to 28, 2001: Linda is a gifted keyboard player and singer. What would it be like to be a very talented blind person? Would I trade my broader mediocrity? Of course, I only see her gift and not her struggle. I sang for her and it was fun. Music is fun for me and writing is serious art.

August 18 to 24, 2002: Bent Angels half hour. Furniture moved 23rd so no time to write. Will I be able to write in my new apartment?

September 1 to 7, 2002: Found far benches behind the building. So here I am ready to eavesdrop, but there's just machinery making the weird noises and wind chimes. Wrote about my bench. Moving Around 2 hours.

February 16 to 22, 2003: Radio commentary essays edited for local NPR station Roses, Heatwave, Feeling Fifty, and Plural of Rhinoceros 3 hours. I still don't read well in studio. Using Braille 'n Speak at writers' workshop was odd. I wanted to stop and listen like I could if I were taking notes with a tape recorder. I can write so much faster than people with pens, but I make too much noise and feel too visible. Also, I can't read my work back in the workshop. (No Braille display.) I know people who listen with headphones and speak work back, but I can't.

April 27 to May 3, 2003: Kathy says I can't have the necklace engraved with 300 bylines and counting yet because I'm only at 298. What is my obsession with 300 published pieces? I barely noticed 200. Perhaps I will not make 400?

May 18 to 24, 2003: My brother Mark died in his sleep this week. I knew something was wrong when I didn't hear from him over the weekend and he didn't answer his phone when I repeatedly called. Friday night, he called saying he was cold, but I know now, his building still had heat. The day after Mark's official death, May 20, my radio essay My Parents' Gratitude List ran. It is byline 300. Perhaps Mark or other dead relatives nudged. It must mean I should keep writing. I need reasons and deadlines. Being around other artists and reading others' work gets me working. Potential markets get me working. Morning, sunshine, chirping birds and just enough isolation help. Moving and outside are necessary, too. I am the last of my family left here. I wrote a lot based on Mark's humor. Will I find things to write about now?

September 7 to 13, 2003: Is Bad Diet; Good Diet real writing or ego? 2 hours. Strange to do very long piece in journal form and think it could be published. I need this intimate writing just now. Radio interview for my essay in Cup of Comfort for Women was too much talk about blind people stuff and not enough author stuff. My fault. Practiced for Cup of Comfort reading and wrote intros. 2 hours. Don't have enough balance to wear heels anymore.

May 30 to June 5, 2004: Weeding Braille files. What I need to keep is changing. Why am I still keeping the old procedure manual we wrote for our National Federation of the Blind chapter, and the resource list for the NFB Writers' Division from the early 1980's? Will anyone even remember that I edited all those cassettes?

Good practice though. Don't want to work; just want to plan it. I need too much help from sighted people. Need to learn more technology? Barbara Sher goals not helping. Connections reading audience around ten people felt very labored. But questions afterwards were good. Write a poem a day for a week.

December 12 to 18, 2004: I want security, divinity, to make a difference, and respect from some people. Maybe a book manuscript of radio essays. I'm also collecting the long essays calling that book The Clay Never Hardens. I'm not writing new stuff, although people like this year's Christmas card.

March 27 to April 2, 2005: Sent poetry chapbook Fourth Person Singular for contest. Listening essay 1 hour. Art is not lonely; it is being very present. Art keeps me from abandoning myself. Dorot University telephone poetry class new semester. Revising radio reading service volunteer handbook 3 hours and it's different having to edit with other people. Put six notebooks of clips into big safety deposit box along with list of what I've published. I need tangible accomplishments. No one can take or misjudge them away.

February 26 to March 4, 2006: Major rent increase. I must make more money and work smarter. Kathy has convinced me to do a reading and a writing ideas workshop for Girls' Night Out. They'll pay me. I've never done a workshop, but talking it through with Debbie has helped me decide how and what I'll present. Kathy will print hand-outs and go with me. Kathy thinks I can do this. Can I teach anything?

March 26 to April 1, 2006: 15 people at my workshop with almost no publicity by the promoters! It felt fun and energized. I think they liked it. Do it again someday? $100 was my stipend. Next time, need contract in writing and amount determined ahead of time.

July 2 to 8, 2006: Maryanne will page-format my poetry chapbook for self-publishing. It's now called Leveling the Spin and has 19 poems. Computersmith Enterprises will convert my home-recorded cassette of Leveling to cd, though I do not read well for microphones. I'm tired of waiting for the next book. And all this help showing up means it is meant to happen.

December 10 to 16, 2006: Leveling the Spin has new cover and Kathy and I have proofed, please God, for the last time. I've been slow doing audio but it should be finished soon. Next, I will work on an essay collection. For the year: 19 bylines and 1 performance, 5 mainstream and 14 disability, 15 prose and 4 poems, not enough money as usual (just under $300) but 365 bylines altogether. Amazing that my first piece was published in 1983. Next year, I'm finally getting a poem in Kaleidoscope after trying for five years. And I'm reading my Ice Poems on January 7 as part of a college art exhibit. 3 hours on Keeping an Artist's Journal but it's too long. Some things never change.

Fill in the Blanks

Nancy Scott

Which word do I hear?
"Tongue, time, tone."
Which word is really there?
I listen again through the hiss.
Rewind. Find that line again.
I still don't know
and review the whole, strain
for diction, for meaning,
my ear even nearer to the machine.

Which word do I like?
That's how I'll decide.
Cast aside recorded craft
in favor of the magic
to change the poet's language
into mine.

Farewell Mon Ami

Tanja Heidmann

This poem is dedicated to a dictionary program I ran on my PC. The French "Mon Ami" translates to "My Friend." With Windows XP, alas, my friend cannot be used. I was so distraught that I was inspired to pay tribute to this excellent writing tool.

You were my best friend, and you always helped me out.
When I was with you, there was never any doubt.
You know I really love you, but things are at an end.
So now I have to tell you, "Farewell Mon Ami."

I was so happy when a friend introduced me to you.
I could not believe that all my dreams had come true.
You were the solution for all I have ever asked.
But now I have to tell you, "Farewell Mon Ami."

When problems were difficult you were always by my side.
I thought I couldn't solve them no matter how I tried.
There were moments when I thought I just could not go on,
but with you, Mon Ami, I was never alone.

I can't imagine how life without you will be.
There's just something missing and there's no good poetry
to describe all the feelings I will always have for you,
still I have to tell you, Farewell Mon Ami."

I'll always keep you with me. No, I'll never let you go,
because I'm hoping that someday someone will know
what to do to make our relationship grow again.
But now I have to tell you, "Farewell Mon Ami."

Squashed Baby Pigs

Writing Childhood Memories

Tara Arlene Innmon

In the depths of our hearts, we often feel tugs from the old and the young that make us appreciate the past and the present. The experiences of my life shaped me into who I am now. I want to go back into my childhood and bring back that little girl and write her stories in her voice. I also want to include the adult I am now who thinks she has learned some lessons.

I sit down to write this essay, but little Arlene, the child I was, tugs at my arm. Little Arlene intrudes into the writing whenever I, the adult, write about her. Even now she complains, saying, "Why do you have to write an essay? What the heck is that?"

I tell her, "I'll get back to you as soon as I'm done. It won't be long."

She wraps her arms around her chest and glares at me. "You'd better tell it right," she warns.

As a child I followed my mother into her garden, down to the basement, and in her kitchen. I told her about the things that interested me: what someone said in school, what happened on TV, or what one of my brothers just did. I knew she wasn't listening. I vowed that when I had my own children I would sit down, face them, and really listen to them.

I wasn't able to do that. Food had to be cooked and dishes had to be done. My son's chattering exhausted me. He persisted in telling me stories just as I had told my mother. That child's voice has to come out and eventually find a listener.

The child's voice is not especially reliable, but does it matter? As I followed my mother around the house telling her the stories of the things I did when I was out in the world and away from her, I embellished my stories to see if she would turn around and look at me and say, "Really?" with interest in her eyes rather than the bored, tired look I usually saw. Once I got caught.

I was leaning against the sink in the crowded kitchen, with its green linoleum, and my mother was stirring something in a pot on the stove. I really wasn't supposed to be in there. Maybe she would like to hear about what happened during the week I'd been with Becky, the neighbor girl, on her grandparent's farm in Montevideo? It was the only time I'd been on a farm, and I loved it. My career choice at the time was to marry a farmer and have many kids and play with them in the barn and up the trees in the woods. My mother had grown up on a farm and looked bored and distracted as usual, as I spoke. What could I say to make the story more interesting? She had told me before that sometimes a mother pig would roll over and crush her babies.

"A mother pig had babies."

"Oh?" she said looking bored at the clock hanging on the greasy wall in front of her.

"Yeah, and the mother was really huge and she turned to her other side and some of the cute pink babies got killt"

She turned and looked at me, "Really? That happened at our farm, too. How many were killed?"

My heart pounded. She actually listened to me. "She had a lotta babies, I don't know how many, but three of them were squashed flat!"

"That sounds terrible."

"Oh it was. I cried, but Becky didn't. She said she's seen that before."

Later that day, Becky came over to see if I could play. My mother said, "Becky, I heard about the baby pigs that were killed when the mother rolled over them. That's too bad."

Becky told her, "That didn't happen." They both turned and looked at my red face.

When I told the story that way, I saw the squashed pigs, and I still can. The ten and under child experiences fantasy the same as the "real" event. The adult reliving memories sometimes slips into the fantasy she may have experienced as a child.

Once at a workshop on writing from movement, we did an exercise that involved lying still and then moving as the body directed. I wiggled my feet, but suddenly, Arlene was wiggling my feet. She said, "Memories come from wiggling feet, barefoot berries and dandelion stickers." We were in my grandmother's backyard. At the time, I was losing vision from glaucoma and couldn't see my handwriting, so I used a tape recorder to write. I turned on the recorder, but before I could get it all down, she ducked under the willow and said, "Willows cover, hiding, peeking out." I kept wiggling my feet to keep her going, and crawled under the willow branches to join her. She popped out again saying, "Next to berries, luscious berries, poisonous to birds!" She ducked in and bounced out again and again in delight.

With my cumbersome adult body and tape recorder buttons, I tried to keep up, her words screaming through the tangled yard. I shaped those words into a poem, but how much changed going through my adult vocal cords and vocabulary? How much did I forget, she spoke so fast, and how much did I inadvertently direct with my knowledge about her future?

As a writer in the first memoir draft, I let the child have her way, and I write what she says in my mind. Her world is small, she only partially understands things outside herself and she doesn't know the future. I know the troubles she will get herself into, and I squeal, "Aha!" as connections are made. I write down these nuggets of insight as they occur. They get stuck in between the child's words, jarring a reader and confusing him as to which narrator is speaking, the child or the adult. Weeding out the adult voice from the child's and deciding when to allow the adult to have her say, without interrupting the flow, becomes the baffling job of revision.

My mother, the adult who couldn't listen well to me, is now a part of my adult self. Not only couldn't I listen to my children, but also I am unable to listen well to little Arlene every time she speaks.

When the child hunches over, looks down at her tightly fisted hands, and mumbles, "I don't want to remember this," the writing gets hard. Who is speaking? Is it little Arlene, my fantasy-writing assistant, or the grown-up Arlene who knows how it will all turn out?

And what about the reliability of the adult voice? What can I say about my making things up now as an adult? I sanction the adding of details of events and conversations I don't remember as a necessity for the sake of creating an interesting story. I don't squash pigs anymore, but my mother is dead and I'm still looking for a reader to turn and look at me and say "Really?" with interest. Besides my uncanny ability to be inventive, I also am trying to remember things that happened almost fifty years ago. Now I look at those vague memories through the filter of therapy and the experience of raising my own children, perhaps remembering their childhood voice more than my own. Perhaps my own children are reflected in little Arlene's proddings.

And what about the squashed pigs? If I stretch the metaphor as I stretch the truth I can talk about how my mother squashed little Arlene's voice and, yes, her spirit, flattened her so she could grow up, and be less annoying to other adults.

I came out of school believing I couldn't write. The Scandinavian culture in which I was raised in the Midwest tended to have that effect on children—preferring silence and work to self-expression and creativity. "Flattened, kilt," the writer's voice in me could only whimper out a poem or two for many years, and silently scribble its complaints in diaries, never to be shared.

What did this squashing do to the child's perception of self and stored memories? This sounds bitter and hopeless. I am not. I'm excited and hopeful about my writing. I admit, the more I write the more thinly I stretch the "creative" in "creative nonfiction." I started out with the naive belief I would only write what I truly remembered. That's not fun and not interesting to read. I want to let both the child's and the adult's voice fly like a hot-air balloon set free. Then, during revision, I can pull those voices back in again, deciding what stays and what doesn't.

My goal is for the child and her feelings to be understood and appreciated. I've learned my lesson about getting caught in the act of a clear lie. If little Arlene and I sometimes see those squashed baby pigs in our minds' eye, we are very careful about sharing it.

PART FOUR
Leveling the Field

A Preview

Are we all really created equal? What happens when we realize the smooth terrain is getting bumpy? We don't have all the tools we need, and no one can remove all the barriers. Race, geography, gender, and disability receive support from advocacy groups and government programs. But we don't always have time to wait for promises. Sometimes we take picks and shovels in-hand and demonstrate our determination. Our success gives us confidence, encourages others, and establishes our value to society in a way no one can deny.

Who Needs Help?

Janet Schmidt

"Money, money, money," is the answer to the question, "Why would a visually impaired woman work as a research assistant?" I tried being a waitress once. I quickly learned customers didn't like wearing their coffee. Being a cashier or sales person wasn't an option. When you can't see two feet in front of your nose, working as a restaurant hostess is definitely not a reasonable pursuit.

With the aid of technology and volunteer eyes, being a research assistant was within the realm of possibility. Meaning, I could probably do the job if I cut my sleep back to four hours a night and placed my social life on hold.

Consequently, while earning my Certificate of Advanced Graduate Study in School Psychology at the University of Massachusetts in Boston, I worked as a graduate research assistant for the chair of the department.

"Janet, you have to go with the volunteer to the library. A volunteer doesn't do the student's work. And you need to learn how to use the library," the secretary at the Disabled Students Center informed me in a superior, haughty voice. Well toots, I was using the library before you were born.

Being severely visually disabled, I often used the services of a sighted volunteer or paid someone to help me with my library research. The Disabled Students Center at UMass was my resource for volunteer assistance. A request for help had to be placed through the center's secretary. Now there was a woman who knew her power and used it.

I wanted a volunteer to locate journals on a specific topic using the Psychological Abstracts. Then pull those journals from the stacks for me. My reasoning: If someone else did the leg work, I'd have more time to write up the results of the research. As Ben Matlock was wont to say, "Ain't nothing easy."

Quite often, those very people who are supposed to provide assistance to the disabled make things more difficult—I guess they think it's for our own good. Keeping my sights on my goal, which was to earn my CAGS, I determined not to alienate the seemingly diabolical secretary. It would only impede getting the assistance I needed, so I jumped through her hoops.

This same wonderfully benevolent woman was also the overseer of the permission forms professors filled out for special accommodations for a disabled student to take exams. One of my professors chose to use his own format. Handing it to the "queen," I was informed, "I can't accept this. It isn't on the correct form."

"The professor told me he wasn't going to use the other form."

"Well, Janet, when you get to be as old as I am and you have a child, you won't let a professor push you around."

"I don't argue with graduate school professors." And I'm old enough to be your mother.

"Oh, I thought you were an undergraduate." Just then the director came out of his office and told her the professor's format was acceptable. Graciously the secretary grabbed the paper from her desk. Stomping over to the file cabinet she yanked open a drawer, thrusting the document into it, she slammed the drawer.

The secretary assigned a volunteer whom I will call Armand. We met in the library lobby in front of the elevators. When we arrived in the reference section of the library, I took him to the Psychological Abstracts section. I told him which years of the tomes to pull. We seated ourselves at a table. As he leafed through the abstracts reading the names and locations of the journal citations, I wrote down the ones I wanted. During this process, he never removed his left hand from his jacket pocket, making it rather awkward for him to turn pages. That's strange. Why doesn't he use both hands? I kept this question to myself.

When we finished perusing the abstracts, Armand and I went to the stacks to find the journals I required. He retrieved them using only his right hand, placing them in a neat pile on the shelf. At last the cloud of denseness lifted from my brain. Oh, for crying out loud now I get it. I asked, "Do you want me to carry the journals?"

"No, I can do it." He scooped them up in his right hand, tucking them in the crook of his right arm. I don't remember how we managed the elevator. He escorted me to the adaptive computer lab for disabled students. I used the specialized, low-vision equipment to read the journals and entered my notes into a computer that enlarged the print on the monitor. Literally speaking, I never saw Armand again.

The next time I needed volunteer assistance, I placed my request with the same personable secretary. She assured me she would find someone to help me. The day I required the help, I called to confirm the time to meet the volunteer. "Janet, I haven't been able to find anyone to help you because of finals study days." I may have groveled. I really wanted the help. Somewhat later she called back, "Janet, Wheeler will help you." He happened to be the director of the Disabled Students Center. How did I rate the big gun?

We met in the library lobby and proceeded to the reference room. I hadn't a clue about Wheeler's disability. I observed a very long straw protruding from the top of a large plastic container, from which he often sipped. The container was attached to his wheelchair arm. I soon discovered he had minimal use of his hands. Wheeler operated his wheelchair with a joystick. This would have to be a real team effort.

Leading him to where the psychological abstracts were shelved, I told him which volumes I wanted. He scanned the tomes, "Janet, on the third shelf start at the left and count over to the fifth volume. Pull it out and place it on my lap." After this little exercise, we discovered the only surface high enough to accommodate his wheelchair was the end of the reference librarian's desk in the center of the room.

The next obstacle was to figure out how we could access the written material—the teamwork was better than a three-legged race. I propped the books up so Wheeler could read them. He perused the index, telling me what page to turn to giving me some sense as to where to open the book. I turned pages until Wheeler told me to stop. He read the abstract to me. If it was a useful article for my research paper, I would note the information necessary to locate the journal in the stacks.

I need a cigarette right now. This is taking forever. Having not yet quit smoking, my body cried urgently for nicotine. "Wheeler, I have to take a break."

"I do, too." He pushed some levers on his chair and proceeded to become horizontal. Our unusual behavior gave me the feeling we were gathering quite an audience.

Standing on the steps of the library consuming the smoke and nicotine of multiple cigarettes, I felt panicky. I'm never going to finish my research. This whole process with Wheeler is taking too long. But I have to. I will.

Wheeler and his chair became upright upon my return. We went to the stacks. I walked and he rolled between the shelves. I read the name of each journal on my list. Wheeler scanned the shelves. We went back to the counting game: "Janet, go up to the top shelf, count over three journals from the left, pull that journal and place it on my lap."

"Okay."

We finished. He accompanied me with his lap full of journals to the adaptive computer lab. After placing the books in my work area, I escorted him to the library lobby because he couldn't press the elevator buttons. Chivalry of the feminine version certainly isn't dead yet. Is this what they mean by the saying, "You scratch my back, I'll scratch yours"—figuratively speaking of course?

Brainerd entered my life when I took my first summer course. Summer programs are so short and intensive I knew I had to find some reliable, consistent visual assistance after my initial experience of a no-show from one of the Disabled Students Center paid aides who was supposed to help me photocopy some materials that couldn't be removed from the library reserve area. He gave me a lame excuse—no pun intended—when I called the center to ask him why he hadn't shown up. I nearly burst into tears, his attitude was so flippant. How on earth was I going to make it through the course with this kind of non-help? I wanted to tell him to haul his butt over to the library, but I didn't.

I discussed my difficulty in getting help for my library research with the Adaptive Computer Lab director. "I'm willing to pay someone."

"Why don't you ask Brainerd if he has the time?" With a decided lack of enthusiasm, speaking in a lethargic manner, he agreed to take on the job.

After he left for the day, the lab director enlightened me as to his behavior. An auto accident caused severe right brain damage during his second year at college, where he'd been majoring in computer science. A metal plate was surgically implanted in his right hemisphere. Neurological damage caused his thought processes and verbal responses to slow considerably. Some had been deleted. Brainerd's vocational rehabilitation counselor asked if he could spend time in the lab as a volunteer. Perhaps he could use what computer skills remained to assist the disabled students. The counselor didn't know what else to do with him.

I arranged to meet Brainerd several days a week at the lab in the early morning. The first day when he arrived I said, "We are going to work in the library."

"Okay," he said. After hanging up his jacket he sat down.

Brainerd's specific neurological idiosyncrasies dictated the breaking down of every task into simple one-step directions. He plodded from one step to another. I relearned the meaning of the oxymoron, "less is more." I slowed down giving him time to process directions.

All right, next step, "Brainerd, come on let's go to the library right now." We sauntered to the elevator. He moved about as quickly as the fabled tortoise.

At least the psychological abstracts had finally been computerized. The glitch was they were not yet available in a low-vision accessible format.

Brainerd entered my topic, Soft Neurological Signs. I hoped he wasn't offended by this research. I really, really needed his help. As each abstract appeared on the monitor, he read it to me and I decided whether the journal article it referred to was useful. "Okay, Brainerd please read it slowly so I can write it down."

"Oh, I can print out the information." Where did that bit of knowledge come from?

The following day was my all time favorite: "Brainerd, let's go up to the stacks and get started." We did. At one point, we came to the end of a row of shelves abutting a railing. Brainerd said, "This is the end of the row. The journal isn't here." Leaning on the railing, he looked down on the floor below.

Next step, "Brainerd, turn around, we are going to return to the aisle and move down a row." He hopped up like a rabbit turning to face me at the same time. Retracing our steps to the aisle we moved on to the next row. He caught on.

Brainerd suggested, "We can photocopy the articles instead of carrying all of the journals to the lab." Wow! Where did that come from?

"Is there a copier nearby?"

Brainerd said, "Yes," remaining where he was. Oh, yes, I needed to tell him the next step.

"Brainerd, take me to the photocopy machine." He did and just stood there. "Brainerd, where do I insert the money?"

"You don't do it that way." And he just stood there.

"Brainerd, what do we need to operate the machine?"

"You need a card."

"Where do I get the card?"

"From a machine." I think I'm going to scream.

"Brainerd, where is the machine?"

"Over there."

"Please take me to the machine and show me how to use it?" Now brace yourself.

Brainerd told me we needed to count the number of pages we would be copying. Then I had to purchase a card to use in the machine covering the exact amount of copies we were going to make. How had he managed to retain this bit of information when so much stored mental information had been destroyed? After counting the pages he led me to the card machine.

"Brainerd, what do we do now?"

"Put the money in the slot."

"Brainerd, how much?"

"Two dollars."

"Brainerd, I only have large bills."

He said, "They'll change your money at the lobby desk."

"Brainerd, I don't want to go all of the way down there. You know what the elevators are like. Do you have two dollars?"

"Yes."

"Would you please loan me the two dollars?"

"I need them for the bus fare to get home."

"I will pay you back. When we go down to the lab, we'll stop in the lobby. I'll get change."

"Okay." He just stood there. Now I am going to scream.

"Brainerd, please put the money in the machine and get the card for me. I cannot see the directions." After he got the card, we returned to the photocopier. He stood there. "Please make the copies I need. I can't see how to operate the machine." Finally, we returned to the lab with the photocopies.

Brainerd used a minimal amount of words to communicate. He didn't go beyond a concrete answer. Talking on the phone with him was quite an experience.

"Hello, Brainerd, this is Janet."

"Hello." Silence.

"You worked for me last summer at UMass." Pause. Silence. "Would you be able to do it this summer?"

"Yes."

"Brainerd, can you meet me at the lab on Monday at eight o'clock?"

"No."

"When can you meet me?"

"The first bus leaves here at eight o'clock."

"When does it get to UMass?"

"8:30."

"Brainerd, will you meet me at the lab at 8:30?"
"Yes."
"Okay, I'll see you on Monday at 8:30."
"Good bye."
"Good bye."

Mirrors, Memory and Madness

Mixed Genre—Prosetry

Andrea Pulcini

Seeing my reflection in the glass partition
separating the nurses' station from the patients,
pacing back and forth in my bathrobe and slippers.

Caged like an animal in this farcical place they call a Psychiatric Ward. Not a prisoner of theirs. Nor a prisoner of time.

I'm a prisoner in my own freaking mind. I took a wrong medication, opened up and saw the future and the past. The memories flooded in way too fast. I couldn't take it all in. Too much information, all channels coming in at once. Before self-incarceration and all the medication, I now can see that I had been running in circles.

Moving way too fast,
always ahead of myself,
not in the moment.

Thinking that my visions or dreams were all my doing.
Knowing now that a lot of it was my will, not
realizing that my thoughts and words were
changing things on the outside of my shell,
affecting others as well!

dreaming memories,
remembering the future
to forget the past.

Realizing that I've been
moving in circular patterns,
covering the globe,
seeing, finally, that I am still me, everywhere, still
attracting the same kinds of people and drama.
Seeing me in everyone I meet.
Knowing that every living being is just
reflecting certain aspects within myself.
Putting someone down is akin to
putting myself down.

Change is a real bitch.
Once you know who you are not,
It gets easier.

Why Should God Bless America?

Andrea Pulcini

America the beautiful, America the freed,
America the wasteful, the needy, the greed.
America the sunlight, America the rain,
America the sinful, the hateful, the pain.
America the proud, America the brave,
America the intolerant, the spiteful, the grave.
America the rich, America the poor,
America the wrathful, wanting more, more, more!

America the hypocrite, America the insane,
Don't do as I'm doing, just do as I'm saying.
America of the diverse, America of the same,
America of the righteous, America of the lame.
America of diversity, yellow, orange, red,
Armed forces, policemen, terrorism dread.
America of ghettos, and the avenue of stars,
Afraid of landing in the courts, longing to land on Mars.

America the tortured, America of the tamed,
America of the brainwashed, and always inflamed.
America of convictions about what's right and what's wrong,
From too much information, watching television for too long.
America that kills doctors in favor of pro life,
America going out in the hood with a gun and a knife.
America the opulent, America overdressed,
America the frightened, the shamed and the oppressed.
America the uninvolved, America asleep,
America the lazy, America, what the bleep?

America I love, America I hate,
America that diets so we won't be overweight.
America strives for thin and fit, constantly working out,
America wants to be Botoxed from both within and without.
America is split, but can reunite once more,
If you're a Democrat marry a Republican, if you're a prince marry a whore.
I love all of America, the sex, music and drugs,
But the drug companies take advantage of us, they're turning into thugs.

And what ever happened to a state's right to govern?
Did it fall into the oven? Get eaten by a coven?
Were leaders tagged by McCarthy? Let's bring back McGovern.

America is powerful in all shapes and sizes,
Sometimes good, sometimes bad, only God criticizes.
So lay your demons all to rest, for none of that matters.
We all have them, we all know, it's just like "Shoots and Ladders."

Remember that game when you were a kid?
Going up, then down backwards, then forward till you did
Get it right in the end, if you were able.
Life's a game like that, or is it a stable?
I think it's a movie with men like Clark Gable.
There's drama and pain, laughter and shame,
Like in a book, music or on Cable,
Life will surprise you, make you think twice,
Like a microorganism you find on your table.

There's a way to play nice, it's right here and right now;
So don't be a pansy, don't be a cow.
Be a dragonfly, and zip and then zing;
Be a panda bear, or any damn thing,
That you want to be, just tell me your wish.
The world understands that we don't have to fish.

America, play nice, America, play fair.
Their toys? Our toys? Why can't we all share?

Her Day Versus My Day

Brad Goldstein

For six months after my stroke, the only time I left the house was to go to therapy or to accompany my parents, relatives, or close friends somewhere. It wasn't because I was afraid of falling or getting hurt. It wasn't because I couldn't drive, because there was a bus stop right outside my development. My reason was embarrassment. I didn't want to be seen.

After eight months, I finally gathered the courage to leave my house alone. I got on the bus and went to the local mall, first to the computer store, then to visit the store I worked at before my stroke. I couldn't speak well enough to be understood, and still can't for that matter. Instead I use a machine to type into, and then I hit "speak" and the machine speaks the words I typed.

I started to get hungry, so I stopped at the food court. I sat down to eat and noticed two middle-aged women sitting at the next table. What brought my attention to these two ladies was that one of them had a loud, high-pitched, shrill, irritating voice that I'm quite sure, under the right circumstances, could shatter glass. She spoke with a New York accent, and waved her hands and arms around like she was conducting an orchestra or trying to signal a plane.

"How was your flight?" her friend asked.

"Yesterday was the most awful day in my entire life," she responded as she threw back her head and rolled her eyes.

I wonder what percentage of people actually believes that when they say it. By the way, when someone starts out by telling you, "yesterday was the most awful day in my entire life," excuse yourself politely, maybe say you have to use the restroom. Then climb into your car and drive away. If the person doing the bitching drove you, call a cab. Trust me, you'll live much longer.

"So we arrived at the airport an hour early to do our bags and go through security and, of course, our plane was delayed an hour and a half. So we just had to wait at the terminal. I got up and complained to the flight attendant at the counter three times."

Can you believe they made her and her family sit in an air-conditioned building, *for over an hour*? Those bastards!

"So the plane finally arrives." The plane was just an hour late. "And I get stuck with the seat behind some four-year-old who is screaming and kicking my chair during the whole flight."

She should actually consider herself lucky. I always get stuck between the reeking drunk who belches during the entire flight and overweight women with bad body odor. You'll never find a scented candle with that mixture of aromas.

"Then to make matters worse …" "Oh my God, you mean it gets worse?" "Jamie, my youngest, is whining that his ear is hurting him. So we finally arrive at Fort Lauderdale airport. The plane lost our luggage." Can't you just hear the violins playing? "We finally got our luggage this morning!" Do I hear trumpets? Thank goodness. One more day without her luggage and she would have had a nervous breakdown.

Let me compare my worst day with hers. I went to sleep on January 12, 2004, around midnight, but before I did, I took some Tylenol and my allergy medication because I had a mild headache. I woke up at four o'clock in the morning. My headache was much worse, my speech sounded garbled, and I was extremely dizzy. I didn't call 911 or wake my parents, a mistake I will regret for the rest of my life. Because I had anxiety attacks in the past and the symptoms felt quite similar, I didn't want to make my parents pay for another visit to the hospital.

I awoke at eight in the morning, and by that time, my speech was completely unintelligible, and I felt very weak. It wasn't like a virus or the flu. My head felt achy, sore, heavy, and empty. This wasn't normal, and I knew it. Despite all my efforts to stay awake and go get help, my eyes closed and I began drifting back to sleep. I hoped all these symptoms were just a result of being tired.

When I next woke up, at approximately ten, my body wanted more sleep, but something told me if I didn't get up and go for help, I might not wake up again. It took all my effort just to roll over. My body felt like a bag of rocks. I managed to get one of my legs off the bed and onto the floor. When I tried to stand, my leg immediately collapsed from the weight of my body and I came crashing down to my knees. I crawled to my door and tried to lift my right arm to turn the doorknob. Much to my dismay, my arm just stayed at my side, like the arm of a corpse. I used my other arm and hand to turn the doorknob, which proved to be difficult, since that arm remained partially crippled from my brain tumor when I was six. I managed to turn the knob and saw my mother standing behind the kitchen counter making her morning breakfast.

My body wobbled from side to side as I desperately tried to move forward toward her. With her help, I got back to a standing position. She asked what was wrong, but I could only respond with incoherent grunts and moans. I motioned for her to give me a piece of paper, which she did. I wrote in big scribble letters, "can't move arm, can't move leg, can't talk, please help." She leaned me against the counter and ran to wake up my father. We called my cousin, who is a pharmacist, and asked him which hospital we should use. Despite being scared, I was actually laughing uncontrollably during all these events, yet I felt no reason to be amused. Later, I learned that uncontrollable, inappropriate laughter can be a symptom of a stroke.

All three of us rushed to Fort Lauderdale to the hospital. We filled out their forms and waited forever before I was taken into the emergency room. Finally, various doctors examined me, and authorized tests. After reviewing the results, they gave my family a diagnosis. At only twenty-five years-old, I, Brad Goldstein, had suffered a stroke.

Yet, despite all this, January 13, 2004, was not the worst day of my life. Before my parents accompanied me to intensive care, kissed me goodbye and then left the hospital, my mother asked me if I was scared. I could not speak, so I used a board they gave me with all the letters of the alphabet on it. I spelled out "No."

"Why not?" my mom asked.

I used the board to explain, "I am only twenty five years-old. I could not have had a stroke. This all must just be a bad dream." I was in such a state of denial that I believed this without a doubt in my mind. I believed that any minute, I would wake up at home in my bed. My body would be as it always was, and all of this would be a fading memory.

The day after was the worst day of my life, because on that day, it became real. I could no longer deny it. Do you think that lady at the mall would like to trade worst days?

The reason this lady got me so miffed is quite simple. I want to live this lady's life where the biggest problems are some minor inconveniences on a flight to my winter vacation. Because, after all, that's just what they were; minor, annoying, insignificant inconveniences. Yes, they're stressful, yes, they're frustrating, but we all have to deal with them. However, we live through them and put them behind us. And, after all, I still have her inconveniences if I take a trip where everything doesn't fall in place as it should. I just add hers to my own. What if we switched roles? I would gladly walk a mile in her shoes, wait in the terminal, or efficiently complain about lost luggage without having to use a machine. Would she as willingly spend one hour playing my part?

Perception

Gertie E. Poole

Perception is the act of recognition using the senses or the mind. The way a person "sees" an object or understands a situation is unique and perfect only in the mind of the perceiver.

Take the phrase, "Only the strong survive." I've always had trouble with that one. Tyrannosaurus Rex was strong and didn't make it. Whole empires were strong and powerful, yet they collapsed. Strength has nothing to do with survival. A truer phrase would be "only the adaptable survive." If you can't adapt to climatic changes, new viruses, be able to defend yourself against all enemies, tolerate new levels of pollution, invent machinery to aid in procuring and manufacturing needed commodities, and govern the populous in a reasonable manner, your chances of survival are slim.

Persons with disabilities learn all this early on, as it becomes an immediate mandatory change in their lives. There's no question of willingness to do so. Adaptability is crucial, perceptions are altered, and the drive to survive takes a prominent priority.

Being blind, I've found new ways of "seeing." I rely on the rest of my senses to pull the weight of the one I've lost. I can boast that I see things no one else can see, and I delight in that. Ground landscaping lights turn into wonderful large green turtles that only I see. Everyone is as beautiful and as young as I remember them to be. I've had one-sided conversations with trees, sat in countless laps of people when I thought the seats were unoccupied and made a lot of friends that way.

The trick isn't to dwell on what you've lost, but to make what you have left work to your advantage. It all boils down to adaptability and how you can substitute other senses and change your method of perception. I know every piece of cookware I own solely by the feel of it. Articles of clothing are found the same way. A taste of anything tells me all the ingredients, but all good cooks know that, sighted or not. I can smell rain before it hits the ground and sense that something is in front of me before I charge headlong into it. I'm still not sure how I can do that, but it may have something to do with echo sonar, like the dolphins use. I can overhear almost every personal conversation in crowded restaurants, can hear traffic accelerating or slowing down, and the haunting call of an owl miles away. I can even hear visitors before my dog does, and she's embarrassed by that.

I won't complain about losing my sight. So many people are in situations that are more difficult and have found their own solutions to problems. Everything changes whether we will it or not, and the key to surviving is to do the best you can, accept the help offered to you, use everything you have in order to survive, and survive well. Wisdom is gained by learning new methods of conquering obstacles that stand in your way. Compassion is gained by wondering how the rest of the world ever survives when they are only using the sight given to them and not all of the senses to capacity, the way we do. It's all a matter of perception.

Rising from the Dust

Gertie E. Poole (Fiction)

Genre: Historical Fiction

The rising sun illuminated the clouds of red Alabama dust chasing the hearse down the winding dirt road. A small gathering of people watched its approach as it moved slowly and methodically towards their neighborhood, obeying every traffic sign so attention would not be drawn to it. The driver, dressed in his best dark uniform hat and coat, glanced around, making sure he remained unobserved by the local police. Dark clouds loomed overhead, covering the bright sunrise, and threatening an early morning thunderstorm. A deep low rumble announced its approach. He hoped he would get everyone inside the hearse before the cloudburst.

Crows clung on the power lines like black clothespins, watching and waiting. They resembled old women in church or a jury waiting to pass judgment on them all. Their occasional caw pierced the unusually quiet morning, assaulting everyone's ears.

On the creaking whitewashed boards of their front porch, five-year-old Mary Louise stood with her mother and brother, George, waiting with a few of their neighbors for the car to arrive. Her eyes grew wide and she squeezed her mother's hand.

"Momma, that's a funeral car. We're not going to ride in that, are we?"

Her mother silently nodded and Mary Louise took her hand back and wrung it as her legs began to shake.

"I can't ride in that, Momma. It's got haints in it. I'm ascared o' haints."

Her mother scowled down at her, then looked back at the dust heading their way. "Oh, there ain't no haints. Dey either stayed where dey died or went to the graveyard. Dey don't stay in the car, Mary Louise, so stop acting foolish. Stop fidgeting, you hear me? I just pressed that dress and you're getting it all wrinkled. I gotta get to work and you and George got to get to school. They ain't no haints in there, child," she whispered as she held up a hand, feeling the first drops of rain.

Mary Louise began to shift from one foot to the other, pulling on her dress. "Are you sure, Momma? Are you sure? I don't want to ride in that car at all." She turned to her older brother George for help.

He didn't seem to care. He just stood there with the other men. They all seemed different today, taller and invincible. There wasn't the typical horseplay and sarcastic comments they usually threw at each other. It was quieter, except for her cousin, baby Abraham who was howling in spite of his mother's gentle rocking on the old wooden porch swing.

Mary Louise backed up a few steps to talk with George and whined, "I don't see why we have to ride in there just 'cause Miss Rosa didn't want to stand up. Why can't we take the bus like we always do?"

George reached out a hand and cuffed her and she whirled on him, her little fists clenched, but she stopped as he said in a low serious voice, "You better never let Momma hear what you just said. Ain't none of us going to ride the busses. It's a boycott, Mary Louise. Don't you know what that means?"

She shook her head that she didn't know and gave another quick glance to monitor the progression of the funeral car.

George pulled her closer and bent low to talk confidentially. He whispered, "It means none of us are going to pay to ride the bus because we don't like the way they treated Miss Rosa. It means we don't like the way they treat us at all and we're going to stick together so things will change."

She rolled her eyes at him. "Change like having to ride in a funeral car like that?" she screeched as she pointed to the hearse that had just parked in front of the house.

Their mongrel dog scurried out from under the porch and barked at its intrusion. George gave her a push in the direction of the people who were climbing in the back door of the shiny black hearse.

"Yeah, like that, unless you want to walk to school in the pouring rain, because we ain't taking no more busses."

She felt herself being pushed along and balked every step of the way. Her mother lifted her up, handing her their small tin lunch bucket and directed her where to go. She pointed to the right side.

"Scoot back over there, Mary Louise, and you hush now and sit still."

She did as she was told, but covered her eyes with her hands so the haints wouldn't get her. Squeezing her eyes tightly shut, she could see large splotches of white. They were haints, for sure. She could hear the adults talking as she bit her lip, cringed, and wished she had a choice in the matter. Haints were all around her now; she could feel their presence and smell their sickeningly sweet perfume. Her mother had been wrong. She would rather have walked in the pouring rain.

"It was kind of Mr. Thompson to let us use the hearse," she heard her mother say quietly to the driver.

He responded, "Well, not too many of us have cars, and we're using every one. We got more bicycles now, but with all the rain that's on the way, it'll be hard on some folks."

Another voice said with conviction, "We'll do whatever we have to do. There's a meeting at the church tonight. Reverend King is speaking. Tell everyone you know. We're expecting a large turnout. The time has come for us all to stand together."

Mary Louise sat behind the wheel of her Mazda at the green light, waiting for the funeral procession to finish passing through the intersection. Every time she saw a hearse she remembered that terrifying day back in 1955, huddled up against George and packed tight as sardines in the back of Mr. Thompson's donated hearse. She had been too young to realize the part she had played in the bus boycott, and she had to admit she hadn't participated willingly.

Looking back over the years, she understood how the camel's back had been broken and the time had indeed come. The next few decades were charged with issues and emotions. So much had happened after that. Events unfolded, changing the course of many lives. She nodded at the funeral procession, remembering the ride that transcended her into a new dimension, but swore she would never ride in the back of a hearse again until she had to. Rubbing the goose bumps on her arms, she was surprised at how long fears survive. But then again, dreams last a long time, too.

Indian Summer

Mary-Jo Lord

I'm almost nine and Laura is three when we pile into Dad's '71 Pontiac to drive to California. Mom and Dad sit up front, and I ride in back with Grandma and Laura and the squeaky cooler. We leave before daylight, eat at Howard Johnson's, and sleep at the Holiday Inn.

There are real Indian reservations in New Mexico. We stop to use the bathroom at a gas station, but Dad has to buy gas, or we can't go in. I ask why, and Grandma tries to explain. I still don't understand.

"Why don't they want Indians to use their bathrooms?" I want to know. Mom tries to hush me. "Don't Indians buy gas?"

We swim in the pool at the next Holiday Inn. Mom buys snacks, and says that peanut butter and cheese crackers were ten cents for her, and fifteen for the Indian boy behind her in line. I eat my crackers and wonder about Indians.

I still remember every state between Michigan and California—dark early mornings in motel rooms with connecting doors and sunny afternoons in warm swimming pools. Along the way we saw the Hoover Dam, a crater, and the Grand Canyon.

Dad kept meticulous track of mileage. Grandma stuffed Kleenex in her ears while Laura used my shoelace to clean her navel. Some nice people at a church in Arizona gave us ice-cold water to drink and let us use their restroom. There was one nasty bar bathroom that Dad wouldn't let Laura use.

I was amazed by the total silence of the desert. One day Mom and I "went pee" behind a cactus. Grandma never took off her sweater, even in 120-degree heat.

Today I put eighty-five cents in a vending machine and buy peanut butter and cheese crackers. I still remember that road trip as if it were last week, but mostly, I think about the Indians who were forbidden to use the filthy gas station restroom, and had to pay five cents more for peanut butter and cheese crackers.

Bound by Blindness

Texas School for the Blind, 1957

Marilyn Brandt Smith

Melinda stole the sugar bowl tonight,
We stayed in study hall till almost eight.
With cinnamon and bread in secret flight
We ate it all down by the campus gate.

I never thought when I set out from home
About the boring hours after class.
The lengths to which we go astonish some,
"Don't break the rules, don't chance the sure harass."

I see myself a teacher years from now
And wonder, will I know a girl like me
Who needs to know the when and where and how,
But wants her mind and body to be free?

We'll find a prank tomorrow to contrive,
It keeps our creativity alive.

The Best First Job

Marilyn Brandt Smith

"You can't go down there with all those crazy Cubans!" my mother challenged me when I told her about my job offer.

"Sure I can," I laughed. "The Dominican Republic is a different island. Besides, Mr. Hernandez promised they would get us out in an emergency."

The year was 1962. Kennedy was president. After three months of applications, interviews, and soul searching, I had reluctantly realized school administrators in Texas did not believe a blind person could manage a classroom. That was very disappointing since I had just spent four years at a teachers college and one semester in a successful student-teaching placement preparing to teach.

When I heard about the Peace Corps, I wondered if, by getting some experience abroad, I could convince the doubting Thomases back home that I was worth hiring. "Why not?" I considered. Yes, I would ask what I could do for my country. Since I didn't know how long it might take them to process my application, or whether they would have any interest once they did, I entered graduate school.

I had just come back from the dining hall after lunch one Wednesday in October, when I was called to the phone in the office of my dorm. "This is Andres Hernandez," his voice informed me. "I'm the Peace Corps director in the Dominican Republic and we need a teacher to help the director and her staff build a better program at the School for the Blind here in Santo Domingo. I just saw your application. Are you interested?"

In record time I dropped out of school, took the Civil Service exam, applied for a Social Security card, got fingerprinted for a security clearance, and packed winter clothes for a two-month stay in Vermont, the first stage of training.

I studied Spanish at the School for the Blind and in college, so I wasn't worried about the language. Since the Dominican Republic was close to the United States, my parents and some friends could visit me during my vacations there. I couldn't wait to board that plane for New England, even if it did mean a change in New York City.

There were twenty-five single men, three single women, and two couples in our Peace Corps group. I was the first blind person accepted into the Peace Corps. One of my friends from school was going to team-teach with me. The others in the group were to establish credit unions and cooperatives. Those of us who passed all the training evaluations would become the fifth group assigned to that country. As our group bonded, those of us from the segregated South found new friends among the African Americans in the group. We welcomed the opportunity to be together as equals. We didn't speak much about the strife brewing in the South, but we gladly discarded old teachings and embraced the new brotherhood we felt.

We received every shot known to the medical profession, studied language and culture, and learned economic development techniques. By Christmas, we were ready for a short visit home before more training.

The first two weeks in Puerto Rico were spent at an outward-bound camp near the rain forest to toughen our bodies and test our courage. We tackled survival swimming, rock climbing, and camping alone overnight. Then my teaching partner and I were sent to San Juan, the capital city, to spend three weeks at a rehab center for the blind while our friends studied local economic development. Harry Belafonte entertained our group once. He wanted to meet with me privately because he had questions relating to oncoming glaucoma. I had to work hard to stay focused on his concerns, because what I really wanted to talk about was his wonderful calypso music.

At the final selection meeting, we learned that three people in our group had not been approved. One was my teaching partner. The gossip of the day—the unspoken question on everyone's mind—centered around whether I would go without my friend. There was never a question in my mind.

On the day we arrived we had a short meeting at the Peace Corps office where we were introduced to Andy Hernandez, the Peace Corps director in the Dominican Republic. I went to the School for the Blind alone, was introduced to the director and some of the students, and was taken to the room I would call home for the next year and a half. Large, colorful flamboyant trees shaded one of the balconies adjoining my room. That balcony became my classroom. No heaters or fans were necessary, but I had to sleep under mosquito netting.

They had tried very hard to Americanize life for me in some ways. The next morning I was served corn flakes in a box—with a bowl, no milk, no sugar. We had been warned to avoid milk and beef because of Tuberculosis rampant among many Dominican cattle, so I dared not ask for it. After breakfast I had a phone call from the Peace Corps office.

Sandra, the other single girl in our group, was going to be assigned to teach with me. Since there wasn't a single female in our group with whom she could be teamed, it was a logical placement. I appreciated her willingness to work with me in a field for which she had received no training, and I was delighted I would have a partner after all.

In addition to teaching the classes—English, math, geography, and history—we held dances, played Braille Bingo, popped popcorn, went swimming, and exposed the students to a much broader slice of life than they were used to. The afternoon siesta quickly became a welcome respite in our daily schedule. Olga, a blind Dominican woman, learned Braille in Canada and came home to teach it at the school. Orlando lectured twice a week on history and culture. A chorus teacher came twice a week to lead a sing-along we all enjoyed. That was all the structure there was to the program. Even the director did not know what to buy, what to teach, or how much to expect of the students. She said it was up to me, if I was willing to organize and implement the changes.

One of the first tasks I undertook was to inventory the materials available for teaching. There were no mathematic or geographical aids and no books with multiple copies. The school hoped I could obtain some special financial assistance from the American Foundation for the Blind. They sent me to New York with $200 to spend on materials.

I purchased maps, cubarithm boards and tiles, signature guides, games, and some sewing aids. A Caribbean conference was planned for the following year. They needed to see results in order to believe the government of the D.R. would stand behind its commitment before they could guarantee assistance.

Sergeant Shriver—the U.S. Peace Corps director—and his wife Eunice (Kennedy) visited my school. When he asked if there was anything special I needed, I asked for fiberglass canes. I had learned to walk to some local restaurants, and knew it was important for the students to begin independent mobility training.

Our students ranged in age from six to forty-six. There were ten females and twenty males who were all housed at the school. I divided classes according to learning ability, not age, because that was the most efficient way to teach. "Here is your island," I told them in Spanish as I touched their hands to a tactile globe, "And here is my home in the United States." I traced their fingers across the water to Texas. Then, on topographical maps, I showed them Braille-labeled countries over several continents, always returning to the globe for the final spatial perspective. Math was something for which many would have little practical use in their lives. But pretending to shop for food and clothing or to make a monthly budget took their minds to places they had never dared to go.

There were two couples at the school who wanted to know each other much better than administrators would permit. We tried to encourage the idea that, with personal skills training and job opportunities, blind people could plan successful lives together. There was sadness in the voices and the eyes of the students when they thought about their futures compared to those of blind people in the United States.

Three of the young men had a band with an accordion, a drum and a guiro. They sang in harmony which reminded me of Conjunto Mexican-American music in Texas. We learned the Merengue, the favorite dance of the country. It was usually played by an orchestra with lots of brass. Like many young blind men and women, the students loved their radios for music, news, and baseball.

Food at school was institutional but adequate: goat, chicken, bananas, and always rice and beans. Their coffee was not for the fainthearted. However, when Eva called, "Fresh pineapple! Fried yuca!" we ran for the kitchen. There were a few local restaurants where we could indulge in a travel warp back home for a meal.

When our buddies from training came to town for supplies, we frequently shared our experiences. We were planning a weekend visit to Los Tres Ojos, a collection of caves and caverns that were a big tourist attraction, when the world was stunned by the assassination of President Kennedy. His was the mind that created the Peace Corps, and we shared his dream for a better world. The wind had been taken out of our sails. The resiliency of youth prevailed, however, and we came to realize that now we must be more determined than ever to keep his vision alive and appreciated. The school honored our country's tragedy by not holding classes on the day of his funeral. We listened on our Sony portable to the Voice of America.

During school vacations, and in order to attend educational conferences, I was able to visit other islands. Puerto Rico, St. Thomas, and Curacao were rich with native cultures. I have always loved the beach, but the warm Caribbean water attracts sharks. We had to be very careful about the times and locations for our swims. One of the first lessons we learned was to avoid sitting under a coconut palm. Nobody wanted a coconut concussion.

During the summer, we were able to visit many of our students and learn about their home environments. Dirt floors and fabric room dividers were common. We realized that attending school must have been like a "rags to riches" adventure for many. The school was only five years old, and some feared that one day it might not be there for them.

We were anxious to encourage job training for our students. Felicia wove purses and mats from cabulla, a native fiber. We helped her to increase her output and develop a market. For some reason, it was difficult to get the other women interested in learning that craft. Andres took a cart along the seawall selling candy and gum. We found him a bigger one. We attempted to get teacher training for Hilda. However, we met with resistance—not only because of her blindness, but because she suffered from a seizure disorder. She was medically controlled, but the stigma was too much for them to disregard. Manuel had a job at night answering the phone in a radio station. He was one of few people at the school who could speak passable English, and he hoped to have a radio show one day.

In 1961, the long-suffering Dominican subjects of a despotic dictator, Rafael Trujillo, finally manned a committee effort to assassinate him. His successor only lasted seven months before he was ousted in favor of a triumvirate military government. This transition took place during our service in the D.R.. There was some controversy about whether we would be sent home because of the unrest. In the end, we were deemed to be humanitarian and not political in purpose, so we were allowed to stay. There were nights when we saw military trucks passing the school from our balcony, and we knew conflict was inevitable. We were in a restaurant when a bomb went off in the men's room, in a theater when rioters attacked the door. When we came out, we made our way through a cloud of tear gas. No one ever tried to harm us. We were young and brave and, perhaps, naive. In hindsight, I wonder at the risks we accepted. Somehow, at the time, it seemed right.

The director of the school was thrilled when Lady Bird Johnson visited us. She brought us a tape recorder and spoke Spanish to the students. We reminisced about Texas.

Geer, a new blind Peace Corps volunteer, came to the school during my last year. He taught cane travel, woodworking, and independent living skills. He brainstormed with the men about jobs they might be able to perform.

After I left, other volunteers came to the school. Their facility has been expanded, and they have better materials and some trained professionals. I kept in touch for a while with students from the school and with volunteers in the D.R. I sent American music to the students at the school. They loved the top American rock songs, and I had introduced them to the folk sounds of Peter, Paul and Mary. They sent me chocolate and banana chips when they could. Even now, when I play tapes of their band or of the national anthem, I'm there in spirit.

After teaching and helping to build a program in the Dominican Republic, I realized I didn't have to teach in public schools. There were plenty of people to do that. My best efforts would be directed toward helping people whose special needs I understood better than many of the sighted professionals planning programs for them. I chose to accept a scholarship at Texas Tech, in a Master's degree program for rehab counseling. I worked in Washington, D.C., in Utah, and in three locations in Texas. Each position was rewarding in its own way.

The summer I returned I spoke to the National Federation of the Blind convention about my experiences. This organization of blind people was instrumental, that year, in forming a worldwide coalition promoting better opportunities and understanding for all blind people. I'm glad my success encouraged the Peace Corps to make this opportunity available to other people who are willing and able to serve despite various limitations. Blind people in developing countries need all the support we can give them. My hat will always be off to the volunteers who serve in the Peace Corps, and to the administrators who believed in me and supported me. Through that experience I learned as much as I taught, and I received much more than I gave.

Acceptance

DeAnna Quietwater Noriega

See me, open your eyes and really look:
I was the child sitting alone on the stairs
While other children played a ball game in the yard.
Because I couldn't see to play, I learned to love books.

I was the young girl who washed her hair on Friday nights,
Because the boys who carried my heavy Braille books at school
Never guessed I loved to dance and go to movies.

I was the young woman holding my newborn infant,
With my heart full of wonder and joy,
While nurses talked about me as if I weren't there,
Speculating about how I could ever care for that child.

I was the young mother sitting alone in the school cafeteria
Because the teacher didn't expect me to come to the mother's lunch
And assigned my child to serve behind the counter.

I tell you these things because I want you to understand,
I am not a disability, I am a person like you.
I laugh, I cry, I sing and dance.
I cherish my friends and family.
I want to be a part of my community and world.
I don't need your pity, I only ask your acceptance,
I only need you to open your eyes and see me,
Not as a dysfunction but as a person.
A human being just like you.

Something About Sailing

Sanford Rosenthal

Recently I had the pleasure of traveling from my home in Fort Lauderdale through Alligator Alley to reach Naples, where there was an annual sailing regatta for persons with disabilities. It was a weekend event with several participants, so I had to wait my turn before joining the fun.

The accessible dingy sailing boats are designed not to sink even if totally filled with water. When catching the wind, the boats can heel far to port or starboard. If the wind is too strong, then the craft can take on water. There's nothing to worry about, though, because letting out the sail reduces the force of the wind. The rudder is controlled by a joystick, which can be manipulated to point the right direction.

Everyone wears life vests, so tipping over really isn't an issue. Also, the boats have long keels, to minimize the chance of tipping over. The real reward is the chance to be one with nature. At least that's how it is for me. Others may have different motivations.

Broward County Parks and Recreation in Fort Lauderdale, Florida, provides leisure activities for special populations. I became a participant in the tandem bicycle program a few years ago. We meet in different parks about every two or three months.

Blind cyclists peddle from the back seat and are called stokers. The volunteer cyclists sitting up front are called captains. The surrounding environment can be much better appreciated through close contact than from just reading about it. The narration from the captain, and the sounds and smells, the breeze and the bumps, make the experience come alive in a way that no words on paper can do.

Our group has also gone kayaking in Dania Beach. We used small two-man kayaks. It was an adventure that transcended time as we skirted the mangroves in West Lake. The only clue that we were in the twenty-first century was the sound of the cars when we paddled close to the bridge that brought the water through the inlet to West Lake from the Dania Bay.

In Naples, while still waiting to sail, I met the mother of a forty-two year-old man who was in the singles race by himself. He was helped down the dock with his walker and then got behind the familiar joystick. Although a brain hemorrhage necessitated relearning how to talk, walk, and eat, sailing was something that he had learned for the first time. He said he can't get around without assistance any other way, but this is something he had learned to do alone.

It's obvious how much gratification the participants enjoy, because we keep coming back. He, like many there, reveled in his independence while taking in the sun and the wind. He left his walker at the dock. Others left wheelchairs. Theoretically, I was supposed to leave my fear. It didn't work out that way. There were white caps due to the strong winds. Waves brought water into my craft. The first partner I had agreed with me: The best place for us was back on the dock. He didn't communicate any confidence to quell my fears, but I will never be so quick to quit again.

Later, I decided to enter the doubles race a second time. A thirteen-year-old volunteer named Samantha became my sidekick for the duration. She was more skilled at sailing than most people there. We raced for two days and ended up with enough points to take second place in the doubles division.

Picture yourself there, adrenalin pumping, water everywhere, and someone at hand to keep you oriented. What a feeling! The boats are matched for classification. No one has an unfair advantage because of the build of his boat. You do all you can by pulling in or letting out the sail. You turn in different directions to capture the angle for speed in relation to the changing wind. Suddenly, you may hear something from behind. It's a sound from a sailboat. You're nervous and then realize it's your own boat as you start to pick up speed. You try to find and stay in the groove they call the "sweet spot." It allows you to increase your speed. The wind tugs at you, but if the sails are full, you're ahead of the game. You need some sighted assistance to know whether the sails are full. You have to turn three times around three buoys that are placed in the water in the form of a triangle.

Then you hear that sound again. This time, it's the lapping of water on the bow of another boat. He's gaining on you. How can this happen? It has to do with momentum. That's why, before the horn is sounded to start the race, you see all the boats going back and forth before the starting line. The idea is to build up as much momentum as possible. It's more advantageous to begin from a moving position than from a standstill.

When you think you have done all that you can, and it's the final 50 feet, you hear something different. It's like an echo. You know someone is gaining on you. This other sailing boat is coming up on you quickly. They had the benefit of a gust of wind that didn't reach you. Wind can be a fickle friend.

You're about to pass by the spot where the gatekeeper will blow the horn to signify the end of the race. Then the other boat nudges ahead of you by about five seconds before you reach the finish line.

This is indeed what happened in one race. In the other four, Samantha and I finished first. There were 10 boats in each race.

For those interested in terms, there's tacking into the wind. You zigzag about thirty degrees off the center to the left and to the right when the wind is coming at you. When the wind is behind you, it's pushing you. Sometimes, the wind comes across the bow. All these scenarios provide for forward movement as long as there's some wind.

There definitely is "something about sailing." I'm sure that whether you were a Phoenician, Conquistador, or might be sailing one-hundred years from now, the same age-old exhilaration is there for the taking. Rich or poor, everyone can participate in sailing after taking a few sailing lessons. Sun block and a wide-brimmed hat are also helpful.

When I was talking with one of the ladies at a recent regatta, explaining my reaction when my boat capsized, I told her I knew I was in trouble when I saw those fish in the bottom of my boat. She corrected my explanation, pointing out that since I was blind, I couldn't see them. I told her I felt the fish nibbling my feet. She understood that, and it didn't distract from the point of the conversation. Blind people use "watch TV," "saw a movie," and "looking forward to seeing you" as part of our everyday language. When people question us, it's like a reminder that we are different. These bridges of understanding need to be crossed, but there are some days when we need a break from being always on-call as the advocate. These new friends have given us a chance at outdoor activity beyond our reach, and we want to build relationships, not complicate them.

I spoke to my sailing instructor Vincent Peritore about the prospect of pushing the envelope for myself a bit further. We will be investigating some technological products to see if GPS, sonar, and wind directional gadgetry might help level the watery playing field a bit more. An enthusiastic participant who also sails at Tiger Tail Lake with me is profoundly deaf. We need to continue thinking of ways to communicate better with him. The technology being developed today makes the outdoors accessible with safety and fun for everyone who wants to be one with Mother Nature.

Making a Difference

Sanford Rosenthal

I have experienced disability, and advocated for acceptance on many different playing fields. As a child of ten, I was diagnosed with Retinitis Pigmentosa, which meant I would lose the rest of my sight around the age of thirty-five. I could see then, so what did that mean to me? I tried to "pass," and got away with it all too well. When I couldn't keep up with blackboard work at school, couldn't do my assignments as quickly as the other students, or couldn't mimic or follow demonstrations, I was assigned to a "slow learner" group. Since I didn't want to call attention to myself, I didn't protest. How much better off would I have been if a counselor, a partially sighted role-model, or a doctor had helped me come to grips with my future?

I'm grateful for the memories from those first twenty-five years. I was able to drive. I earned my Bachelor's degree and took a job in a hospital library dealing with print books and records. By the time I was twenty-six, my vision was failing, and I couldn't drive safely. I decided to try a guide dog, and on my first day back from training, I encountered discrimination. My ticket was not honored at an Elton John concert in Madison Square Garden even though I had a card from the guide dog school saying it was the law to let a blind person into public places with a guide dog. Didn't people who could see care about my needs and my rights?

I willingly took on the cause for the disabled, and became much more assertive than I anticipated. McDonald's, a well-known health club, and famous theaters and playhouses in New York City locked horns with me. I had the right to bring my dog. It took lawsuits, human rights commissions, and negotiations to work out the differences, but I gained some ground in every case. Signs were posted acknowledging the rights of the blind who used service dogs. Special arrangements could be made for accommodations with only a phone call. New York taxi drivers watched as one of their own went to court because he refused to pick me up. This was many years before the passage of the Americans with Disabilities Act. Some probably said I was an angry young man. I didn't want money or pity or fame, I wanted change.

Hawaii had a quarantine law which required service dogs, as well as other pets, to remain in captivity for several months. When I moved there, I used the media, an attorney, and government officials to attempt to get the law changed. Consumer organizations for the blind were not in accord, although everyone realized the policy was antiquated. The appeal, in a California court, never materialized. It took another twenty years for enough pressure to be brought to bear to remove this restriction.

Later, my focus grew broader than the issues involving guide dogs. In Atlanta, ten years ago, I wrote the editor of a newspaper column in an effort to gain support and understanding. I had been denied membership in a dating service because of my blindness. I was not allowed to use the church bus grocery shopping opportunity provided to other residents in my apartment complex. Bus drivers refused to call out stops, which they were required to do by law. I asked my fellow Atlantans to help us by expressing their disapproval when we were denied accommodation and acceptance.

Agencies and organizations whose purpose is to assist the disabled sometimes don't get the job done very well. In Georgia the rehabilitation services agency gave me a cane which was much too heavy, and hard to manipulate. I purchased a carbon graphite cane on my own that worked much better. How did that slip-up happen?

In Florida, where was Student Services when I needed them? I wanted to earn a Master's degree in social work. That particular university had never admitted a blind student to that graduate program, and my application was rejected. Eventually the director of the program vetoed their refusal, and I was admitted. Readers were hard to find. Shouldn't that have been one of Student Services primary efforts on my behalf? I was able to find and hire my own, and have tried to assist other universities in understanding the need and the difficulty when blind students need to read "on the spot" material which could not be recorded in advance.

Newly blind or disabled people often don't know what they need in terms of training or specialized equipment. Rehabilitation specialists tend to want us to fit the same mold. Yet, many of us know what we need, or what we want to do with our futures. If they would only ask us, options could be explored from both sides of the equation.

Thirty years after facing my visual loss I am still active in the advocacy movement. It takes a great deal of energy to carry the banner for that long. However maturity has shown me new strategies for intervention and coping techniques. Sometimes compromise must be tried along with the more flamboyant media, governmental, and legal avenues. We need the fervor youth can bring to our cause when their rights are denied. But we also need the wisdom and the maturity from those of us who have trod the path for several decades. Together we can make things happen.

Recently I participated in a political race in the first district in my community. Although I was unable to unseat the incumbent, I believe I left a good image with the public of a disabled person taking a stand on community issues not related to disability.

When speaking to classes in schools, I am able to show them my talking watch and my cane. They ask questions like, "Does anyone ever make fun of you?"

I honestly tell them, "Yes, I sometimes hear people talking about me when I walk past, as if I were deaf and blind." Then I explain how I handle various situations in order to educate without making anyone, including myself, angry.

I was glad to add my support and praise when the Broward County Parks and Recreation division sought media coverage for its program for the disabled. Sailing, tandem biking, rock climbing, and kayaking provide us with experiences we wouldn't be able to enjoy unless volunteers and professionals leveled the field a little for us. We also meet other disabled people in our community, and gain a better understanding of their capabilities and needs. I'm always glad to help try to find solutions when accommodation is needed. Often the use of technology is the answer.

Our planet is a jewel in the universe. We have found no other place we can call home. We owe it to subsequent generations to make it the best it can be. If we become more in tune with the needs and desires of all mankind, we can set the stage for changes which will allow everyone to fulfill his or her maximum potential. We can't promise the absence of disability. That is not within our power.

I personally believe the decision to confront me with blindness as a young man was based on a calculated assessment of my needs and strengths. In retrospect, I wonder, if given the full complement of physical abilities enjoyed by my associates, would I have grown into the man I am today? Would social work and advocacy have been my objectives? Would I have pursued graduate degrees?

Not only are we fortunate to call Earth home, we are lucky to live in this age when many aspects of disability can be minimized through technology broadening the choices we can make for our lives. Our choices determine how well we take care of ourselves, our community, our nation, and our planet and each other. Toward that end, disability is a torch which some of us have been asked to carry.

There is great diversity within our minority group. Some are content to be resigned to disability, others resent it so much they appear to always be angry. Many take their abilities to amazing heights carving out a respectable and comfortable existence. Many of us learn by sharing experiences and working together.

A word to the wise is often not enough to change a misunderstanding. Marches, petitions, and lawsuits sometimes gain enough attention to force a change. When the answer is "No" to inclusion, and the ears that need to hear won't listen, a collective movement can act as a springboard for new approaches and solutions to disability issues that open doors, eyes, and ears.

Secrets

Nicole Bissett (Fiction)

Dawn Bennet put on the finishing touches of her makeup and paced the living room of her studio apartment. She stood before Lorette Robins, her best friend from childhood, who was lounging on the couch. It was Saturday night, and Lorette was there to offer moral support.

"Well," Dawn said, clearly fishing for compliments.

Lorette smiled. "You look great," she said.

Dawn smoothed her black pants and straightened her red sweater. "Am I too informal?" she asked.

"Like I said five minutes ago, no. You weren't too informal in the other two outfits you put on tonight, either."

"Yeah, yeah. I know, I'm a pain. I just want to be sure."

Dawn had already changed twice. The first time, she wore her favorite blue dress but thought she looked like a church secretary. The second time, she wore a new pair of jeans and a big green sweater but decided it was too casual.

"Should I just call this off?" Dawn waited for Lorette to say yes. No such luck.

"If you don't meet him, you'll never know if it will really work out."

Dawn stopped pacing and flopped down on an armchair opposite Lorette. "You're right," she admitted. "I just don't know if I can go through with this. I hope it doesn't matter to him."

"It won't matter," Lorette assured her. "Not if he's the great guy you say he is. Just give it a chance."

"I hope he doesn't think less of me when he finds out."

"If he thinks less of you, he's shallow, and you wouldn't want him anyway. I just don't know why you wouldn't tell him. Telling him would have taken away some of this tension."

Dawn shrugged. "I guess I should have. I just didn't want it to be all we talk about. That happens, you know."

"But if it was all you were going to talk about, then you could have found out before tonight."

"I know, I know."

Three months ago, Dawn had been seeking a source for a story. She had to interview someone who represented the other side of a skirmish with a local teacher's union. The only one she could locate was Jack Slade, a public relations representative for the state department of education who worked out of Los Angeles. Jack gave her an interview, and afterward, they communicated by phone and emails on the quiet. They talked of politics, religion, their dreams. Everything except … one significant thing.

Two weeks ago, when Jack began pressing her to go out with him, Dawn explained that it was against the ethics of journalism to date sources. That was no lie, and it served as a good excuse. If the Gazette knew she was meeting him, she'd be fired. But that was the least of her worries.

Now she had things on her terms. He saw an attractive picture she had taken before her world turned upside-down a year ago. She hoped that image wouldn't change after tonight.

At twenty-six, Dawn had forged an admirable career in journalism, working at the city section of the East San Diego County Gazette. She was proud of this aspect of her life, after all she had been forced to overcome. Jack knew her as a competent career woman, but he didn't know the most obvious thing. Too many people treated her with less respect when they knew.

In the end, despite all the concerns, curiosity and strong attraction won out. Jack had a three-day weekend and convinced her to meet him if he came and stayed at a hotel. This would be her first date in a year and a half.

Dawn sprayed on some Rare Gold, her favorite perfume, and brushed out her waist-length blond hair. At five-foot-five, she had a slender figure with curves in all the right places. She hadn't smiled much in the past year, but when she began talking to Jack, things started changing. The mere thought of him could bring a smile to her face. Dawn wondered, as she went to her closet for a jacket, if she would lose that after tonight.

"I feel nauseous. I better cancel."

Lorette rose from the couch and went to her. "You're fine now," she insisted, putting a reassuring hand on Dawn's shoulder, "let's just go."

The January night felt like true winter, with a chill that was becoming more characteristic of California by the year. It felt good to sit in Lorette's car and bask in the warmth of the heater. Too good.

"You're gonna be okay from here?" Lorette asked as she directed Dawn to the door of Laurie's Diner.

Dawn nodded. "As okay as I'll ever be. Think I should change again?"

They both laughed. "Into what? You didn't bring anything."

"Into someone else."

"You'll be fine."

Dawn pulled her collapsible white cane from her purse.

"Thanks a million," she said. "I'll call you if he turns out to be Ted Bundy."

"Don't say that!"

"Okay, okay. Here goes nothing." She opened the door and waved goodbye.

The small diner was warm and had the atmosphere of a cozy living room. Dawn went to the front counter with her cane, and a woman approached her there. When people saw her cane, they were often anxious to assist—whether she needed it or not. Tonight, she needed it.

"Hi there," she said. "I'm Carol, a waitress here. I believe I'll be serving you. Are you looking for Jack Slade?"

The question threw Dawn off guard and she felt her face grow white. "Uh, well, actually, yes." Dawn was sure the pounding of her heart had to be audible.

"He's been waiting for you. Here," she offered her elbow. "Grab an arm and I'll take you right to him."

With a trembling hand, Dawn took Carol's elbow gratefully. She didn't want Jack to watch her negotiate the restaurant with her cane. Knowing her luck, she would run into a table and knock over a drink.

"Dawn, I'm here."

It was unmistakably Jack. Dawn would know that voice anywhere. It was strong and confident, yet soothing. She had come to associate it with good humor and depth of character.

His tone suggested everything was all right, but Dawn wished she could see the look on his face. Surely he saw the cane under her arm. Surely he had to think something was strange about her holding on to the elbow of a waitress.

It seemed Carol and Jack shared some kind of knowledge between them. Though she couldn't see them, Dawn sensed they were exchanging knowing glances, or smiles, or something.

"Here he is," she said.

Jack stood and took Dawn's hand. His hand was rough, as if he was accustomed to physical labor. His grip was firm and warm.

"Thank you," he said to Carol. "Now I have to do something about this twit."

He often teased her this way on the phone, and it occurred to Dawn that he knew. Furthermore, he seemed amused.

"You're more beautiful in person than in the photo," Jack said, letting go of her hand to pull out a chair for her. "You didn't tell me you were going to be this beautiful. Was there anything else you forgot to mention?"

Dawn laughed nervously. "I'm sorry," she said.

Jack placed a reassuring hand on her shoulder. "Sit down," he offered.

Dawn collapsed her cane, put it in her purse, and sat beside Jack.

"You know," he said, "you really didn't have to keep your blindness from me. Why did you?"

Dawn removed her coat and placed it on the back of her chair. "I didn't want you to think of me as different. I haven't let myself get emotionally involved with anyone since I went blind a year ago. I guess I was too afraid."

"Were you afraid with me?" The amusement was gone from his tone and replaced with concern.

"Very," Dawn admitted.

Jack took her hand between his two. "What did you think I would do if I knew?"

Dawn shrugged. "It wasn't so much that I thought you'd decide not to meet me. Like Lorette said, if you were going to react that way then you would have been shallow and not worth meeting."

"Well put."

"Well, I was more afraid you would just look at me as blind instead of Dawn. People do that. They can only relate to me in terms of blindness, and they don't know how to talk with me on any other level. That's something I'm still adjusting to, and it gets old fast. I couldn't take that from you. I didn't want you asking how I did my job, or how I cooked, or dressed myself and all that stupid crap, before we'd even met in person."

Jack was quiet at first, then suddenly laughed out loud.

"What's funny," Dawn asked, annoyed.

"Just so you know, since we're into exposing truths, I've known you were blind for two weeks now. I just figured you did these things somehow."

Dawn was stunned. Two weeks ago he had started pressing her to meet him more persistently.

"How did you find out?"

"I called the Gazette and told someone named Cathy I was interviewing with you, and she told me you had already left with your driver. Since I had been suspecting something was up for a while, I asked her why you needed a driver, and that's when she told me you were blind."

"That Cathy," Dawn said, "what a mouth. Not that she was supposed to help keep the secret, but …"

"The point is, it wouldn't have mattered if you had told me when we met on the phone. I happen to work with a guy who's blind. I see how he does things."

"You mentioned that."

"Last week, right."

"To get me to tell you."

"I couldn't get you to bite."

Dawn's face reddened. "I'm sorry."

"No harm done," Jack said. "It was just a waste of fear on your part, and I could have put your mind to rest."

Then a thought occurred to Dawn. "Why didn't you put it to rest, then?" she demanded. "If you knew for two weeks, you could have done that."

Jack laughed. "Well, that's true, and I'm sorry. But I thought I could get you to tell me. When you didn't, I wanted to see if you would really go through with meeting me."

For a moment, Dawn felt annoyance, then, finally, peace. Everything was falling nicely into place.

"I just haven't dated since I've gone blind."

"It's okay," Jack said. "I'm honored to be your first blind date."

They both laughed.

"Would you be offended if I asked you a question?" he asked.

"Probably no more offended than finding out that you've known about my blindness and didn't choose to tell me."

"How did it happen?"

"My blindness?"

Jack nodded. Then, remembering Dawn couldn't see his answer, he said, "Yes."

"Macular degeneration. It took my vision away slowly, so I had time to adjust, but I've had a harder time adjusting to people's attitudes and dumb misconceptions."

Carol approached their table then. "I see you two hit it off just fine," she said.

"You could say that," Jack said.

"Ready to order?" Carol asked.

They ordered dinner, and ate slowly. When the shop closed at ten, they walked hand in hand on a nearby beach and talked until the chill of the evening was more than they could stand.

Dawn felt safe with Jack. He didn't seem uncomfortable guiding her when they walked.

He stood five-feet-ten, with light-brown hair and hazel eyes. Lorette had described him when he sent his picture, so she knew he was handsome. Jack smelled of cologne or soap, as if he had just taken a shower before their meeting. The package in person was even better than on the phone, and Dawn found herself more attracted to Jack as the evening wore on. She wondered if he would kiss her on the beach, but he didn't.

He drove Dawn home at 11:00 PM, where they talked on her couch until 3:00 AM. Dawn felt good discussing her feelings about blindness, and her adjustment to it, with Jack. She inwardly cursed herself for keeping this side of her life from him.

At 3:00, Jack rose to leave.

"Why don't you stay?" Dawn suggested. "On the couch, that is. It's three in the morning."

"No. We arranged what we arranged. I'll call you tomorrow morning when I get up, whenever that is, and we'll have breakfast."

He took her into his arms, and the two finally enjoyed their first kiss. It was tentative at first, then grew deeper and more passionate. Jack was on the stocky side, which Dawn liked, and his embrace was strong and protective.

"Goodnight," he said when they parted. "I'm going to leave before I change my mind about staying."

"Smart move," Dawn said.

At thirty-four, Jack had already endured a painful divorce, and he needed time to rebuild his life. Tonight had been a painful reminder for Dawn that there was still much she had to come to terms with, and she needed time for those adjustments.

For the first time since the day the doctor told her she would soon be totally blind, Dawn felt happy—no, elated. She knew dating a source would be frowned on at work, and she would be fired if her editor found out. But she wasn't going to let work take this chance for happiness away. Jack hadn't been in the story's photograph. Few people knew of his presence in her life anyway.

For the first time in a year, she felt like an attractive young woman with possibilities to live for, not just some blind wonder whose only life was work.

She could hardly sleep when Jack left. A ton of bricks had been lifted from her shoulders. She had conquered yet another hurdle. Now it was possible to see herself on a date and perhaps even married. There had always been a question in her mind about that. Better still, there were no more secrets between them. It appeared, at least from Jack's perspective, the big secret wasn't really so bad. As for the rest of her concerns, they would work themselves out in time. Now that she knew he could accept her blindness, she was sure of it.

Oh, Thank God I'm Blind

Albert Cooper

Since the dawn of time man has struggled with accommodating those with differences and accepting people with disabilities. There are no standard sizes, shapes or colors that guarantee anyone success in the human race. Men have destroyed each other, and nations have suffered from strife over the issue of equality for all. What makes the United States a great nation is we are a melting pot.

Late at night when I get a quiet moment alone, my heart, my soul, and my spirit want to cry out to the universe. I am a visually disabled individual, a native son of Georgia, with certificates, awards, and a college degree. This is not unusual for a disabled person.

I am concerned about the negative attitudes toward disabled persons in this wonderful nation of ours. A few issues rest heavily on my mind.

First, when a major tragedy occurs, conscientious, concerned individuals establish a movement to raise money, and provide food and clothing to assist total strangers in their time of need, putting aside their discrimination, hatred and prejudice in this mean old world. At that time, without any consideration, the wolf and the sheep lie down together without danger. The major focus is about trying to rebuild lives in a time of emergency. No one seems to care if those who need help belong to a minority group and those in need gladly accept help regardless of the source. Disabled people are just as likely to offer support at this time as to need it. Hurricanes, apartment house fires, and terrorist attacks bring out the kindness in people. Why is it when the crisis is over we go back to the same old ways?

Second, the government spends a lot of money on the rehabilitation of convicts. Some are guilty of child abuse, physical, emotional, or sexual abuse, possession of an illegal drug with intent to sell or use it, murder, rape, or theft. We all make mistakes and everyone deserves a second chance. The federal government tax deduction program encourages companies to hire former prisoners by providing fifteen-thousand dollars for each hire. Coworkers and businesses look beyond their former crimes and hire these total strangers. What a noble idea.

Now the true issue can be addressed. Why do these companies, and the people who work next to former criminals, object to hiring or working next to disabled people? Why is a record of previous criminal activity acceptable and a physical limitation not acceptable? I would like society to explain this to me. We seem to forget the disabled individual does not choose to be disabled. Yet, employers and coworkers feel no burning need to give them credit for their rehabilitation or offer them a second chance at employment.

Three-fourths of the individuals who become disabled as a result of job-related injuries have suffered from someone's carelessness or company negligence. It is time for Dr. Martin Luther King, Jr.'s dream to be realized. A person should be judged on his character, not his skin or his disability.

Often the hatred and bigotry in this world are hidden in a closet. Some bigots think they have found a loophole in this dark closet. They slip in and feel secure, and discriminate against a neighbor. It is very simple to throw a rock and hide one's hand in the dark. While standing in the dark, everyone can be anonymous. It is easy to discriminate against someone who can't hear, see, talk, walk, or stand up to fight back. How much strength or audacity does it take to fight against an individual who is disabled? I shed sorrowful tears for these individuals who cannot keep an open mind. Many are caught up in issues based on selfishness. They don't understand the damage, harm and worry they cause, and they don't seem to care.

No one should misunderstand the sentiment inspiring this article. I totally support the need to help disaster victims and rehabilitate criminals. My concern is that we start showing the same respect to disabled people. The disabled must be allowed and encouraged to work. But businesses and coworkers often think of them only as strangers who are different in some way. Community leaders forget promises and disappear when elections are over.

In this new century we need to face and address the biases, judgments, and negative attitudes about employing disabled workers. People must be judged on their capabilities, expertise, skill, and talent, instead of their disability. I hope and pray the concerned citizens of this wonderful nation of ours will take a few moments to think about this situation, and speak out on these serious issues.

The following is my desire and request: let companies make a policy of employing the disabled, by hiring at least two disabled people per company. Target the disabled community in search of qualified workers. It takes a great deal of strength to overcome biased attitudes against individuals who may appear to be different, but every now and then we need to take a reality check and stand up for what is right.

Early in the morning, all through the day, and especially late at night, my heart, soul and spirit cry for Dr. Martin Luther King, Jr.'s dream to be fulfilled. From time to time, it takes a tragedy or a miscarriage of justice to make us wake up and be aware of how unfair human beings can be to each other.

Sometimes people must really get close to a problem before they can grasp its significance. But life finds ways to teach lessons, if we only take a few moments to reflect. We can use prayers and smiles, and hope to change the minds of bigots.

Whenever we look for justice in life, we turn to the most famous blind symbol of all, Lady Justice. Now isn't that funny? Ha, ha. Everyone truly wants her to be blind, and base her decision on just the facts. Her disability doesn't affect anyone. That's why, as I reflect on the world's troubles today, I can only stand up with pride and say, "Oh, Thank God I'm blind!"

Sight with the Mind

Michael Coleman

British spelling retained.

I myself have been a wandering butterfly. Though blind, I have travelled around every country in Western Europe and some of the eastern countries, and I speak a number of their languages. To me, a language is a window into another dimension. It's a form of sight with the mind.

Because of bias and prejudice, we're often blinded to reality and actually don't perceive what's truly there. Many think all Italians are gangsters, all Germans are Nazis and all blind people are beggars and musicians, etc.

I'm an adventitiously blind person because I became blind through accidents. There's a great difference between a congenitally blind person and one who becomes blind during his lifetime. The former does not comprehend perspective.

Nor does he even know what colours are. Consequently, he has a different way of thinking. This doesn't mean he is inferior but merely different.

I myself find it exceedingly frustrating that a blind person is expected to be extremely talented musically. My music is in relationships and the window to personal contact is through the spoken word. Each language I have learned has provided a new way of seeing, a new vista, a new form of sight.

The A's for Success

Bobbi LaChance

I am blind! Who ever said, "Life is fair"? There are some things in life's journey we take for granted. And when they're suddenly gone, all we can do is grieve for that which was and that which never will return. We may want to throw a pity party, but believe me, it won't help. Or we can play the blame game, which doesn't help, either.

I developed a formula. I call it the six "A's." The first three are Acceptance, Attitude, and Actions. By using this formula, I have a fulfilling life.

The first word is Acceptance. You can't deal with a problem until you face it. I couldn't change the diagnosis of blindness. I couldn't control it. I couldn't fix it. So, I learned about it. One of the nagging questions I had was, "What does blind look like?" There's no specific look. Blind people's eyes have as many looks as there are hair colors and hairstyles. Many blind individuals' eyes look normal. They move like those of a sighted person. Some blind people lack the ability to focus and appear to stare.

A person is considered legally blind when their corrected vision is twenty-two hundred or worse, or if their peripheral vision is twenty degrees or less. Only 10 percent of the blind population is totally blind. The rest of the blind population's vision ranges from only light perception, to being able to read large print. Some blind individuals wear dark glasses, but some don't. In researching the causes of blindness, I discovered that diabetes is the leading cause of blindness in the United States. I could be your neighbor, your sister, or a shopper in a store.

The second word is Attitude. A change of attitude for the newly blind individual is difficult. How can you feel positive about yourself when you can't see where you're going? Being blind doesn't mean the end of your life. You just learn to do things differently. I'm not saying it is easy. But it is possible.

At one point in my life, I went into a department store to make a purchase. Upon arriving at the cashier, I used my check overlay to fill out my check. The cashier asked me for my driver's license. I backed away from the counter where my guide dog was in the sitting position and remarked very sweetly to the cashier that I drive my guide dog very well. Then I produced my state identification card. Some other person might have been very upset over the cashier's request, however, I find humor and grace resolve many difficult situations.

You have to have a place to start. There are some great rehabilitation centers in all parts of the country. I was lucky to get immediate placement at the Cleveland Sight Center in Ohio. A sixteen-week course helped shape the person I've become today. At the center, I learned to type, read Braille for labeling and marking, and cook. I even applied my cooking skills in a snack bar. There were classes in arts and crafts to develop better sensitivity and coordination.

In mobility, they give you a white cane and teach you how to use it. You learn how to cross a street safely, how to locate doorways and elevators, and how to use escalators. There are lessons on how to get on and off a bus. These things are all important to help you retain your independence. You want to say, "I can't!" But you have to learn you can, and how to do it safely.

There are tears of frustration and tears of joy. You worry about your image, knowing you are always on display. People are curious by nature. They are also afraid, often thinking, "I could never do that!" But they're wrong. Survival is a basic instinct. There is an inner strength in all of us that we can tap into.

I had an excellent mobility instructor. He inspired and helped me overcome my inadequacies and fears, allowing me to get past some very embarrassing moments.

I got on a city bus to go downtown one day and asked the driver if there was a free seat. He said, "Over there!" Not knowing where "over there" was, I veered to the right and ended up sitting in a gentleman's lap. I'm sure my face was as red as my sweater. I was sputtering an apology, when he whispered to me, "I haven't had a young lady sit in my lap for years. Wait until I tell my wife!" We both chuckled, and he assisted me to the seat across from him.

Acquiring a sense of humor helps you get through those difficult and awkward moments. People take the lead from you. I remember once at my sister's house, I ran into the dining room wall. I hit it hard enough to dislodge a picture. My sister came in, all flustered, and I said, "I knew you wanted to remodel. I was just getting you started early!" I had a whale of a headache, but I kept smiling. If I had reacted as if I were hurt, she would have felt responsible. Instead, we discussed making a larger doorway. A positive attitude can save your backside or your head—and your pride.

The next "A" is Actions. How you conduct yourself when you are out in public is important. Do your homework. If you are asking directions, remember the general public can see. They'll give you sighted directions unless you're specific. You could ask directions to the bakery, and they'll offhandedly say, "It's the third store on the right." If your eyes look normal, they'll assume you can see. You need to say, "Excuse me. I'm blind. Could you tell me where the bakery is, and how many doorways until I reach it?" This will help them to give you useable directions.

Your memory is one of your best friends, so work on increasing it. I always try to remember to thank anyone who gives me assistance. The above three "A's" have helped me survive.

The second three "A's" are just as valuable. They are Alternative, Ability, and Assistance.

My six-year-old daughter was very upset because she didn't believe I could be a "room mother" for her first grade class. I knew I couldn't supervise nineteen children for a party, so I talked with her teacher. I brought cupcakes, which I had baked, and served them to the children with Kool-Aid. I was a co-Sunday school teacher and a co-Brownie leader as well. It's not what you can't do, but what you can, that's important. When you hit a barrier, don't stop with, "My blindness won't let me do that." Look for a different way to do it.

The next A is Ability. I wish they would take away the "dis" in disability when they discuss peoples' limitations. Blind people have many strengths and abilities. People compliment me and say I do very well. But I work at it all the time. I dismiss failure and can get very miffed when I can't complete a task. If you can't take lemons and make lemonade, then add lime and make a new drink. We all have the ability to be creative.

Assistance is next. Everyone needs a little help, but pride can get in the way. Just use common sense. Sometimes, assistance makes our lives much easier. Be gracious. In general, most people have good hearts and want to help. Unless you ask, they may think you have it all figured out.

For thirty-five years, my system of "A's" has worked for me.

PART FIVE
Honoring Nature's Pride

A Preview

Dorothy really wants to stay in Kansas this time, but that prairie wind is strong. A lifelong gardener fears he must be satisfied with memories. Then he learns the rewards are still there. He just has to change his approach. Frogs, crabs, snakes, and spiders share what they've learned about making careful judgments.

Prairie Wolf Wind

DeAnna Quietwater Noriega

The prairie wolf wind howls outside my door.
He thrums signboards and snaps off the branches of trees.
He pries at roof tiles and knocks over trash cans.
He huffs and he puffs and says he'll blow my house down.

It isn't built of straw, nor made from sticks and twigs.
But I hope he doesn't start circling round and around.
Cause this old trailer home might take a notion to fly.
But it has no wings or landing gear,
And would be much the worse for its flight,
When it comes on back down.

The Frog People's Choir

DeAnna Quietwater Noriega

White Buffalo Calf wandered alone at the edge of the herd. Grandmother Spider saw his loneliness. She paused in her spinning to ask gently, "Child, why aren't you playing with the other young folk of your kind?"

He answered, "The others say I can't play with them because my coat is not the same as theirs, Grandmother."

"Bring them here and I will tell them a story," she instructed. This is the story she told:

It was in the early summer when Big Green Bullfrog was appointed the director of the choir in a beautiful pond in a high mountain valley. He had a rich, deep bass voice and all agreed he should call the young folk together for tryouts to join the choir. These were the young frogs who had just acquired legs and left their baby tadpole tails behind. Their voices were high and sweet. Most of them were vivid green and their skins glistened emerald and jade in the sun.

Some had speckles of brown. He decided these spotted ones would spoil the look of the great frog choir. In his deep bullfrog voice, he demanded they leave and take their ugly spots elsewhere. Only those who shone with beautiful green skins like his own could sing in his choir. Sadly, the spotted frogs plunked into the pond and swam off.

Wise Old Turtle watched the unhappy young ones gather on the far side of the pond on a large moss-covered ledge. She did not think them ugly. Were they not as the Maker of All Things made them?

Crane moved silently along the shore thinking how delicious fresh young frogs tasted. Against the light browns of the sandy bank, the bright green frogs were easy to see. With a snap of her bill, there were a half-dozen less potential members for Big Green Bullfrog's choir. Everyone else jumped back into the water with a splash.

The next day, Big Green Bullfrog decided he would test the young voices in the shade of some green rushes and ferns further from the edge of the pond. His new choir members would not stand out so brightly against the lush green foliage. He was pleased with their sweet young voices, but before they had time to really warm up, Snake slipped between the stems and gulped down more small green frogs from the soprano section. The choir fled to the safety of the pond once more.

Big Green Bullfrog was very angry. "How can I have any kind of a choir if I don't have enough high voices?" he cried.

"What about those little frogs with the lovely brown speckles?" asked Wise Old Turtle. "Last night, I heard them singing by themselves across the pond. They have sweet voices, and I think the Maker of All Things put such pretty marks on them to make it harder for Crane to find them when they sit on mossy stones. You only looked at how they were made differently from you and never even listened to them sing."

Big Green Bullfrog was ashamed. He could see now that The Great Spirit, in his wisdom, marked these young frogs as they should be. Green frogs were harder to see on green lily pads, brown spotted ones could sit on mossy speckled rocks, and both would be safer from the sharp eyes of Crane. Though some were green and some were spotted, all could sing sweetly in praise of the Maker's gift of life as frog people have loved to do throughout all time.

We cannot always tell why the Creator of All Things chooses to make one of his children differently than another, but we can be sure he has his reasons.

What If

Marilyn Brandt Smith

If I could see fire,
Wonder, would I be less or
more afraid of it?

If I saw lightning
It would spoil the bold surprise,
Of the thunder clap.

Whose Ice

Marilyn Brandt Smith and Nancy Scott

You're not my mother's ice.
It came in big bags
she beat on the floor
turning rocks into gravel
for old-timey ice cream.

You're not my ice either.
Mine comes from its maker
in symmetrical shapes
ready for blending
with berry, lime, or grape.

You're clumpy, bumpy stuff.
Sun and salt chase you.
Scrapers send you packing.
Hot water thaws you in car locks.
Shovels and choppers shift blocks.

You hate our shoes
with treads and tacks
that crunch and crack
as we attack
these sheets you lay down.

We slip and grip the gate that's stuck
and we check twice with grinding teeth
make sure that stubborn outdoor faucet's off
while you expect to stay for ages,
weeping only when you leave.

April Lilacs

Nancy Scott

This is more than sipping spring,
more than the fluke
of two days over eighty.

Purple scent waves
in time grown full and short
though days grow longer.
The debutantes flaunt
a month early,
scorning Mothers' Day in favor
of blooming before
the last frost.

By May first,
petals fall unheard,
unhurried but too fast
once we notice
the scent is gone.

Roses

Nancy Scott

Barbara, my across-the-hall neighbor, planted the rosebush twelve years ago. "It'll look nice and you can have roses to bring in the house," she promised.

I knew nothing about plants and flowers. If the bush had to depend on me, it would die. I left it alone and didn't touch the flowers till the last big summer drought. That was the year the mysterious tomato plant took root and thrived among the weeds and possible poison ivy in my flowerbed.

My Italian neighbor, Mrs. S (who lived across the fence on my other side) and I marveled at and checked on and discussed the progress of the tomato plant.

Tomatoes and fall roses miraculously appeared together with little help from me. I told Mrs. S I never took the roses because I didn't help with the bush and so didn't deserve the flowers.

"No," she said in Italian-accented English. "You take. They die if you no take. They smell nice in your house."

I hadn't thought of it that way, and I took the roses in with the tomatoes. After all, I did water the tomatoes. The roses and tomatoes were both amazing. I began cleaning and weeding the flowerbed.

Over the next few years, I clipped huge roses for my kitchen table. I even planted tomatoes a few times. (Peppers once, too, but that's another story.)

But this year, I decided to stop caring. The neighborhood was changing. Mrs. S had finally moved. I was the only person on my half of the block who had lived there for more than twenty-five years. The newcomers had no attachment or loyalty to the area.

It was time for me to move. As part of my separation process, I didn't weed the flowerbed. And I didn't check for roses.

On a hot July second morning, I was out walking at 8 AM. I had inquired about an apartment in a large complex that would be more secure but very different from what I'd known. The walk was habitual and I wasn't paying attention.

I walked by the rosebush and my left hand brushed against petals. Petals? Now? It was late for roses. I stopped. There were a few dried up roses, but right in the front of the bush, I found three open flowers. I bent to sniff. They smelled wonderful and would, I knew, smell even better in my kitchen as they dried toward potpourri. I brought them in.

I wasn't meant to miss these last roses in this place. I wasn't meant to stop caring. I must be grateful for this reminder and take it with me as an omen of good luck. Maybe, wherever I end up, I'll plant a rosebush and not lose this link to a past and a future that still needs tending.

Livy's Hiss-Story

Roger Smith

Hello. My real complete legal name is Olivia Scarlet Snake. But most of my friends just call me Livy. I'm an eight-foot, forty-pound Colombia red tail boa constrictor. My story, therefore, will be written "constrictly" from my point of view. We snakes have gotten a bad rap, and I want to change some attitudes.

People have watched too many movies in which my friends are always the villains. Every time there's an unfortunate accident involving a human being and a snake, the news people come up with this incredible and sensationalized story that's longer than I am. We understand that our human counterparts can never be satisfied to just crawl up in a tree and peacefully hang out like we do. The media never report the reasons for accidents. Usually a snake is caught out in the wild and has not been domesticated as yet, or the snake has been starved or physically injured. Never mind the fact that your dog or cat would most definitely be capable of attacking under similar circumstances, and sometimes will.

My first real memories are of being owned by a high school kid who sold me when he turned sixteen and got into cars and girls. It's just human nature for a young man to be more excited about having his girlfriend on his arm than having a girl snake on his shoulder. Getting sold and then resold is something we snakes have to get used to. We don't mind as long as our new owners are good to us.

This family let me roam all around the house and did not get all bent out of shape. Sometimes I did, though—like the time I fell asleep under a recliner that was occupied. I felt those springs move and did a quick figure eight to get the heck out of Dodge.

When people came over for dinner, I had fun. My owners had a skinny little dog, and I didn't think they fed him enough. I'd wait for everyone to get seated, sneak a look from some hidden corner, and try and guess which person might be more shocked if they felt me. Then I would creep over and climb up on the unsuspecting person's leg. Surprise! Their plate would invariably end up on the floor, and the dog would have a great meal. More than once, that act got me carried back to my cage, but it was worth it.

One thing that bugged me was that the family never gave me a name. In school the kid was studying "self identity" in psychology class. He would sit there rubbing me as I wrapped around his shoulder while he read, but he couldn't call me anything special. I was a little hissed. Should I give him an anxiety lesson with a little nibble or a less than gentle hug? Naw, I'm just not that kind of snake.

Not long after that, the guy sold me. I was in a pet store for a short while, and then one day, my current owners came in. It was love at first sight. Most people admired my pretty colors but passed me by. These folks held me, all three of them, and didn't seem to care about my looks. My new owners, the Smith's, had held a rat snake at an "exotic pets" show in Florida. They didn't know diddley squat about snakes, but they sensed that I was gentle and they were after a new adventure. They purchased a thirty-gallon critter tank where I was to live. I was really afraid that I would be stuck in that thing for the rest of my life. But before long, they built me a really nice cage, more like a condo. It was glass that went up over a bathtub, and it had all kinds of trees and shelves and stuff for me to climb around on. I missed roaming through a house, but this was almost as good.

One night, they had put me in an old tub to soak. I slithered out, and got myself all wrapped up around a drainpipe, and I mean, I was really tight. I think I could have gotten out, but they didn't. They called a plumber friend, and he came over and they spent hours trying to figure out how to get me out of that mess, while I laughed at them. The only problem was, I had just eaten a dumb old rabbit a few days before that, one that I didn't half want anyway, and boy, it sure was hard to laugh and digest at the same time. You see, I am a rat eater. I'll eat a rabbit if I must, but I don't like all that fur. Anyway, after a while, they went down stairs, and the plumber was poking around on the ceiling with a saw and a drill. Let me tell you that nearly scared me skinless. I mean, just try and get the picture. Here I am stuck on this drain pipe with my head down on the floor, and there they are down below me, about to drill through the ceiling, and I can't even talk! The plumber was afraid he might cut me, Ouch!

They came back up stairs, cut some pipes, and finally got me out. After that, the plumber actually held me. Later when he went to work at City Hall he put my picture on his desk, and now the mayor knows me by name. Because of all that my master got a nickname. Now everywhere we go, they call him "Snake Man."

The next spring, Brigham came into my life. He is this really nice hunk of dude snake, and before I even knew what was happening, I was, what do they call it, with child, oops, with children, fifteen to be exact. It was a drag, it took away my appetite for several months, and it seemed to happen every two or three years. Finally I said, "No more." Ellen was here, let her be Mom so I could get back to my rats. At one time there were fifty of us, not counting the children.

The Smiths have two pythons who are bigger than I am. They are really nice snakes, and the male even has sort of a crush on me. I know this because when we are in the cage together, he will climb up to where I am, and put his tail around me. It's okay though, Mel is a charmer, and I sort of like it when he snuggles up to me, but I wouldn't tell him that; wouldn't want him to get his head all swollen up and get it stuck in a water bowl. Besides, that female python, Keeni, short for Zucchini, is the biggest darn snake/squash I ever saw, and I sure wouldn't want her to get after me.

Trust is a big part of snakes and humans getting along. I know that when my mistress rubs my head she won't hurt me, and she knows that I like it and that I will not bite her. Most people wouldn't dare to trust me like that. That boy of theirs doesn't hold me that often, but he pets me a lot. He usually brings me my dinner. Believe it or not, I only eat about every two weeks. One time, not that long ago, I think I scared him a little. I had eaten a rat, and he was checking my cage to see if there was still one left in there. I wanted another one in the worst way, and his hand smelled like a big fat rat, so I showed him my teeth just, as they say, to make myself perfectly clear. I wouldn't have bitten him, like I said, I'm just not that kind of snake. Truth is, I have never bitten a soul in my whole snake life.

When I'm getting carried anywhere I love to latch on to something like that tall bookshelf with their bumpy books, or worse yet, the ham radio tower. They hang on to my tail but sometimes have to get a ladder. Just about the time they get to me I give them a big hug and a lick. See, it's kind of like a game we play. I like it when my master cuddles up to my mistress when he is holding me. I can sneak around and get a part of myself around her too. Talk about a close family.

We have a lot of fun at snake shows and pet shops trying to sell all the children. I don't think they meant to go into business but what else are you going to do with a bunch of baby snakes?

Here's a puzzle: My owners act like they're opaque all the time. For you two-legged folks I need to explain that in snake-speak, "opaque" is a stage before shedding when our eyes get covered with old skin. We don't eat because we can't see our food or anything else. These people don't look or act anything like us, but they sometimes run into things. I keep looking for people skin, but I swear, they never shed. Besides, they eat all the time just like that other family. They have a nice motor home that's been customized with heated storage bins for us reps, but they hire someone else to drive it. Tell me they're not opaque!

Friends and helpers avoid us at first, but they often eventually ask to hold us. I've had my picture made with people who couldn't wait to show how brave they were. They're surprised I'm warm and leathery because they expected cold and slimy. They're fascinated watching me chase something furry around a cage, and they love the "rolled-up sock" look when I crawl out of my skin. My master has some relatives and business friends who squeal and carry on if they see me. I can feel the vibrations when they scream or run across the floor. That's sort of like hearing.

There is one special friend who is always on our wavelength. She doctors my scrapes or burns; sometimes I stay on the heat rock too long. When I get congested, I whistle when I breathe and she always knows how to make me feel better. Maybe she's a doctor?

My owners are always having people ask them if I am poisonous. I am not. Some of my brothers and sisters are, but they don't belong in homes. They are cursed with a dangerous weapon that makes it almost impossible for people to love them.

One lady said we should all be dumped on the freeway and run over by the first truck that passes. If there weren't any of us, rodents would eat up all the grain. I wonder how that lady would like breakfast without her bagel. Sometimes in spiteful dreams I wish she were a fat old rabbit, trying to dodge trucks on the interstate. Maybe, on the other hand, she would make a fine stew. Hey! Keeni, that big python, just "woooves wabbits!" Oh, there I go, thinking like a human again.

When people make remarks against us, they are often just ignorant. We let them pet us if they want to, and we hope that they—or at least their children—will become more open-minded, and realize that all we are after is a little love and respect. If we hiss, we are just scared. We also hope that people will learn not to be so selfish with the space on this great earth. We all live here for a reason, and there is plenty of room. If one of my brothers or sisters should stray into your yard, or onto the road you happen to be traveling, don't beat him up. Let him live free, just as you do.

I'm getting to be an old gal now. These last twelve years have been a super slither with some wonderful rep companions and three opaque humans who have treated me like a queen. My master takes me and some of my cage mates to schools so young people can learn what we are like and ask questions. They have often been taught that we are mean. I am glad to be a part of changing their attitudes. He tells them not to touch a snake's head until they know her well, but to be willing to let that snake tail wrap around their wrist in order to build trust. Stroke my scales like you would rub a cat. I can't purr, but when we know each other well I might lick you if you want me to. That means we're really friends.

The Visitor

Bobbi LaChance

There came a tap, tap tapping, at the window pane.
I listened, then faintly heard it again.
A tap, tap, tapping this seemed rather queer.
I peered at the window, the night seemed clear.
Content in my rocker, I continued my book,
Another adventure with a cop and a crook.
Then into my story came that same tapping sound,
I gazed through the glass as I turned around.

On a branch in the moonlight what should appear
But a shadowy figure with a snow-covered ear,
Two small bright eyes looked right in at me
Then, catching me watching, disappeared in the tree.
Was this an illusion? Why not check it out.
I knew I saw something, what was this about?
The ground all around was blanketed in snow,
If something were there, where did it go?
I cracked the window an inch or two,
And returned to my reading for something to do.

Then a tap, tap and a soft mewing came,
Quietly I listened, there it was again!
I returned to the window, opened it wide,
Lifted the screen, a creature jumped inside!
It huddled in the corner right near my feet,
My heart turned over, it skipped a beat.
The creature shook from whiskers to tail,
Snow flew around like a whirling gale.

I knew my life was about to change,
Though this wee creature looked a bit strange.
Once she was dried, she was fluffy and white,
She had all my attention, what a beautiful sight.
Two wide blue eyes looked right at me,
She wanted to be friends, that was easy to see.
This tiny kitten, maybe six weeks, no more
Was a warm furry ball on my bedroom floor.

Since she came to me on a cold snowy night,
I named her Crystal, that name seemed just right.
At night on my pillow she'd always leap
Purring lullabies till I fell asleep.
Now when the branches tap my window panes
I realize how much my life has changed,
I remember my gift from that snowy tree,
And all the love Crystal brought to me.

New Horizons

Ernest A. Jones

The sun shone brightly through the crystal clear atmosphere as I walked up the gravel road. Large Tamarack, Douglas Fir and Ponderosa Pine stood like sentinels along the trail and up the hillside. The stream, which ran close by, bounced merrily as it dashed over large boulders strewn in its path, oblivious to the fact that soon it would be buried in ice and snow. I kept a lookout for a deer, but the only animal life I found was one old porcupine waddling across my path and a couple of ravens flying noisily overhead. The deeply rutted road, hardly more than an old logging trek, snaked up the valley as it followed the stream. Coming to a fork, I left the creek behind as I started up the steep climb. I heard the wind as it brushed through the trees, heard the ravens calling to each other, and a squirrel chattering from a nearby tree. But otherwise silence reigned.

"Ah!" I whispered as I rounded a bend and stopped where I took in a panoramic view of the rugged terrain. To my left, I looked through a narrow ravine to the valley far below. I saw what could be described as a patchwork quilt as green pastures vied with the dull yellow of a harvested grain field and the brown of several plowed fields. I saw a couple of houses and even an old weathered barn, its once red siding faded by years of harsh weather.

What I came to see lay to my right. I saw one hill after another, each decked out in a splash of glorious color. I stood, just drinking in the view, knowing that for me, one day this, too, would be gone. I desperately wanted a picture in my mind that could never be blotted out. I beheld splashes of red, orange, yellow, and green covering the hillsides. For the Tamarack, otherwise known as the Western Larch, fall is the time to really show off. These trees wore brilliant gold and orange as they hovered between summer and winter. Scattered between these bright trees were the green Ponderosa Pine and Douglas Fir. Lower in the valleys stood the yellow birches, crimson maples, and green cedars.

I drank in this beauty, from the valley below to the azure blue sky overhead. Soon those beautiful Tamarack trees would stand stripped naked, while winter blasted them with bitter cold ice and snow, waiting for another spring to once again bring them to life with first a touch of light green changing to a dark summer green. Could there be any place more beautiful?

Refreshed, I returned home knowing I would always remember this scene. Maybe the doctor was right. But nothing could take this picture away from me, not even fading eyesight.

The next day, I decided to take another walk up the road. I wanted to make one more effort at reaching the lake. The trail was seldom used, because the main entrance lay on the other side of the hill, but I had to try.

The afternoon was growing old as I headed out. Turning down what used to be a road I found many small trees growing in the path. I needed to be careful, as branches swept low over the trail. Also, I found fallen trees lying across the old road. Suddenly my head cracked into a fallen tree trunk. I stopped, reaching out, measuring the difficulty of continuing. I gently rubbed my head with my hand but could not find any bleeding, so figured I would be fine. I crawled under the tree and again started down the overgrown logging road. But I found the path hard to travel as the brush and small trees became ever thicker. I was afraid a branch would catch me in the face and I would lose the contact lens in the only eye with any eyesight left. Then how would I find my way home? No one knew where I was. My wife only knew I was walking up the gravel road.

Thus, with the shadows growing long, I turned around and headed for home. In the growing dusk, what little vision I had was greatly decreased. If I had trouble seeing in bright light, I was virtually blind in the dark. I was concentrating on my feet when again I cracked my head into the same fallen tree. This time I felt a sticky fluid slowly running down my head and forehead. But I reasoned it was not serious and, after ducking under the tree again, started down the trail. I hoped to get in the house and clean up before my wife saw me, but she was waiting for me when I opened the kitchen door.

"What happened?" she cried.

I tried to act like it was nothing but she wouldn't listen and hurriedly pushed me into the bathroom. With a cloth and warm water she proceeded to clean my face, forehead, and even my ear. From her expression and few words I guess I looked a sorry sight. Fortunately, the injury was minor, but I had a sore head for a few days.

That night as I lay in bed I grew depressed. Why did this happen to me? Why must I suffer blindness and thus lose out on a great nursing career? Life just wasn't fair. Still, as I brooded, I felt peace come. I could do it. I would show the world I was no quitter. I would still be useful. After all, I could still do anything I wanted, except drive our pick-up and work as a nurse. I drifted to sleep knowing tomorrow would be a good day.

Dorothy stopped the car in the little used parking lot. "The trail is right ahead of the car," she said as she opened her door.

Opening the passenger door, I stepped out onto the small parking lot. With a quick flip of my left wrist, I felt my cane expand and click into place. Using my left hand, I followed the side of the car to its front.

"Ready?" she asked.

"Ready," I answered as we set off. Finally, I was going to the lake, but today we were taking the main trail.

We had only walked a short distance when some leaves brushed my face. Stopping, I reached out to pick a leaf. "This is a maple tree. I think it's an Oregon maple or big-leaf maple as some call them. See how big this leaf is with its five jagged points."

Swinging my cane to my left, I heard it hit something hard. Carefully, I moved toward the object and found the large trunk of the maple. "Hey." I said, "Is this what I think? Is this a licorice plant?"

"It sure looks like one," my wife answered as she moved to stand beside me, "but you're the expert, not me."

The lower trunk of the large old maple was completely covered with a layer of moss, which felt as soft as any expensive carpet of today. Small fern-like plants grew through it. I gently worked through the moss, finding the swollen tubular-like roots of the small plant growing on the tree trunk. Carefully I removed a two-inch section of root and, after breaking it, handed her one piece. I wiped the dirt and debris off my section of root and took a bite. "This is good licorice."

We returned to the trail, walking side by side, for the trail here was wide and smooth. Deftly I swung my cane with my left hand. We did not speak for a while, walking hand in hand, enjoying our closeness. From overhead came the songs of many birds. Some, like the crow, did not have melodious songs, but still their cries added to the restfulness of the day. The leaves rustled as the wind blew through them, and occasionally we felt the breeze brush our faces. The afternoon sun warmed us, and we didn't hurry.

I reached up as another tender branch brushed my face. "This is cedar. The cedar is another great aroma of the woods. There must be water nearby, since the cedar tree needs surface water to live, as it does not have a long tap root."

"There's a little stream just a few yards past the cedar, but the water is moving so slowly we can't hear it," she said. "Really, I guess it's mainly a marsh area."

The trail grew narrower, so I stepped behind my wife, trying not to strike her legs with my cane. With a loud squawk, a large bird flew from an upper limb of a nearby tree.

"What was that?" I asked.

"I'm not sure but it's a large, mostly blue bird. It just landed over across the lake. It has long legs and a long neck and is wading in the water."

"Oh, that must be a great blue heron. It sure startled me, and I cannot say much for his singing," I added with a laugh. "His cry sounded more like what a six-year-old lad might sound like, given a voice of a sixty-plus-year-old man after taking a hefty dose of cod liver oil."

"Is this a huckleberry bush?" she asked.

Reaching out my hand I answered, "It does feel like one but if it is, there are no berries on it. What I really like are the small red huckleberries that grow over on the west side of the state. Do you remember them?"

"I remember them," she replied. "They had a tart taste but still were sweet."

With a laugh I continued, "I remember some great pies made out of the red huckleberries. A friend once told me one could not make a pie with the red huckleberries, so I set out to prove him wrong."

"That was foolish of him," she laughed. "I remember other times when you were told you couldn't do something. You always prove them wrong. Remember when they said you couldn't grow corn and tomatoes where we lived, because it was too cold? It only took you a couple of years before you proved them wrong. In fact, we had extra tomatoes some years."

We continued on our way and, with a start, I felt warm sunshine, telling me we were out in the open. The trail changed from dirt and gravel to grass.

"We must be there," I said, pausing to soak in the peacefulness that lay around us. Then hand in hand, we walked through the grass to the water's edge. I bent down and put my hand into the water. "Burr, that's cold! Is there anything to sit on, maybe an old log or large rock?"

"There is a log right over here." Then catching herself, she added, "I mean it's over to your right about a dozen feet. Here, let me help you."

We sat on the hard log, worn smooth from many summers and winters. I sensed a large object behind me and reaching back, I found a huge tree trunk. Feeling its rough bark, I said, "This must be an old fir tree."

Turning to face the lake, I leaned back against the large tree, enjoying the lingering sunshine bringing warmth to body and soul.

We sat in silence for several minutes, allowing the peace to fill us. We could feel the tension of the past busy days fall off like snow melting on a hot day. We heard ducks and geese on the water and birds in the trees, while from high overhead came the shrill cry of a red tail hawk. Just to my right, I could hear a stream as it entered the lake. The water made a gurgling sound as it bounced and rolled over and around the boulders in its path.

The sun was dropping rapidly, and would soon be gone behind the western mountains. I knew we should be going but still we lingered.

"Hear that?" I asked.

"Yes, what is it?" she asked.

"It's a loon," I replied. "It sure has a mournful cry. It sends shivers up my spine. We'd better head home as it will be getting dark soon."

Rising, we felt the cool breeze brush our faces, another reminder the night was upon us. The many songbirds were settling down, and the ducks and geese were finding rushes for a safe rest. Across the water, we heard the loon crying and from another direction came an answering cry.

We were only about halfway to the car when my wife stopped. "I can't see a thing! It's grown dark so fast. I'm not sure I can follow the trail in the dark. I should have brought a light."

"Here, follow me." I guided her behind me, telling her to hang on. Carefully, but still fairly fast, I tapped out the trail. I cherished the feeling of being needed again. Maybe it was dark, but so what. This was not new for me. I tried to make sure the tip of the cane didn't get stuck behind some rock or root, and although it happened several times, I stopped quickly and swung the cane a little higher. We walked on in silence, each enjoying the moment at hand.

"I see the car," she said. "The moon is reflecting off it. We made it!"

"Of course we did," I replied. "Were you afraid?" I thought about adding, "Sometimes the sighted are the handicapped," but decided this was not the time to tease, so I remained silent. I lingered a little longer, knowing I should get in the car but still waiting. For several moments, we waited as more cries floated across the countryside.

I slowly opened the car door. "Listen," I said as a howl echoed across the land. "Hear that coyote? I like to hear them howl. Their cry haunts me, sort of scary but still peaceful," I said as I climbed into the car.

Settling back in the car seat I felt good. Today I had enjoyed life. Today I had been really needed again. Maybe being blind was not the end of a good life, but just the start of a little different kind of life. Life would go on. I would reach out, always seeking for New Horizons.

Growing a Garden

Ernest A. Jones

I grew up working in the family garden. Neither weeding nor hoeing is a favorite task, but they're necessary. When I entered nursing college, another student told me, "You won't have time for a garden."

"If I don't have time for a garden," I told her, "I won't have time for my nursing, because my garden helps me unwind and actually refreshes me." As an adult, I've always had a productive garden with many flowers, fruits, and vegetables. The physical work tones my muscles while, at the same time, taking me away from worries and stress.

My next-door neighbor often comments on how lovely my garden is, while her garden is full of weeds and struggling plants. The difference is, I spend two or more hours a day working in mine, and she and her adult family find this work too hard. While they moan over their weed patch, I use my hand rake and keep working, loosening the soil and pulling out the weeds. This may be hard work at times, but I find it rewarding, especially when we eat the produce of our labor. Try eating sweet corn only one hour from the garden. Or how about a thirty-two pound watermelon, its luscious juice blessing your taste buds.

My garden is twenty-five feet wide and seventy-five feet long. I do all the planting and watering, and most of the weeding and harvesting. Round black soaker hoses made from old recycled tires use low water pressure to water only the row—and not the aisle between the rows. It's easy to follow this hose to plant and care for my flowers and vegetables.

Two years ago, I tried something new. The potatoes had to be dug up because the vines had died and gophers were busily eating the crop. On a warm morning after digging up one row, I was dripping with sweat, filthy from the dust, and discouraged. Many of the spuds had been eaten or chewed on. I decided to stop, planning to return very early the next morning before the day grew warm.

That evening, a crazy thought hit me. I couldn't get rid of it. "Okay," I said out loud to nobody, "I'll do it." Why not work late instead of early?

The evening was lovely, and the heat of the day had vanished, replaced by a refreshing coolness. I was comfortable wearing my walking shorts and a thin cotton shirt. After placing several empty boxes on our back patio and grabbing the digging fork and two large buckets, I headed to the garden. I sank the digging fork near the first hill, turning over some beautiful spuds. Hill by hill, row by row, I worked. After taking the full buckets back to pour the potatoes in the boxes, I returned to do more digging. The gophers had just started to eat on the potatoes, so I saved most of the crop. It was 11:45 as I entered my house that night. The harvest was in, the crop saved, and after a fresh shower, I slept just fine.

For many years, I tended more than a dozen beautiful rose bushes that I kept trimmed and healthy. I gave them all to my brother after I grabbed a handful of thorns one time too many. Because of my fading vision, I thought the bush another shrub. Why, with all the increased knowledge in horticulture, can't experts come up with a thornless rose bush?

Eventually, I stopped growing flowers. I no longer enjoyed them, except for my daffodils. They are a great sign of spring. No matter how cold or how long the winter, I know they'll bloom, showing a mass of lovely golden heads—a promise of better days ahead.

Just a few years ago, I started to include more flowers in my yard. I planted a row of geraniums in front of our house and a short row of sweet peas along our front fence. Maybe it was the aroma I enjoyed from these flowers. Maybe it was because the neighbors talked about their beauty. Maybe it was just knowing how much these flowers pleased my wife. Maybe it was a little of all the above, but I've included flowers in my planting every year since then.

Their fragrance helps me enjoy my labor. As spring daffodils fade with the warming days, the geraniums, sweet peas and petunias take over. The rows of gladioli and zinnias add beauty and color to the green foliage of the vegetable garden, while calling hummingbirds and other songbirds to our place.

Last spring, I planted two Cheddar Pinks in a small flowerbed near our outside clothesline. One day while hanging out the laundry, a lovely sweet fragrance drifted to me from those flowers. This year, I hope to buy another dozen Cheddar Pinks to spread their aroma over more of our yard.

Why should I allow blindness to rob me of this joy? Our yard has around three-hundred feet of flowerbeds, most are two to three feet wide. There are borders of flowers and mulch along both sides of our driveway. I take care of all of these.

I hear some people say, "I'm not strong enough to work out in a large yard." If you have strength enough to walk or wheel yourself out on your deck or patio and carry a pitcher of water, you can grow many beautiful flowers and some vegetables in large pots. Check with your local nursery or garden store for choices and planting tips.

I enjoy a soft green lawn. I even like mowing, for there's something rewarding about changing a ragged field of grass into a smooth green carpet. But when people could tell who had mowed our lawn just from the way my fading eyesight caused me to miss patches of grass, I decided it was time to leave the mowing to someone else. We bought a riding mower for my wife who actually enjoys taking part in the upkeep of our yard. I have several blind friends who still mow their lawns. Because they have small yards, they have worked out a way to keep their lawns looking nice. But in our large yard, a sighted person must do the mowing.

Having fun and helping nature share her beauty and bounty make me glad I didn't give up my lifelong hobby because of blindness. The physical and mental rewards of working hard, then tasting, touching, smelling, and sharing the results of my labor, are enough to keep me gardening year after year. Don't be afraid to try something new because of a disability.

Shore Wars

Gertie E. Poole

Dolphins danced in the bright orange sunlight as the coast came alive on a brisk Atlantic morning. The sound of the impact as they crashed back into the water blended with the pounding surf on shore. The wind buffeted seagulls like spirited kites over the ocean. In the tide pools below, several hermit crabs scoured the lines of shell and rock for tasty morsels. Turning over pebbles, salt-frosted sea glass, and half angel shells, Buster came upon a rather large shell. It was intact, roomy, and in excellent condition. He thought it might be suitable for a new home.

Glancing about guardedly, and confident no one was watching him, he eased out of his shell to try the new one on. Knowing he was vulnerable without his armor, he hastily shifted shells. He carefully inspected the inside spirals and found it to be much larger on the inside than he originally thought. Disappointed that it was too bulky for him to haul around and not very comfortable at all, he sighed and, wriggling free, reached out for his good old home he had left next to the new prospect.

Panic gripped him and he angled his eyes all around, not seeing his shell. He stretched out as far as he dared with seagulls flying overhead—their keen eyes wouldn't miss a naked hermit crab. He frantically felt the silt for any sign of the shell. One of his eyes spied a movement off to his right and there was his home, dragging down the beach. It had been stolen while he afforded himself the luxury of new house shopping.

Reversing to anchor himself into the clumsy oversized shell, he took off in pursuit. He had to get it back! It was heavy work hauling the newly acquired shell and Buster huffed with the strain, neglecting to see the momentary darkness of the shadow that passed over him.

He didn't realize he was under attack, since he had the criminal in his sights now. The seagull descended upon him in a furious assault of beak and wings. He tucked in and scuttled for the clump of windswept sea oats, trying hard not to lose sight of the culprit who stole his residence. Plunging himself into the soft sand within the oats, he buried himself and hid from the hungry bird.

Discouraged at not finding the crab, the gull took off for better prospects and Buster swiftly resurfaced and tore out of the saw grass, heading straight for his target with determination. Splashing in a tide pool, he dodged the larger crabs who were notorious for their bad temperament. He could not lose sight of his one and only possession.

Fiddler crabs snapped huge claws at him, raking the cumbersome shell he had been compelled to use. A sharp strike from one of the larger crabs forced him into a roll until he collided with the soft sand dune. Reeling from the blow, he rolled back upright and, frantically searching, found the villain a few yards ahead of him. He poured on the speed but was kicked carelessly by a beach-goer carrying a large cooler and an uncooperative umbrella. The huge shadow had crossed over him like an eclipse, but it was too late to dodge out of the way. The reckless kick had propelled him into the surf and hindered his attempt to catch the fiend. Pulled with the incoming tide, he swam in a frenzy to reach the shore before the hoodlum escaped with his home.

Footing was precarious as he pushed the loose broken shells out of his way, trailing a stream of water from his heavy shell, and regaining top speed. Hampered by an obtrusive piece of driftwood, he launched himself upward, clawing at the crevices to support his weight. Decayed pieces of grey driftwood flaked off as he tried to grip the sturdier strata in between the worm-eaten sections. Cresting the top, he tucked in and plummeted to the sand, immediately engaging his claws to dig deeper and move faster. He strained, reaching a pincer out to barely touch the shell that had once been his.

The thief twisted around, and thrust a menacing claw at his eyes and Buster ducked and countered, bravely snapping back and wielding his claws aggressively. Locked in battle, they tugged and spun out into the shallow tide pool, drawing the attention of the gulls milling about the dried seaweed.

The largest of the flock pounced on the renegade hermit crab and tossed him onto the dry sand. Grasping the kicking crab in his beak, the seagull began pounding the shell on the rocks to dislodge its inhabitant. Buster lost no time in fleeing and he took shelter behind the rocks. Digging in, he turned his anxious eyes away in horror and cringed at his foe's misfortune.

Ripping the offending smuggler out of the coveted shell and making a snack of him, the gull flew away. Buster turned his frightened eyes to the sky for a moment and then bolted to claim his prize. He quickly changed shells and scrambled into the safety of the surf for a well-deserved respite. He sat very still for a moment, realizing he could have easily been the one who perished instead of the unfortunate crab that had committed the crime. He backed into the cool darkness of the familiar shell, leaving out only the tips of his claws as he bubbled in relief. There's no place like home.

The Team

Roger Smith

"Hang on pup, I'm coming." Cold, doggy nose-kisses nudge my arm as I reach for my shoes and shut off the alarm. Finley is ready for a trip to the back yard and his morning snack.

He is my second Yellow Lab—my fifth guide dog over the past thirty-four years.

"Smell that wood smoke, boy?" I ask with envy as Finley returns to the porch. "Someone has a fireplace going. I'm glad it's winter. After I drink my coffee, we'll head up to the hardware store. The basement door isn't closing right. It must need a new latch. It's a great day for a brisk walk. We'd better enjoy this weather before the snow makes your job a lot harder. Wish you could've known those fellows who came before you."

When I trained with my first dog, a gentleman in our group dropped out in mid-program. "Why did he do that?" I asked my instructor.

"He left because what he really wanted was a machine, not a partner," I was told. "The team concept didn't work for him, and wouldn't have worked with any dog, because he expected perfection."

I've always wanted the public to understand that these guys and gals who work with us are not bred or trained to be cookie-cutter predictable. They are dogs, when you come right down to it, and we can't expect them to act like humans. Each has days of feeling bad, not sleeping well the night before, being afraid, getting frustrated while trying to complete a job, or getting hungry when someone else is eating something that smells good. Just like us, they sometimes get distracted by something on the fringe of their main focus. We can't learn each others' languages, but thanks to memory of commands and gestures, and mutual feedback, we can communicate quite well.

I want to forego the "me first" approach we usually use to show the special services these dogs can perform. How can I show you feelings and humor from a dog's perspective? They tell me with whimpers, licks, wags, and groans, what pleases them, and frustrates them. If my dog isn't ready to go, doesn't eat enough, has accidents, or can't work a regular route, it's time for me to serve him, and get him some help. I do my best for them, and they do their best for me. That's what makes it work.

Tracy's Tale:

I was Roger's first guide dog, a seventy-pound male Golden Retriever. We all came from the California and Oregon schools called "Guide Dogs for the Blind."

I went through training twice because I wasn't quite sharp enough to be trusted the first time around. When Roger took me back to Lubbock, Texas, I found out about cold weather. Roger's wife, Marilyn, also blind, brushed and fed me just as much as he did, and although I wasn't required to protect her when we walked together, I did the best I could. I crouched beside pianos he tuned, slithered under Greyhound seats when they went traveling, and made myself useful in various work situations.

Once, when they left town for a long time, they hid some sterling silver under the house. While down there, they became disoriented. They called me and I went to the trap door and whined so they found their way out.

I was there when they brought "Baby Jay" home from the hospital and when they picked up newly adopted Karolann at the airport. During the summers, we visited relatives in Kentucky, and Granny Smith gave me a slight weight problem with leftover mashed potatoes and biscuits. When Roger decided to go to college, I learned the whole darn campus—and got a lot of attention in the process.

Their eye doctor noticed my clouded vision and put me on the table in the regular people's ophthalmology clinic to examine my cataracts. My vet didn't object. He might have done surgery but bone and lung cancer came along too soon, forcing me to give up guiding.

It was tough for me when Roger went back to California for my replacement. I almost stopped eating. Roger took me out the night he came home to show me he still loved me. In less than a month, I went to sleep.

Skelly's Story:

My original name was Burke. I was another Golden. Roger thought that name seemed too brusque, because I was a playful fellow, so he changed it to Skelly in honor of my trainer. My puppy raiser took me to college classes with her, so I fit right in with Roger's lifestyle. I learned two colleges and four public school systems where Roger taught. In my spare time, I liked to pull the bark off of trees and eat it—I paid the price later. When we lived in Appalachia, I sometimes slipped into folks' houses and helped myself to leftovers.

When we went to the beach, I loved to dig up seashells and bring them to everyone. I barked at the big waves and chased the tide as it went out. The family could take showers, and sometimes they could sneak me in with them. I was a salty sandy mess!

Roger credits me with being the best guide and most intuitive dog on his team. He did a lot of training with kids and future special-education teachers. I thought it silly when he wanted me to guide a person who could see but who wore a blindfold to try to figure out what it would feel like to be blind. I wouldn't treat them like blind people. I ran them into stuff, as if to say, "Take off that silly blindfold and let me get on with my business!" Some guide dog schools discourage us dogs using our memory to try to guess (anticipate) where our blind handler wants to go. But Roger loved it. Once I took him back to a phone booth he hadn't used in five years, and I was right, that's where he wanted to go.

They gave me shots and pills for allergies and thyroid problems. All of my bad habits—chewing on rocks, coal, and tree bark—caught up with my esophagus in a big bad way. The final damage came at Christmas time when I found a hidden stash of chocolates meant for the kids' stockings and pigged out. I was supposed to see the vet the next day, but I just couldn't hang in there that long. It was a sad day for the Smiths. Because of teaching obligations, it would be the next summer before I could be replaced.

The First Yellow Fellow:

Everyone liked my name: Zeb. I was a big fellow, about ninety pounds. Probably the worst thing about me was my habit of stealing food. Once I wrecked Thanksgiving by consuming a whole pecan pie, but guess what? I didn't get sick. There was an ongoing war between me and that Mandy cat who thought she owned the place. I hated to go out in the rain and sometimes embarrassed myself and my family when I couldn't wait. I guided by the book, but I don't think Roger ever trusted me the way he trusted my predecessor, Skelly. Once I gave him the "Stop" signal when he got disoriented on a bridge. But he was going to have it his way, so he stepped off a four-foot ledge. I didn't know what to do, so I jumped off on top of him, licked him, and kind of asked, "OKAY, buddy, what now?"

Roger taught some preschool kids who had trouble with language. He wanted the kids to get me to bark when they asked me to, so they would be encouraged to talk. They would say, "What does a dog say?" and I would put on a show that made the teachers in nearby rooms peek through the door to find out if everything was okay.

One day at school, I took Roger into the ladies' room by mistake. It's supposed to be his job to check out the door, but he was being lazy, and maybe I was ready for a little excitement. The cute girl in there was washing her hands, and after she got over her initial shock and Roger apologized, she asked, "Since you're already here anyway, may I pet your dog?" He took off my harness and we played catch with a magazine she was carrying.

I learned three different school campuses in three different towns. One high school dealt with drug problems. The kids got it in their heads I was a drug dog, and Roger might be working under cover. The principal told Roger not to tell them otherwise. It was the only school where the kids let me keep a low profile.

I had a crush on another guide dog about 10 blocks from home. Roger sometimes went down there and did something with computers with her mistress. Fran and I played in the back yard. On Valentine's Day, Roger took Fran some milk bones in a heart-shaped box and said it came from me. One day before they got the new fence, I sneaked out and went to see her. But that got me in trouble, so I didn't do it again.

When the family moved to Louisville, they chose a four-level house, and arthritis finally made it too tough for me to work the stairs, much less work the hilly neighborhood. Coming back from the grocery store one day, Roger had to carry me and the gallon of milk up the hill. Time for a replacement? She was a feisty young thing. We loved being together during the rest of my time here.

Moments with Moo:

Guide Dogs considered making me a breeder. However, I was a big woman, ninety pounds or better. They thought my pups would all be big. The Smiths say I would have been a great mom. I have mixed feelings. I wouldn't have wanted to miss out on life in this family.

Roger always wanted a girl dog. Guide Dogs told him he could change my name. Who ever heard of a Black Lab named Marmalade? We all settled on Mamie and somehow it got shortened to Moo. Give me a break, I'm not a cow, but as long as they're calling me to dinner, I'll answer to anything. I love to eat! I'll bite the hand that feeds me! Now, we get carrots in the morning instead of milk bones. They're longer, I don't bite any fingers, they're less fattening, good for our teeth, and for our breath. I say "our" because my replacement is already here. You see, folks, guiding frustrated me. Don't ask me how I ever got through training. It's true, I needed to learn two neighborhoods in six months time. His other dogs managed it, but I got hopelessly confused.

I love to tease cats! The first week, I tore a tie-down chain out of the wall so I could chase a cat up two flights of stairs and stare him down on top of a file cabinet where he thought he was safe. The cats had to go.

I would love to have been a lap dog. Maybe in my next life I can be a poodle. I love to roam the fields when we visit relatives in the country, but I'm glad Roger has a new yellow guy he can depend on to get the job done better than I did. Once I sneaked out and followed them up to Walgreens in the next block. Roger caught me on the way back and made sure I never did it again. I guess my job now is to just keep Finley in line.

Finley's Finest Hours:

I came in the second half of Moo's questionable career as a guide. She's my buddy, and she always beats me to the table scraps and droppings. My 4-H puppy raiser family encouraged me to be a social critter. If there are people on the street, in the store, in another vehicle, and especially if they have doggies, I want to be there. I'm learning not to whine so much, because it drives folks nuts. It's one of those bad habits. Maybe we're not so different from humans after all. I'm also a sniffer, which gets me in trouble on the street some times.

Dog hairs are nightmares for blind folks trying to keep house. But darn it, we just can't help it. Mine are white and Moo's are black, so we can really mess up a carpet or a winter coat. We get brushed, but once or twice they tried the vacuum. I scooted away from it at first, but curiosity brought me back. Now I get vacuumed once a week.

When we head up to the local twenty-four-hour restaurant, I move like there's no tomorrow because a couple of the waitresses slip me some bacon under the table. Roger pretends he doesn't know, because the guide dog schools frown on it, especially while I'm in harness. I don't get us lost very often, and I'm always ready to go. I'm a young pup, and I still like to play "tug of war" with a rubber ring. The baby Tracy talked about bringing home from the hospital is now a grown man. He's my buddy. He feeds and brushes me, gives me my carrot every morning, and gives me a playful romp every now and then.

I hope Moo stays healthy for a long time because she's good company. Maybe as she gets older, I can beat her to some of those table scraps too. I hope I can prove to be as loyal as Tracy, as great a guide as Skelly, as healthy as Zeb, and as good a family pet when I'm not in harness as Moo is. I'm looking forward to lots more good years guiding, guarding Roger against danger when traveling and, of course, being the center of attention.

"Okay, boy," I call. He's off in the living room taking in the sunshine through the front door. "Coffee's gone." I shake the harness. He's at my side and ready to go.

Part Six
Sunday Night Sharing

A Preview

Poets, journalists, publishers, novelists, and teachers share their secrets with us two or three times a month on our Sunday night teleconferences. When we don't have a guest, we share our own work. Recent exercises included: flash fiction, holiday memoirs, poetry, newspaper reports or features, and a story within a story.

As exemplified in the exercises below, a nudge from one of us often results in interesting diversity.

Traffic on our e-mail list complements our Sunday night sessions.

If you are a disabled person interested in writing, or wish to refer a disabled person to our list and conference, send a message to sanfordusa@bellsouth.net.

Section One
The Watcher

DeAnna Quietwater Noriega suggested the following assignment:

Write a poem or story of any type with a main character being a watcher using this scenario:

"The small figure was caught in the glare of the headlights of a passing car. Fine silver-gilt hair gleamed and fluttered in the rush of air from the vehicle. The watcher stepped deeper into the shadows."

The following questions were to be answered within the piece:

"Who is the small figure? Who is the watcher? Why is the watcher on this road or street?"

The following are samples from the exercise.

Rescue

Ernest A. Jones

She was a lovely thing. Her long silky hair draped down, completely covering her shoulders and neck. Although quite small, she was no infant. Her bright eyes didn't miss a thing as she appeared to be searching for something. Cautiously, she moved down the road, unaware that danger lurked in the shadows. She really should not have been out alone at night. She had no business here. Still, she moved along unconcerned.

Suddenly, she sensed a presence, and started running across the road in front of a passing car. There was a squealing of tires as the driver slammed on his brakes, stopping only inches away from her. Quickly, he got out of the car and scooped her up.

"What are you doing here?" he asked. "I am so happy I found you. The kids are crying since you ran away. I have already fixed your cage more securely, so you will be safe from now on."

With this, the man climbed into his car, turned around, and headed for home. His children's silky long-haired guinea pig lay nestled safely on his lap.

Just as he started down the highway, his headlights picked out bright glowing eyes lurking only a dozen paces from where he had stopped. He knew those eyes. "Well, little girl," he said. "Looks like I found you just in time. That coyote would have had you if I hadn't rescued you when I did."

The Walk Home

Marilyn Brandt Smith

I seldom walk this way, but since it's late,
The highway tempts me, offers smoother tread.
Approaching from the woods, my traps all set,
I see that rain has left a silver sheen;

Lights from a passing car direct my gaze;
Am I the first to come upon distress?
Tendrils flutter, motion draws me near.
A child, a wounded dog, what have we here?

Hurry home and call for help from town?
Lift this bundle, see what I can do?
I touch the unfamiliar, pull away,
My God! It's only broken bails of hay!
I murmur thanks, and soon go on my way.

Home Sweet Home

Jennifer Childs

The approaching vehicle startles me as I dash ever so quickly across the road. I'm not sure the driver sees me, but I hope my friend who watches me and waits in the shadows knows to stay there until I'm safely across. When I make it to the other side and am hidden from view, I wait to see if the mortal continues to drive past. If so, I'll motion my friend to come quickly across.

I hear the car pull over and the engine stops. My friend peeks through the foliage at me from the opposite side of the road and snorts in concern.

The driver gets out and, upon closing the door, walks toward the place where she last saw me. What does she think she saw? I'm no prey and never had any reason to be afraid of any living thing. I have no reason to fear this female mortal with the half-elfin blood, unless she finds out about us and tells the human world. Then, we'd no longer be able to live peaceably anywhere.

We've come in search of this forest to find a home. My own was burned down, thanks to a few humans' carelessness, and my friend's home is now a national park where he no longer feels at ease. I know this forest is far from civilization and isn't favored by humans as a gathering place. It's where we can live in peace. Now if only this woman will go back to her travels, we can get on with our search.

I wait impatiently as the woman searches through the thicket of bushes, shrubs and small pine trees. She isn't far from me. She stops, and I'm sure it's because of a ringing we both hear. I wonder if this noise will make her forget about me.

She walks back to her vehicle and answers the ringing phone inside. It isn't long before she starts talking to someone, then starts the car and drives away with only a quick glance and a sorrowful shrug backwards.

My friend Morrogh crosses the road and comes quickly over to me. His golden scales gleam in the moonlight and he snorts, "What was that all about? I thought you said you wouldn't be noticed."

Smiling sheepishly, I whinny, "How could I have known she was half-elven? From what I saw in her eyes, she didn't even know that herself, and if she had only been a mere mortal, I wouldn't have been noticed."

Morrogh shakes his head and tsk, tsks at me for not staying in the shadows till the vehicle had passed in the first place. He stretches his golden leathery dragon wings, lowers his amber eyes near mine and whispers, "Most humans, even if partly elven, wouldn't know what to make of you if they did see you. Why, you're a lovely creature, Terra."

"Of course I am," I whinny proudly. "With my snow white form, silver tail and mane and golden hooves, I'm a vision of magical loveliness. Top that off with my unique, taffy-twisted, rainbow-colored horn, and well, you've got a masterpiece in the form of a unicorn."

Morrogh shakes his head in disbelief at my apparent vanity. Still, he pulls me close in a friendly hug, and we go off toward the forest. He saunters along, swishing his big tail back and forth in merriment, and I canter in jubilation as we approach what we've both been dreaming of, "Home sweet home."

Section Two
Appliance Alive

Jennifer Childs provided this concept as a writing exercise. "Think of an appliance of any kind. Give it life and a purpose for coming to life. Create a conflict and find a way for the appliance to resolve it. The genre is up to you."

The Squabble

Ernest A. Jones

"Man, you're so slow. Why do you take so long anymore? Maybe I will dump you and use the stove."

"Well, maybe I'm getting tired."

"Tired? All you do is sit there all day long. Why should you get tired? Does sitting there make you tired?"

"Okay, maybe I am bored. How often do you even think about me? Come on, be honest now, just how often?"

"Think about you? Now why should I think about you unless I am trying to get you to do a little work?"

"That's it. Work and more work, but never any thanks. How would you like to never be thanked or even appreciated?"

"But you are just an appliance. Why should I thank you? I must be going crazy to even talk to you. What would Dorothy think of me, talking to an old appliance? Why, I remember the day we brought you home. You were so stylish, and you gleamed as we unwrapped you. We just knew it was love at first sight. You really showed us love, too. But now you seem to be in some dark recess and we have to shout to get you to respond. Also, little jobs that used to only take you thirty-five seconds now take you nearly three minutes. So what is wrong?"

"Have you ever thought of the aging process? Are you as young as you were when you brought me home? Look at yourself. Wasn't it you who drove the car that brought me here? If memory serves me right, you were quite handsome then, sporting a sound body, never fat but not skinny, either. You, too, used to be busy all the time. But I notice that even you have slowed. You're skinny, and because of your fading eyesight, my face was marred."

"Hey, leave me out of this. Also, who marred your beautiful face? It wasn't me and you know it."

"No, it wasn't you, I will admit, but my face was marred because of you. Because you could not see my face clearly any longer, a nice lady put high-rise dots all over it. Oh sure, you did not put them on me, but you sure like to feel them. Admit it, don't you like to feel these bumps?"

"Yes, old friend. These bumps help me operate you. Otherwise, I would ignore you completely. I can take these bumps away. If you want, I can smooth your face and remove all those dots. But remember, if I do, I will never be able to help you do your work again. You will be completely worthless to me then. You will still sit there, but will remain idle all day and night. In fact, you may even be carted off and hauled away, leaving your empty space for a new one of your kind, one who will be happy to do anything I ask—and do it fast, too."

"Might this really happen? Am I getting that old? I'm not ready to die yet. So what can I do to change this?"

"Well, my little friend, you cannot stop the aging process. Age is creeping up on you, but life isn't over yet. Sometimes the later years are the golden years. So do not fear. You're slow, but I'm not ready to kick you out yet. It's true, a newer model might be more handsome and trim, and surely would do the job much faster. But I think I'll keep you. But for a start, you can stop complaining."

With that, the old microwave rang its bell and its light burst forth like the dawn of a new day. "You won't be sorry. I will do my best. Also, I do not mind my face being covered with those high-rise Braille dots. Really I don't. But can I rest a few minutes now before I have to return to work? Twenty-four years is old for a microwave." The old appliance lapsed into silence.

"Okay, I'll let you take a rest. But be ready to help when it is near dinner time." With this remark, I threw the appliance ads in the garbage.

Wake-Up Juice

Marilyn Brandt Smith

"Put down your pipe and turn off the ball game, this is something you need to hear." Mrs. Claus stood beside Santa's recliner trying to get his attention. "It's December fifteenth, my dear, and the elves are protesting again!" Finally, Santa got to his feet. "Besides," she pouted, "Rudolph stole my blush this morning to fancy up his nose, so now there are reindeer hairs all over it. Yuck!"

"Now, now," Santa soothed, "About the blush, we'll just give it to him. I'll buy you another, but hide it well. What about the elves?"

"Just listen!" Mrs. Santa interrupted raising the window between their quarters and the workshop.

"No more toys on Santa's sleigh, until Santa gives more pay. We want coffee and Blue Cross, or we'll find another boss!"

Ruffling his beard and scratching his head Santa sighed, "It's the darn commercial coffee pot we bought on eBay, isn't it? It's not working again?"

"I told you we couldn't get it serviced up here," his wife admonished, shaking her finger in disgust.

"What shall we do?" he ruminated. "It's not just the coffee now; they've brought up all those issues we've been avoiding for the past few months."

Mrs. Claus closed the window and came to stand beside her husband. "Well, we can't avoid them any longer. But if we could get them coffee," she proposed, "I think they might call a truce until we get through this Christmas rush."

"There's nothing wrong with me, you guys," came a croaky voice from the kitchen, "I should be working fine. You must have done something wrong."

"Holy smokes, Clara!" Santa laughed. They walked into the kitchen and gave the commercial maker a glance. "You didn't tell me it could talk!"

The little light at the "Brew Settings" menu winked at him. "I can't get any power," Mr. Coffee complained. "Without electric juice, I can't make wake-up juice, get it?"

"This is incredible," Mrs. Santa pondered as she opened drawers and cabinets looking for the manual, "Why didn't you talk to us before?"

"Because you always got me going," the appliance giggled.

"I'll call in Thomas," Santa concluded, "He's good with those trains and Game Boys and such."

"No, no, no! Those run on batteries," his wife laughed, "We better get Virgil. He assembles those kitchen gadgets the ladies want, and they work on electricity."

Virgil had to be enticed. "I said no more work and I meant it," he grumbled. But after an offer of extra cookies, he agreed to have a look.

"Oh, here's your problem," Virgil smirked after twisting and turning a few knobs and switches. He started pointing. Santa grabbed his glasses and leaned toward his helper. "There's a break in the power cord, right where it goes into the machine, so of course it can't work."

"It didn't come with an extra," Mrs. Santa commented. "How can we make it work?"

Mr. Coffee spoke up, "You've got all those appliances in the workshop. Can't you find one out there to fit me?"

"Sure we can!" Virgil smiled, clapping his hands. "Want me to run and get one?"

Mrs. Santa quickly served up a 50-cup pot and put another on to brew. Virgil took coffee and cookies for all the elves out to the workshop with her blessing.

"Thanks buddy," Mr. Coffee called from the kitchen as Virgil bid the Clauses good day.

So, if on Christmas morning your new coffee maker mysteriously arrives with a missing power cord, just remember, it went for a good cause, and don't be surprised if it can tell you exactly what happened, and maybe even what to do about it.

The Misadventures of Sassy and Lulu

Jennifer Childs

My name is Lulu. I'm eight-years-old and well loved, even though I get a bit dusty now and then. I have a lovely yellow shade made of soft cloth, an ebony ceramic base with gold inlay, a golden enamel fixture, and a bright 60-watt bulb to light up my owner's lives. Don't be silly—of course I'm a lamp. I was just another inanimate object until one Friday when I heard my owners tell their cat, Sassy, they'd see her in a few days because they were leaving for the weekend.

Although they provide for her needs, that Sassy, she's such a typical Siamese. She caterwauled for a while after they'd gone, then finally settled down. That night, Jennifer left a message on the machine for Sassy, which started her caterwauling again. Since it was so dark in the apartment, I clicked myself on to bathe her in light and give her comfort.

Sassy stared at me and meowed curiously but with a hint of suspicion, "Mother isn't home to turn on lights, so who's there?"

I tilted my shade to her in greeting and said, "Don't be afraid, Sassy. My name is Lulu, and I'm your owners' lamp. I'm just trying to make you feel better."

Sassy clambered up to the end table and sniffed me. "Stop, that tickles! Ooh, I never thought a lamp could be ticklish."

Sassy lay down at my base and purred contentedly, "Why have you never done this for me before? I love the warmth. It helps these old bones of mine." We had a nice conversation about why lamps and cats should be friends before Sassy fell asleep, and I turned off.

Saturday was boring for me, with nobody home. Sassy chased imaginary floating things through the apartment, and cat-napped all day. That night, I turned on again, and we talked until she fell asleep.

Sunday morning, I heard Sassy jump down from her perch in another room. She jogged by and meowed, "Hello, Lulu, it's a fine day isn't it? I'm happy because Jennifer is coming home."

I was happy, too, in a way, but also sad because being animate would surely come to an end for me. I mean, I can't be talking while humans are around.

Sassy caught my attention when she slipped through the narrow opening into the closet where her litter box was kept. With a gleeful backward kick she disappeared inside, and before she realized her mistake, the door closed and latched behind her. I heard her meowing fretfully inside, and I said, "Hold on, Sassy! Let me figure out what to do."

She worriedly meowed back, "Okay, but please hurry. They won't be home for a long time."

I tried talking to the door to see if it would just open itself, but it didn't budge. Then I asked the TV and the stove to help, because they're both close to the door, but they just sat there, lifeless and unresponsive.

I was agitatedly pacing from one side of the end table to the other, when I accidentally unplugged myself. Wait, I could still move and still feel the pulse of electricity running through me. I quickly plugged myself back in and considered this new option. Could I make it across the couch to the floor and over to the closet and still get back in time to plug in?

I had to take that chance. Why should Sassy have to stay captive in that closet? I pulled out my cord like a whip, jumped over onto the couch and bounced all the way across to the other end before leaping down onto the floor.

"Hold on, Sassy!" I said, "I'm coming to help you."

As I reached the door, I aimed my cord at the knob, turned it, and yanked as hard as I could.

Sassy purred happily, "Thank you, Lulu." As the door swung open and she was set free. She and I hugged as only a cat and a lamp can, and then I felt my electric adrenaline start to ebb. I realized I wasn't going to make it back. "You saved me, Lulu. Can't I do anything to save you?" Sassy yowled sadly.

I tilted over and lay down on the floor. "Sassy," I said in a weak, fading voice, "I hope you don't get punished when Jennifer finds me on the floor, unplugged. I would hate for the blame to fall on you."

"Don't worry, Lulu. I'd take the fall for you any day. Isn't that what friends are for?" As Sassy smiled down at me, everything went black.

At 4 PM the family came dashing in. Up Sassy went into Jennifer's arms. After a hug and a kiss, she began purring. She had become spoiled by those conversations with Lulu, so the last few hours had been miserable. Jennifer noticed the lamp on the floor and, without a word, picked it up, put it back on the end table, and plugged it in.

Softly she said, "Sassy, we have a surprise for you. You see the pet carrier we brought in with us? Well, it contains something just for you."

Sassy trotted over anxiously to the carrier, and inside, she came face to face with a cute little multi-colored Siamese kitten. They exchanged some friendly sniffs, then the kitten meowed, "Hi, I'm Lulu!"

Sassy shook her ears in disbelief and said, "Hello Lulu, I'm Sassy." And that was the start, or perhaps the continuation, of a beautiful friendship.

Section Three
Spontaneous Safari

This journey began with Sanford's fable in response to a writing exercise about making a mistake. Then, Ernie picked up the thread and told us about some elephants who were his houseguests. Janet posted some elephant poetry she found on the Internet on our list-site. Marilyn announced there was a contest to name a newborn elephant at the Louisville Zoo. Heather took a classic elephant poem, and applied it to the disability community.

Come travel with us through the results of this spontaneous safari.

MBS-ED

The Mistake

Sanford Rosenthal

In a daze, Kimba stumbled past the tree limb he'd knocked to the ground. He was thinking how great the familiar pulpy taste was as he'd worked his tusks into the bark.

Suddenly, there was an unfamiliar buzzing and stinging. He didn't understand what was going on, nor did he have time to. The only thing he could comprehend for now was that there were a bunch of little guys coming at him from all directions. At first, there was a pleasant relaxing buzzing sound that didn't seem to warrant his attention. Then in less than five seconds, it grew in intensity to the kind of sound he sometimes heard when there was thunder and lightning. "No," he decided to himself. This wasn't like that, either. It was more like a whirlwind. He decided he had spent enough time classifying this dilemma, because at the same time, his giant ears and wildly flailing trunk were fighting a losing battle with the swarming insects.

He knew one thing for sure. It was time for Plan B. This plan was invoked often in the jungle by all its inhabitants. Everyone seemed to know it, without knowing why. The plan said: When in doubt, get out.

Kimba was on the move before he could even remember telling his giant feet to start. Beautiful Bertha knew, before the tree fell, what was to come. She tried to warn him, but he didn't listen. Kimba loved this wise elephant that he considered to be his woman, but also resented her for being right all the time.

Now he was paying the price for not listening. It suddenly dawned on him why Bertha had backed up more than one hundred feet. Yes, Bertha was right again.

He surmised, "These must be those new bees discussed by the elders the other night, and they didn't appreciate the way their home was knocked down."

Kimba ran hard for a while but slowed his pace when he started breathing heavily from exhaustion and the waning excitement of it all. Bertha could hardly keep up. She knew not to try and talk to him. Kimba was pouting. A couple of hours later, they emerged from deep within the jungle to find their favorite lazy flowing bend in the river. In the cool of sundown, Bertha coaxed Kimba into the water and took some big gulps of air through her nose. She knew how to suck the water in this way for the shower Kimba needed. Kimba started to cool down, as Bertha's trunk became a magical hose, soothing all the places where he was stung by all those nasty little guys.

Bertha felt as though she'd burst if she didn't get a chance to say what was on her mind. She couldn't contain herself anymore. "You shouldn't have continued eating that tree when I told you there was a bee hive there."

Kimba retorted, "I couldn't believe those little guys could affect me in any meaningful way."

"That's the trouble with you," Bertha said. "You're thick-headed. Always thinking size and power are everything."

Kimba started to shove her but suddenly realized what he was doing. It would be foolish to make a second mistake while trying to correct the first one. Then, for the first time Bertha could ever remember, she heard him say, "I think I made a big mistake."

She said, "You seem to have made quite a few lately, like not thanking me for trying to warn you."

Kimba said, "I'm sorry." Then he nuzzled her while planting a giant of a kiss on Bertha's cheek. She was lost in thought, as she spun her tail around, thinking about the silly cliché in which elephants are never supposed to forget about what they learned. There was a part of her that hoped it might be true. She was content to only kiss him back and not do any more talking.

Temporary Employment

Ernest A. Jones

I want to report about my new job. It's a specialized position. In fact, I fear I've worked myself right out of the job. I had the sole responsibility for bathing two hundred and fifty elephants. Yes, you're reading correctly, I had to bathe two hundred and fifty dirty elephants.

It was about a week or so ago that I bathed one hundred and fifty elephants, from quite small ones to rather large ones. These arrived in the first shipment and showed they had been well cared for. When I was finished, they stood all clean and shiny, some with trunks trumpeting straight upwards, while a few held their trunks in front of them. But they appeared to be thankful for the bath, and all were in perfect condition.

Today I bathed another one hundred elephants that arrived in the second shipment. Poor critters, these had a harder time in transport. It was obvious some of their trainers were harsh on them. Such caretakers should be fired and replaced, because five elephants were badly injured. We had to do surgery on them. Four had been treated so badly that they were completely missing a leg. That's right, the whole leg was missing, as if sawed off and left lying at the beast's feet. But the fifth one was the worst. How she could still hold her head up is amazing. She had her trunk completely cut off, lying at her feet.

Thanks to a good surgeon, we do believe that all five of these beautiful animals will be able to face tomorrow almost as well as the other two hundred forty-five. The surgeon was very good at reattaching the missing limbs, and it's felt they will mend quite nicely. We hope they heal rapidly, and we'll take the wrap off in a few days to make sure. For the next few days, we'll keep these five away from the main herd. For sure, they'll need some special attention and extra food. But regardless, they need not fear, for even if they don't mend perfectly, they'll still be allowed to remain and have a full life.

The other two hundred forty-five are doing just fine, eagerly waiting for new green pastures. I'm afraid they might be in cramped quarters for a few weeks, but they seem contented.

While I was bathing the last hundred and the surgeon was repairing the injured, it was snowing outside—probably a couple inches of the soft but very wet fluff before the warming temperature melted the snow. The snow vanished almost faster than it had appeared. We didn't expose our equatorial houseguests to the pleasures of snowball fights, but they seem to be tolerating the change in climate quite well.

The preceding is what I wrote after cleaning two hundred and fifty hand-carved miniature elephants, all made out of shades of the jade rock. They were later given as remembrances at our daughter's spring wedding. Even though I knew these were hand-carved, I was still taken aback when I beheld the different sizes and shapes. Here we get so used to machine-made items, all pressed in the same mold. But with these, each one was different.

The Blind Men and the Elephant: A Summary

The blind men and the elephant story is a fable-style plea for careful investigation and patience before conclusions are drawn and action taken. It originated in eastern religions. The most popular version, the poem by John Godfrey Saxe, was written over a hundred years ago.

Six blind men, each examine a different part of an elephant's anatomy and stated their findings: a spear, a fan, and a rope were some of the descriptors for the whole elephant by the men who touched his tusk, ear, and tail, respectively. The other three men each individually found the elephant to resemble a snake (his trunk), a tree (his leg), or a wall (his side)—an opinion determined by the part each was touching. Conflicting opinions were never resolved.

MBS-ED

"Think if those men had pooled their resources, as we are doing, how much knowledge they might have gathered and shared with others." Janet Schmidt

Who Are We?

Heather J. Kirk

Perhaps the fascination of our authors with the legend of the blind men and the elephant is more ironic than we first understood. Although most of the members of our writers group are blind, we don't seem to identify with the blind men in the story. Instead, we're the elephant. Whether the elephant is a sum of its parts or a whole first, then divided into various parts, no elephant is exactly like another. Both individually and as a group, we're unique. We're complex. We have many facets to our beings—physically, emotionally and intellectually.

Although we are guilty of compartmentalization when we ask others, "What's your disability," we're tired of having people categorized and judged by labels such as blind, sighted, deaf, hearing, disabled, able-bodied, mentally challenged, gifted, savant, brain-damaged, normal, congenital, progressive, juvenile onset ...

Society in general tends to have a very limited view of how blind people or disabled people live or think or feel. We're often considered as people who can't ever be understood—and therefore never looked at beyond the "tusk." We're kept at a safe distance. Many of us have experienced being ignored in regard to our needs, thoughts, and feelings. In our presence, people ask those with us what we want and how we feel, instead of talking directly to us. Perhaps they believe although the elephant has enormous ears, it's blind after all, and so it can't hear very well. Probably that's why, when there's no one else around and they must speak to us, they yell, talking very slowly to be courteous and better understood.

If you just laughed, you, too, are probably an elephant of a unique kind, and certainly not a "blind man" even if you happen to be blind.

Many people believe they understand us by virtue of the assigned label defining all we are. "Ah-ha! That's a tail."

Whether they can tell the difference between an elephant's tail and a mouse's tail is highly unlikely. A tail is a tail, after all.

The only person in this legend we strive to be is the narrator who understood the wisdom of putting the pieces together and seeing the whole picture.

One of us might approach the telling of a personal legend through poetry, another through fiction, others through personal essays. We know the elephant isn't just a spear, rope, fan, wall, tree, snake, tusk, tail, ear, side, knee, or trunk.

As you read or listen to *Behind Our Eyes,* you'll find we present our own living legend, a book rich with life and hope that cannot be ignored.

"Life's hurdles are like elephants. Damn big, but you can still go around them."
Courtney Gale

Part Seven

Flaunting Full Moons and Fantasies

A Preview

Are our dreams really about insecurity or libido, or could they just be our promises running wild? Can you imagine vision as a handicap? What would you like to send into space? What's in the mind of a witch or a waitress with a surprise up her sleeve? Could you turn a humorous misunderstanding into entertainment for others? We'll keep our curiosity and creativity in stretch mode and leave the nuts and bolts to those digital wizards in the plastic boxes that seem to keep shrinking.

A Witch With an Attitude

Nancy Scott

She knows that spells
are more than stuffing and straw.
It's the planned cat-smile
and the stitched-to-a-point nose,
but mostly it's the gold
lamé hat she flaunts
cock-eyed on the broom;
astride like she's got
the horse tamed
and could take off and fly
whenever she damn well likes.

But just now she's staying,
fingers of her right hand
pointed skyward—
the secret angle to salute
all those angels
who've been telling her
how to be hallowed.
Flash. Fashion.
She dares to win a prize.

Horn of Plenty

Nancy Scott

The mouth is gaudy
with fruit and flowers and leaves;
they are ripe,
blooming green, obvious.

It is the narrow end,
the underneath,
stem and scheme
of wire and moss
that makes me sleepless.

One eye, one finger, probing,
searching for unlisted stars,
an end of the whole of things,
never easily seen
from the top of anywhere.

The Final Frontier

Nancy Scott

I love anything to do with space though I am not brave or healthy enough to go there. Airplanes bother my ears, and I spend most flights white-knuckling armrests to hold up the plane, having great faith in my ability to will good things.

But what if, for five-hundred dollars you could send a pound of anything up, and have it come back to you?

One TV commentator for the winning X PRIZE flight sent up his wedding ring and family photos. A friend said she'd fly costume jewelry and sell it later for megabucks. Another friend speculated about sending written prayers. A third friend said she wouldn't waste her money. My favorite astronomer said low earth orbit wasn't far enough.

I like the ring idea, or any jewelry I'd wear a lot. But I'd probably send copies of my poetry chapbooks to sell for a higher price when they returned. I'd package the books in a silk bag with hearts and stars on it.

Oh, I'd happily pay to have a pound of my faith or my potential prospects go weightless, even for a short time.

Maybe NASA should try this as a fundraiser. It might tempt more people than charging twenty-million dollars to ride on a Russian Soyuz.

What do you think? What would you send?

Please God, Not My Baby

DeAnna Quietwater Noriega (Fiction)

Molly Foster sat nervously on the wooden chair in Doc Taylor's examination room. Gently she rocked her four-month-old daughter in her arms. She tried to comfort herself with the thought that, even though there were some signs of a problem, it didn't mean Jamie would be severely afflicted. There were treatments and procedures. Maybe she was only marginally affected, please God. There was no history of such a thing on either side of the family. Surely she was only imagining things. Mama always told her not to borrow trouble, and here she was, with her heart trying to pound its way out of her chest over something that might not mean anything.

The door to the hall opened. The measured footsteps of the Doc, and the lighter tap of his nurse Velma's shoes, reverberated on the smooth tile floor as they entered the room.

"What seems to be the problem, Molly?" asked Doc as he lightly touched her shoulder; then ran his sensitive hand over Jamie's downy head.

"Doc, I know some babies are more sensitive than others, but Jamie's sensitivity is different. She hates it when the sun is especially hot. It doesn't matter if she is perfectly cool, say, in her bath out in the screened-in porch. She starts to fuss. Whenever we are outside, she hides her face." Molly lowered her voice. "Her eyelids are odd. She flutters them when I touch her. You don't think …"

"Now Molly girl, don't get too worried. Let me have her for a few minutes. I'll do some simple tests."

Doc Taylor lifted the baby from her mother's arms before treading carefully out of the room, followed by the nurse. He took the baby into another examination room.

"Velma, get my photoflashometer from the desk drawer in my office." In moments, the nurse was back, placing the instrument on the table with a heavy clunk. The doc turned the instrument to its lowest setting. As it gave off a hum, he passed it in front of the baby's face. Gently, his sensitive fingers stroked Jamie's satiny cheek, and touched her silky lashes. They fluttered against his touch. "I'll be right back, Velma. I just need to do one more test."

Doc Taylor stepped out the back door. Lifting his face to the warmth of the sun, he reached into his pocket. Drawing out his gold Braille pocket watch, he swung it back and forth in front of the baby's face. She turned her head to follow the swinging object. Her small hand reached toward it, and she cooed with delight.

With a heavy heart, Doc returned inside to tell Molly the bad news. "I'm so sorry Molly girl," he said, shifting the baby into her mother's arms, "your baby is a visioner. She responded to my photoflashometer. Now that just means she perceives light, which isn't very serious. But when I swung my watch in front of her, she followed it with head movements. We can limit how much she is distracted, of course, by bandaging her eyes whenever she is taken outside, or you open a hatch to let air into the house.

"But you know, if she is allowed to use vision to explore her world, she will never learn to use her other senses effectively. She will be dependent on vision for too much. This will distract her from developing normally. It will stunt her mental growth and limit her to only being able to manage during daylight hours, or outdoors when there is sufficient light. But if we are careful, and protect her from light as much as possible, it may not be so bad."

Molly held her daughter close as tears rolled down her face. What would everyone say? How would they treat her precious little daughter? Would she have to live with loneliness and ostracism? What about her education? Would this vision thing, this learning disability, limit her to performing menial outdoor tasks? Would she have difficulty finding a husband because of the fear her condition might be passed on to her children?

Oh, how could such an awful thing happen? Well, whatever it took, Molly vowed she would fight to raise her child as normally as possible. If hard work and love could prevent Jamie's condition from ruining her life, Molly would be there for this little person entrusted to her care.

Jungle Fever in Georgia

Albert Cooper

I was standing in my front yard the other day when a young lady named Consuelo came up to me and said, "Mr. Cooper, I know you're a blind man. I don't mean to get into your business, but I'm very puzzled about something you do. Can I ask you a question?"

"Sure. Go ahead and ask me anything you like."

"Sir, I've been watching you. I've noticed every time you walk out of your house to get in a car to go somewhere, you always stop at the end of your walk and bend over toward the car as if you're looking in there. But it can't be because you're looking, I know you can't see so, why do you do it?"

I turned toward her with a chuckle. "You can call me Coop. That's the nickname I got when I was a little kid. Now, to answer your question, I have to tell you a story. Come on; let's sit down on my front porch so I can explain."

As we walked up the steps I began telling her the following story: It's funny now, but it could have been dangerous then. It's all about people judging each other, and making assumptions based on somebody's race, color, gender, religion, or physical size. You can learn a lot by seeing how people treat each other.

Nobody would have ever thought, fifty years ago when I was born, I would be telling you a funny story about something that happened to a big black blind man. You see, I was a sighted kid who got into all the same kinds of trouble the other kids did except, I was bigger than they were. I got teased a lot. By the time I was fourteen I weighed two hundred eighty-five pounds and was almost six feet tall. My shoe size matched my age for years.

Finally, I decided to turn my size into an advantage. I became the best defensive tackle in the Georgia high school football program. I earned a scholarship to the University of Louisville and played football there. People didn't hurt my feelings about my size anymore. Though I liked the attention I got from playing, it wasn't what I wanted to do beyond college.

In 1981 I was ready for my twenty-fourth birthday. I got up that morning all excited about celebrating with my little family. It was a special day all right, but not in the way I expected. In two hours my life was to change drastically, because I was shot in the face with a twelve-gage shotgun by a man who didn't take time to find out much about me. He was afraid of my size and jumped to the wrong conclusion. After several surgeries I had to face the fact I was going to have to learn to live as a blind man.

Ten years later I was pretty well used to being blind. On my thirty-fourth birthday I decided to have some fun. My cousin called me about going to Atlanta to celebrate. My neighbor, Pap, agreed to watch the house while I was gone. He took me to the bank so I could get cash for the trip. We laughed and joked on the way to the bank. He parked right in front of it.

While I was inside, withdrawing my cash, folding it according to its denomination, and storing it in my wallet, two or three customers pulled up in their cars, and asked Pap to move up so there would be more room for parking. He did assuming he could catch my attention when I came out of the bank and help me find his car. Meantime, he noticed a good-looking woman in a short, red skirt hanging out across the street. His eyes and his mind were on her, not on me.

Unfolding my white cane I exited the bank. Moving down the sidewalk I ran into a man. When he apologized I could tell by his accent he was a white man. He said he hadn't realized I was blind, and he shouldn't have been in my way. I told him it was all right, no harm done. We went our separate ways. Upon reaching the curb, I opened the car door, and got inside. Turning to Pap I said, "Let's ride."

"Help me! Help me! Help me! He's gonna rape me! He's gonna rape me!" screamed a white woman in the driver's seat. She kept getting louder.

I'm sure I was as scared as she was. What was going on? Where was Pap? "Ma'am! Ma'am," I tried to exclaim, but she wasn't listening. I knew better than to try to touch her arm to get her attention.

"This man, he got in my car! He's gonna hurt me! He's gonna rape me!" she hollered.

I could hear car doors slamming. They told me later people were standing around trying to figure out what was going on. People came out of businesses. Traffic was backing up. By this time, I had figured out what must have happened. I decided the only way I could prove to her I wasn't going to hurt her, and the only way I could shut her up, was to get out of the car. I opened the door, but someone immediately slammed it against my leg. I couldn't move. Maybe they thought I was trying to run away from the scene of the crime. I just wanted to get away from the screaming and not draw any more attention to myself.

The woman's husband apparently heard her yelling from inside the bank and came dashing out to save her. He was the white man I had run into when I was leaving the bank. Finally the light must have dawned. He started trying to calm his wife. He told her I was blind and pointed out my cane. She was having none of it. "He's got a weapon! He was gonna rape me! Get him away from me! Get him out of here! Call the police!"

Where was Pap through all this? Why didn't he come to my rescue? I was getting nervous. This woman was crazy.

Finally, the teller who had helped me with my withdrawals, and who had seen everything through the window, came to my defense. She explained to the husband how I happened to get into the wrong car. His wife wouldn't listen to her either.

The traffic backup, the horns, the screaming woman, and the approach of the police got Pap's attention. He came back to the couple's car to investigate. By this time the man had moved and I had hurriedly gotten out of the car. I just wanted them to get on their way and let me do the same. We walked toward Pap's automobile. People in the crowd who knew me started teasing. These black folks thought it was hilarious, but I hadn't seen the humor yet.

"Coop, I didn't know you liked little-old, white women now."

"Yo, I didn't know you were lookin' for white meat these days."

"What's the matter? You got a little jungle fever?"

The police came down to Pap's car to talk to me. They had already talked with the white couple and wanted to make sure everybody was telling the same story. I couldn't understand why those folks who thought it was so funny hadn't tried to help me. That woman thought because of my size and because I was where I didn't belong, I had to be up to no good.

The bank teller came out again when she saw a policeman had me out of Pap's car with my hands in the air. She told them what she had seen. They seemed to be satisfied. I got back in the car and turned to Pap, "Get me the hell out of here."

Pap was laughing so hard he could barely drive.

It was about four weeks before I felt comfortable going back to that neighborhood and bank. I made several calls, thanking the teller for her assistance. Now before I get into any car I stand about a foot away from the door and lean forward to hear voices or to ask questions before getting in.

When people want to hear a funny story about a mistake somebody made because of their blindness, I can always lay 'em in the aisles with this one.

The Working Girl

Janet Schmidt

"A gentleman at the bar wishes to buy you a drink," the waitress told us. We declined.

I was in Worcester to visit with my friend, Myra, and finish an independent study for my master's degree. Since neither of us was an enthusiastic cook, we went out to dinner. The hostess had seated us at a small table under pink lighting in the lounge/bar area. The decor was dark red and black. The ambiance dim and smoke hazed.

After ordering our food, we proceeded to catch up on what we and our significant others were doing as well as the latest literature we were into.

When Myra left the table to use the lady's room, a man in a business suit appeared beside me and said, "What do you say you and I spend the night together?"

"I don't think you can afford me."

"How much would I have to pay?"

"You'll have to ask the madam."

"Where is she?"

"There she is now," I pointed to my friend, Myra, as she emerged from the lady's room. He beat a hasty retreat to the black hole of the bar. I wondered in retrospect if the man proffering the drink and the one of the failed proposition were the same. If so, he possessed the good sense not to try for three strikes.

My next brush with this late-night career opportunity occurred several years later while I was a graduate student at the University of Massachusetts. Three of us had grouped together to work on a class presentation. Dean, one of the project members, was going to pick me up in front of the Harvard Coop in Cambridge. We were to meet the other member of our team at the Boston University Library for a research session. As I stood there waiting for him, a car pulled up to the curb and honked its horn. I was certain Dean's car was red, so I continued standing there. The horn sounded again. I didn't move. It sounded a third time, whereupon I reasoned perhaps I was mistaken about the color of my friend's vehicle. As I opened the door to get in a male voice informed me, "I'm waiting for my wife."

When I related this incident to Myra, she hooted with laughter as she spluttered, "So the man probably thought you were working Harvard Square. Well, that's one way of earning your tuition."

"I don't think so," I replied emphatically.

Is the third time the charm, as they say? Was I destined for night work and not getting the message?

I had chosen to attend the University of Massachusetts in Boston because my area of the world on the Canadian border didn't possess a university with a graduate program in school psychology. Being legally blind, I was condemned to a 12-hour round trip commute by bus. The first half of the ride was on a local bus that meandered along, stopping at a multitude of small towns on its way to a central hub. From there, I transferred to another bus that made fewer stops on its way to Boston.

My husband, Karl, often met me at this "central hub" on my return trip. We then continued home via our own transportation.

While waiting for him, I indulged in tea and crumpets at the terminal lunch counter. One evening, Karl joined me and ordered coffee. As the waitress started to hand me my bill, he said, "I'll take that."

"How nice to have someone pay for you," she remarked.

"Yes, he's a nice person."

The following week the lunch counter was very crowded. I found a seat next to a man who appeared engrossed in his meal. When I ordered tea and an English muffin the waitress from the previous week asked, "Do you want me to put this on his bill?"

"That would be nice but I don't think he would appreciate it."

"Oh, okay."

The man just kept eating.

Trapped

Abbie Johnson Taylor

Surrounded by walls and bars,
I'm not free.
What did I do wrong?

My eyes open.
The stark, unfriendly environment
dissolves
into a bright, welcoming place.
I'm filled with an overwhelming sense of liberty.

Lady Collingwood Models Her Birthday Suit

Mary-Jo Lord

In that dreamy state between
consciousness and deep sleep, I ride
naked on the back of our tandem bike.

My husband, in full control as he
steers us around the corner off Collingwood and
onto Truewood, brakes to
cross Avon Manor. I beg
"Please, let's just go home." We
pass many people. I
wonder if they know I'm
naked. One quick reach forward tells me my
husband is fully dressed.

I separate myself from the
dream and ask, "Is this how
Lady Godiva felt? What
statement am I trying to make?" or
"Am I like the emperor in his
new clothes,
utterly stupid or unworthy of my position?"

We stop at the neighbor's. I
long to ride home and
disappear undercover. I
somersault into morning as a
four-year-old Peeping Tom exclaims,

"She doesn't have any clothes on!"

Spirit Wind

Valerie Moreno

Simply, like a child,
My heart reaches for you
Across the bands of time.

Somehow you've managed
To touch the deepest part of my soul
With yours.

No words spoken,
Miles between us that are deeper than
Those we see.

Still the sound of your voice,
Gentle, resilient,
Lives in my heart unbound.

Maybe one day soon
I will touch your hand,
In the midst of a dream,

Looking up at you,
Seeing your sparkling eyes,
Like stars in a morning sky.

Now, About That New Waitress

Elizabeth Fiorite (Flash Fiction)

Most of us regulars at Sally's Diner thought we knew the new night shift waitress pretty good. She was a looker—and young, too. She told us her name was Barbara. When Mike called her "Barbie Doll," he got served last and found that his omelet and black coffee were cool.

"The name is Barbara," she informed him. So, like I said, we all thought we knew Barbara, okay. But not after last Friday night.

When the 11 P.M. shift from the factory ends, the diner always fills up fast. Mike is standing by our favorite booth, close to the counter. He waves us over. I see Barbara is working the counter, and I give her a little smile, which she returns.

All of a sudden, this new guy, not one of us from the factory, comes dashing in. He runs up to the one empty stool at the counter; leans over it, and in a hoarse whisper, he says, "Bunny!"

Barbara looks up from the glasses she's been filling and drops one of them. You can hardly hear the crash, there's so much other clamor going on, but I'm close enough to hear almost everything this guy is saying. Barbara doesn't even look down at the broken glass and ice cubes on the floor. Her mouth has formed a perfect little O.

The guy says, "Bunny, I've been lookin' for you ever since I got out. You got to come with me. I won't make the same mistake. I got everything figured out."

He starts talking faster. Barbara moves closer to him. Without breaking her gaze, she reaches under the counter for her purse. I try to signal the guys at the booth to pipe down so I can hear what this guy is saying. Later, I tell the police I didn't hear nothin' and I didn't see nothin'. I figure Barbara's got her reasons.

"Your ma's dyin', anyway, and you don't need to be stayin' in that dump with your drunk of a father."

He starts to say more, but Barbara pulls a small pistol from her bag, points it at his chest, and fires. The pop of the gun is barely heard, and by the time the guy hits the floor, Barbara returns the gun to her bag, which she slips over her shoulder as she disappears out the door.

The Lucky Charm

Gertie E. Poole

Razor, a young griffin, flattened his ears and peered up from his notes to watch his twin brother, Laser, frantically dart around their cliff cave home. It was impossible to study with Laser upsetting everything. Why start all this hunting now?

"That's very distracting, you know. Why don't you study instead of driving yourself mad?"

Laser scowled at him and ground his beak. "I'll never pass the Level One testing without my lucky charm. I don't have to study if I can find it. It has great powers. It was given to me by the wood sprites. I told you all about it. You know the charm I'm talking about. Help me find it."

Razor rolled his eyes. "You've searched everywhere already. Twice, in fact. Forget it. If you study, you'll stand a better chance of passing that test without that crazy charm of yours, anyway. Those things never work and you know it."

Laser flung up his fire-red wings. "You don't understand, you never do. This is crucial. This charm really does work and I had it, I know I did. Why isn't it here? Dad is counting on me passing that Level One test today and I can't do it without my charm. Maybe we've been robbed. We must have been robbed."

Razor threw his notes down and trotted over to Laser's sleeping nook. There would be no peace until Laser's latest obsession was found. His beak scraped the floor in his attempt to inventory Laser's belongings. A few interesting rocks, some delicately cut jewels given to him from the dwarves, and his carrying tote which had been turned inside out several times and shaken vigorously in the hunt.

Razor shrugged. "Looks like it's all there to me. I don't think anyone would take that charm and leave those jewels behind."

Laser huffed in frustration. "Except my lucky charm is still missing. Help me move those boulders over there." He pointed with a claw to the heavy rocks positioned at the rear of the cave, used for sharpening beaks. "Perhaps it slid down behind one."

Groaning with the strain of shuffling the large stones, the twins managed to rearrange them so the floor could be examined. It was a huge effort that required both grifflets to back-wing feverishly, rocks locked in their talons. Feathers flew and littered the cave floor, but even though the task was accomplished, it revealed nothing of interest except a sleepy beetle who hustled to be back beneath the pile of rocks again. Razor watched the bug absently, then turned as Laser complained.

"It's not here," whined Laser, his voice reaching a high hysterical pitch. "I'm doomed without it," he added in defeat, as he flopped down dejectedly.

Razor, panting heavily and brushing the sand from his talons, caught sight of the sun's position. "Oh, Good Gods, we've spent all this time looking for your missing charm and now it's time to leave. I didn't finish studying. We can't be late or we flunk automatically."

They hurried to the practice field as Master Argon told the classmates where to sit for the test. They were the last to arrive, and Argon scowled at them and pointed a huge, razor-sharp talon where they would take the exam. A hush fell over the students as the tests were distributed. Some bent eagerly, anxious to answer the questions quickly before their memories failed them. Argon watched over his students—his keen eyes and sensitive hearing would not permit any covert attempts at cheating.

Razor found the first two questions relatively easy and jotted down the correct responses, but knew the remaining answers to the test resided in his notes he left behind, unstudied. Silently, he cursed Laser's superstitious tendencies. Why hadn't he ignored everything except his notes? He raised his beak and risked a guarded glance to his brother.

Laser was a griffin condemned. The ordinarily healthy salt-and-pepper feathers crowned by carnelian wings had faded to a dismal washed-out gray, a normal reaction for a griffin about to faint. Stress brought on color changes that were quite effective in battle, but Laser was waging a war on his own and was already defeated. Why did he put so much faith in the supernatural? A simple talisman—no more, no less. A shiny piece of pressed metal in the shape of a moon paralyzed his brother by its absence. Why wasn't he trying to answer the questions? He wasn't even reading the test. His eyes, clouded, stared blankly into space. Razor gave an internal shake of the head and bent to finish the test as best he could. At least he'd make every effort. He might get lucky.

The pencil point snapped, and as required, he raised a claw for Argon, who trotted over. Razor showed him his pencil and Argon nodded. "All right, get another from your tote." The teacher watched as Razor fished around in the tote's pencil compartment.

To his horror, a small glittering chain with the lucky moon pendant entangled his pencil. He shook it free and surreptitiously folded the tote flap. He winced as Argon left to attend another student. Laser's lucky charm was in his tote the entire time. Laser must have mixed up the totes when he tucked the charm in it. They had neglected to examine Razor's tote bag.

He sank down and with the new pencil, scrutinized the next question. To his amazement, the answer came immediately to him as if he were struck with lightning. He swallowed as guilt flooded his soul. The lucky charm is helping me through this test, and I told Laser it was nonsense. Brilliant flashes of knowledge charged him and he elaborated endlessly on the essay questions. Equations, quotations, the wisdom of the world and infinite information channeled through the charm into Razor's mind, and he wrote furiously. Quicksilver ideas pulsed through him and his claws had trouble keeping the pace as his pencil burned across the pages. He was exhausted by the time the test was turned in.

Afterwards, they relaxed in the fragrant shade of a huge apple tree, laden with ripe fruit. Nibbling at the sweet fallen apples, they waited for the tests to be graded and returned.

"Well, it wasn't my fault you packed it in the wrong tote. It was accidental, and you were the one who put it there. I didn't even know it was there until I needed a pencil. It does work, Laser, I'm sorry I doubted you. I knew everything, even things I know I don't know. It's unbelievable," said Razor, apple juice dribbling from his beak.

Laser snatched the charm from Razor's talons. "I can't believe it. You had it all the time? Let me have it back so I won't lose it again." He tucked it into his own tote with a sigh. "At least one of us will pass. Did you remember the chant and the little shuffle thing?"

Razor's beak dropped open and he giggled with incredulity. "The what?"

Laser snapped his beak in annoyance. Razor was making fun of his charm again. "I told you how it worked, before. It's an ancient wood sprite ceremony for truth. You must do it right. Remember? You need to say this sacred chant and …" He pranced, lifting each back paw in turn and began wiggling his behind.

Razor burst out in laughter. "No, I certainly didn't do that. I wouldn't do that if you paid me. What makes you think Master Argon would allow you to do that ridiculous dance during a test?"

Laser shrugged, digging his back claws in the dirt. "Well, I'd be as inconspicuous as possible. At least the charm would be cast correctly. I don't know what happens if you do it wrong. I guess we'll find out, won't we? You shouldn't laugh at ancient traditions you know nothing about," he hissed, as Master Argon strode up to them, papers in talon.

Shaking his head, he handed Laser his blank paper back with a huge glaring red zero scribbled across the top. "Very disappointing. I can tell you were totally unprepared, Laser. Study hard for the next testing. You should have made an attempt to answer at least some of the questions."

Laser sulked, clutched his failed test, and nodded dutifully. Argon turned to Razor, who stood up, anticipating compliments on his masterpiece. He wondered if he was the only student to ace the difficult test. Chest puffed out and eyes gleaming, Razor began to deflate as Master Argon cleared his throat.

"Well, Razor, you started off all right. You answered the first two correctly. I'm not sure what you were thinking for the rest of the test, or even what test you studied for, but it wasn't mine. I must say, it made for interesting reading, though. Unfortunately, we're griffins and what we study is the art of war, not creative writing. Perhaps you should consider writing a book?" The black and silver griffin gave a short laugh and shook his head at Razor as he handed back another failing paper. "I'm sure, if the two of you study hard enough, you'll both pass next time. You should study together. Oh yes, and by the way, study my subject and the notes I give you, if you want to pass one of my tests."

Razor collapsed on the ground in defeat. All the charm-given answers were incorrect. Every single one of them. Scanning through the test quickly, Razor realized that Argon was right. All the answers were totally ambiguous, rambling drivel that at the time he wrote them seemed like outstanding answers to the questions. Where one question concerned battle tactics, his answer seemed to elaborate on forest growth patterns. Another question on defensive maneuvers was answered with a rather imaginative bit of fairy folklore. Confounded wood sprite magic! He threw his test at Laser and cuffed him, plucking several white crest feathers and sent them flying.

"You and that blasted charm. The only way that charm works is if we don't spend our study time looking for it. You see? It didn't work a bit. This is all your fault. Never again will I let myself be taken in by your foolishness"

Laser ducked his brother's blows and grinned. "I told you. Didn't do the chant, didn't do the dance. Wouldn't do it even if I paid you to," he mimicked sarcastically. "Maybe next time you'll pay closer attention when I'm telling you important things." Laser looked back over his wing at his furious brother as he sauntered away. He sang the wood sprite chant and did the shuffle dance, wiggling his behind, his red-tipped tail flagging in the wind.

Anytime Resolutions

Sanford Rosenthal

Lost—can't find Months Road;
You pick up a hitchhiker, Captain Atmosphere,
Wearing the strangest smile you ever saw.

A sign says, "Weeks Lane,"
But it's not on the map.

Best make your companion your friend.
Have drinks at Days Inn with party-goers.

Pulling out of Hourly Road
You witness a balancing act,
A man on a tightrope with no wire in sight.

Horns blast, replacing reality with much fanfare.
Up ahead, green light turns yellow.
You're sure you can reach it before it turns red.
Officer Minute lets you go
As you promise never to speed again.

You should be elated, but something is wrong.
Your companion is gone, no time to wonder why.
You turn onto Second Street.

Is that revelry in your mind, or all around you?
Was that a siren?
Don't they split Second Street at the next intersection?

A sudden epiphany penetrates your subconscious!
Your last thought is:
"New Year's resolutions are not as powerful
As anytime resolutions could have been."

Part Eight
Angels Watching

A Preview

How well do we take care of each other? Family support makes tough times easier. But sometimes courage has to come from within or from watchful spirits who seem to know exactly what we need.

When That Baby Comes

Nicole Bissett

"You are pregnant," the doctor announced. "I hope you wanted to be." I felt my face lose its color. This was just a routine appointment, and the pregnancy test had been an afterthought. It never occurred to me I'd hear news which would change my life forever. We'd only been married four months, and although I wanted to have a baby eventually, this was too many changes too fast.

I had been blind since birth, so that was not a major concern. Unfortunately, I hadn't been around many babies, and only recalled changing a few diapers as a teen, when I babysat my cousin.

Fortunately, there was a good community of supportive blind people in St. Louis, where I lived at the time. I was introduced to two competent, blind mothers. One of them showed me the easiest way to change diapers. She also served as a good sounding board as I shared concerns, and she offered pointers about rearing a child as a blind parent. I appreciated the support, because people asked more questions than I could answer.

I encountered the worst attitude from a childbirth instructor, who came across as someone who might call Child Protective Services on me. I had read of blind couples losing their children because of ignorant misconceptions about blindness. The fear of that happening to me grew as this woman addressed me.

"When your baby comes," she asked, "who will be around to help take care of it when your husband is at work?" My husband had some usable vision, so she must have assumed he would do everything.

"I'll be taking care of the baby myself," I answered.

"A lot goes into taking care of a child," she informed me. Her tone suggested I was still a child wanting to play house, rather than a twenty-five-year-old woman.

"I know that," I retorted.

"How will you know when the baby has diaper rash?" she asked.

"I can feel it," I replied.

"Not always, but, well how are you going to handle it when the baby becomes a toddler and starts getting into things?"

"I'll hear him. Also, there are leashes I can use, or bells I can put on his shoes." Was I in an interview for a job, with this intruder assigned to decide whether I was qualified to be a parent to my own child? Perhaps she picked up on my resentment, because she stopped her line of questioning after that. Fortunately, as far as I know, she didn't call CPS.

My biggest concern was that I wasn't giddy with excitement over being pregnant the way everyone seemed to expect me to be. I was bombarded with unsolicited advice and fortune-telling on how I would feel when that baby came.

"When that baby comes, you won't get any sleep."

"When that baby comes, you're going to love him more than you've ever loved anyone."

None of this meant anything to me, because I thought my lack of interest in the pregnancy made me a bad mother automatically. Even when he kicked, though I was fascinated at first, I couldn't seem to conjure up feelings of closeness.

The best part of the pregnancy was labor and delivery, even though I was in labor all night. For one thing—and this is a big thing—the epidural worked. Knowing I would find out about motherhood one way or another put my mind at ease.

Eddie arrived on the Sunday morning of February 5, 1995, at 10:28 AM. He was quiet, and that scared me. Eventually, after a time which seemed like an eternity, but was really more like thirty seconds, I heard the sound of his first cries. Suddenly, now that Eddie was out of the womb, I understood that he was a separate entity and had his own voice and personality.

When the nurse placed him on me for the first time, he stopped crying. I was stunned. This little being, which I'd been carrying for nine months, had some idea who I was, and he felt life would be okay with me. He didn't ask how I was going to take care of him. He just needed and loved me unconditionally. I knew then, whatever challenges I would face, it would be okay.

I won't tell you there weren't challenges, but with Eddie's easy-going personality, we made it through them all with relative tranquility. He wasn't a fussy baby, which helped. He seemed to have distinct cries for when he was wet, hungry or tired, and I understood them quickly. The only other time he fussed a lot was when he was teething.

I was fortunate to have a good team of friends and family around, as well as an excellent pediatrician, and a woman from Nurses for Newborns. This nurse came to my home for a year and put my mind at ease about the minor, day-to-day concerns any mother has with an infant.

Eddie only had two diaper rashes. They occurred when he had ear infections and was on antibiotics. The rashes were easy to spot by feel, and I cared for them without assistance.

Using a leash with Eddie was rarely necessary. He quickly learned how far was too far to go and was good about staying nearby. He understood, before he could talk, that he had to communicate his wants and needs to us in different ways. If he wanted my attention, he came to me and tapped me. If he wanted his father's attention, he just pointed.

Ironically, Eddie was notably hurt first in the care of a sighted babysitter, who just happened to turn her back. He hit his head on the corner of a glass table and was cut. Although stitches weren't required, it gave us quite a scare.

Eddie is twelve years old now. He's in the sixth grade, in all honors classes, and making nearly straight A's. With the help of other parents, he just finished his first soccer season and is into martial arts.

People mistakenly assume that, because Eddie's vision is normal, he takes care of me. I didn't have a child for that purpose. Maybe, when I'm old and gray, he can do some of that if I need it. For now, it is important that he respect me as the parent.

Eddie has always had a great sense of humor, and excellent social skills. He is unusually mature and has a strong sense of right and wrong. He has never made fun of other children with disabilities. I couldn't be more proud of him. Needless to say, we've definitely bonded since the pregnancy days. Without a doubt, my life changed for the better when that baby came.

Will You Be My Mommy?

Ernest A. Jones

"Daddy, I don't feel good."

"Well son, it looks like you have the chicken pox. I was afraid you'd get them after being with the other children who were sick."

While I tried to make my son comfortable, I wondered what I'd do, because I had to work the next day. My son didn't like babysitters because of some bad experiences. Still, I knew I couldn't take the next two weeks off work. Then I remembered Dorothy, a friend for more than fifteen years, and gave her a call. My son wouldn't mind Dorothy, for he knew and loved her already, and would not think of her as a babysitter.

"I'll be glad to help as much as I can," she replied.

"Thank you, this is a big load off my shoulders," I said.

Dorothy worked evenings at the local hospital, and I worked the day shift in a Washington State office. I was allowed to leave my job early so she could arrive at the hospital on time, but on her days off, I worked my full shift.

One afternoon when my son felt better, he and Dorothy were playing table games. Suddenly, with no warning, he looked at her and said, "Dorothy, I know who you should marry!"

A little taken aback, Dorothy answered, "Well who might that be?"

He looked at her, surprised she hadn't figured it out, and said, "Well, my daddy of course!"

"Why should I marry your daddy?"

"Well, he's an awful good man and a good Christian!"

"That's true, but it takes more than that to marry. Is there another reason?"

With a gleam in his eyes, he answered, "Sure, I want to eat some wedding cake."

Smiling, Dorothy replied, "Okay, I will bake a fine cake and decorate it like a wedding cake for you. How is that?"

"No," he replied softly.

"Why? Is there another reason?"

He hung his head for a moment, then tipping his face to look up at her, he said, "Yes, you see, I don't have a mommy anymore, and I want you to be my mommy."

Startled by this reply, Dorothy worried that even this young lad might see the flush creeping over her face. However, she remained calm, and after finishing the game they were playing, she started preparing our supper.

It had been a stressful day at work, with several machine problems and staff absences. I was very tired physically and emotionally, when at last I clocked out and left the building. My only thought was to get home, enjoy a nice meal, and just relax.

Looking to the future as I drove home, I also looked back. Eight months ago, my wife left me, complaining, along with some false accusations, that I'd be going blind one day. She took the three children with her. My oldest son, a lad of not quite nine, refused to stay with her, and several nights later, ran back to my house. Finally, a judge awarded him to me, but not before he spent a weekend in the juvenile hall for wanting to live with me. Meantime, I was booked, fingerprinted, photographed, and charged with interfering with a court order. Now he'd be home waiting for me, and Dorothy would have a hot meal ready for us all.

As I pulled around the house to drive into the carport, my thoughts were on resting and forgetting work. But fate had a shocking surprise for me.

Entering the kitchen through the back door, I saw my son and Dorothy at the dining room table. I grinned and called a "hello" to them.

My son looked up and, giving me a broad smile, said, "Hi dad, I asked Dorothy to marry you."

Without saying a word, I hurried into my bedroom while I tried to figure out what response I should make.

For more than fifteen years, Dorothy had been like a sister to me, and I liked it that way. My life had been shattered, and I was not thinking of another woman to share it with—not yet. "Why had he said this?" I pondered. Finally, I returned to the dining room, and nothing more was said about marriage that night. It took me longer than it took my son to realize that Dorothy belonged in our future. I had healing to do first, and I had to know I could trust again.

Dorothy was a friend to me during these lonely months. We remained as brother and sister, neither allowing any serious thoughts. But a few months later, I held her hand for just a moment. My son, watching, went to school and told his teacher, a good friend of ours, that she could be the flower girl at our wedding.

Who needs to broadcast news with a son like this? Today, thirty-six years later, I have never been sorry.

Butterfly

Judith Hendrickx

I wrote this piece after a counseling session for parental loss/bereavement with a young adolescent of thirteen. I am a hospice counselor. Her father was killed only months before. In counseling I also use art therapy and sand tray. She was sitting by the sand tray, arranging a family of tiny dolls, representing her family. She was also sitting beside a large window, with a garden outside. Her silhouette was outlined by light shining in from the window.

I then noticed a Monarch butterfly, hovering on the other side of the window, above her blonde hair. It had been a very long time since I had actually seen a live butterfly, due to my vision loss. The butterfly appeared to be very large, and extraordinarily beautiful. For me, this image was surreal, other-worldly, and all that I could see was the child, the sand tray, the beautiful butterfly; all surrounded and highlighted by beams of light. Did the butterfly represent her deceased father watching over her? Perhaps.

I was touched deeply, and I still am as I recall how moving this archetypal visual/mind/spiritual experience was.

She is sitting at the table, light reflecting on her golden hair.
Golden sand shifts, moves. A sand tray
moves and shifts like time.

Beyond the glass window, butterfly wings flutter.
Wings move, light reflects golden auburn wings.
Light reflects Monarch wings of bright intensity.
Colors of transcendence,
shades of impermanence,
colors of approaching autumn,

Day of the Dead the child reminisces.
Candles glow, reflect a ritual,
reflect time passed away.
Outlined in black, like a shroud of death
wings flutter, beams of light capture gazes.
Oh, wings of time child of phases,
golden-haired child with autumn leaf wings,

For a moment, all time is suspended.
Child of light with wings of light,
she is a messenger of memories remembered as bright,
memories of being Daddy's babe again.

Wink at the Devil

Elizabeth Fiorite (Fiction)

Mary Covelli dried her hands and hung her apron in the pantry. She automatically surveyed the kitchen before switching off the light, stepping into the hallway, and pausing at the half-open door of her mother's bedroom. Reassured by the sounds of rhythmic breathing, she noiselessly padded to the dining room, where she picked up the large envelope containing Benjie's scholarship application forms from the largest stack of mail on the buffet.

Benjie's chances of getting a basketball scholarship to De Paul University seemed promising. He was a junior at St. John's, an honor student, and he earned his own spending money bagging groceries and stocking shelves at Jewel. Tony Parisi, the basketball coach at St. John's, and Benjie's father, Ben Covelli, had been classmates and stars of St. John's High School basketball team in their day.

Both men had gone to De Paul, where Tony continued in sports and graduated with an education degree. Ben had to drop out after two years when money ran low. He worked at any number of jobs (the most lucrative being construction work), took night classes, and graduated the year before Mary and he were married. He was two courses away from his MBA degree and had just been promoted to assistant foreman when he was killed in an accident at the construction site. Benjie was three weeks short of his fourth birthday.

Mary began to muse, talking to Ben as though they were sharing a cup of coffee after a meal or sitting on the front porch on a cool autumn evening, watching for the stars to come out.

"You'd be so proud of Benjie," she murmured. "He's your clone, all right."

Mary wondered if Ben really heard all the monologues she had with him. "He's a natural athlete, just like you, and he's smart, too. I think I should get some credit for that. He'll be seventeen next month. Some days he acts like he's twelve, but then there are times when his maturity scares me."

Mary and Benjie had moved into her parents' ample apartment in Westchester, one of Chicago's oldest suburbs, shortly after Ben's death. Aunt Bea and Uncle Vinnie lived in the upstairs apartment, so Benjie never lacked adult supervision growing up. Mama watched Benjie when Mary started working as assistant librarian at Kennedy Junior High.

When she finally settled in the living room, Mary eased herself into her father's old recliner and turned on the table lamp. How often had her father held Benjie in this chair, headrest reclined, feet elevated, reading him to sleep as he had read to Mary and her sisters years before?

The gentle ticking of the grandfather clock in the front hallway lulled Mary into a peaceful feeling of serenity and well-being. She allowed her thoughts to wander. In two weeks, it would be a year since her father's death. He, too, was taken from her suddenly, without warning, without goodbyes.

Papa and Benjie had been inseparable after Ben's death. Papa, having gratefully allowed his wife to have the leading role in the raising of their three daughters, was challenged, delighted, and rejuvenated to have Benjie follow him around the store he managed, listen to his stories, and bring him his drawings and papers from school, to be proudly displayed on the refrigerator door. Papa had found in Benjie an eager listener, an avid learner, and a repository for the Lucetti wisdom.

When a case of measles kept Benjie from trying out for the Tiny Mites baseball team, everyone told Benjie it was just bad luck.

"It's no such thing, this bad luck," Papa had said, carrying an armload of library books into Benjie's semi-darkened room. "We'll use this time to find out about something we don't know. We don't waste time thinking about what we can't do now. You fall down, you get up. You'll learn; you have to wink at the devil. Next time he'll pass you by. 'That Benjie,' he'll say, 'he's too smart for me!' Now, which of these books do you want me to read first?"

Tears welled in Mary's eyes, but she hurriedly wiped them away with her fingertips, not wanting Benjie to find her sniffling and red-eyed when he came home from practice. The grandfather clock chimed nine bells, stirring Mary from her reverie. She reached for the remote control and clicked on the news, keeping the volume almost at mute. The blurred picture reminded her that she needed to make an appointment with Dr. Sanders. Was it two years ago he told her she had Retinitis Pigmentosa (RP) and to see a specialist? She had given up night driving months ago, but was lucky enough to have teachers and another librarian to ride with when there were evening meetings at school.

Mary had never told anyone what Dr. Sanders said. According to the Merck Manual in the school library, Retinitis Pigmentosa was a genetic disease of the retina, usually causing total blindness. Grandma Lucetti had been blind, but she was also hard of hearing, and Mary had thought it was due to the aging process.

Lisa from Dr. Sanders' office had left a message on the answering machine asking her to call, but Mary hadn't listened to the messages until after five P.M. Well, it would have to wait until Monday. She hoped it had nothing to do with Benjie's appointment this afternoon. He wouldn't have forgotten to keep the appointment. They had talked about it this morning. The bill couldn't be paid until the first of the month, but that had never been a problem with Dr. Sanders before.

Mary heard the faint squeak of brakes and put the footrest down. Benjie would be coming in, and maybe they could start on some of this paperwork. The door opened and then closed quietly. He switched on the kitchen light and soon was silhouetted in the hallway, balancing his book bag, school jacket, and a piece of cake in his hands. He stopped at his bedroom to swing his belongings onto his bed, and then was beside her, wiping chocolate crumbs from his face. "Hi, Mom, where'd the cake come from?"

"Aunt Frannie brought it over. How was practice?"

"Pretty good, I guess." He plopped onto the sofa and started to unlace his Nikes. "We have a few glitches to work on, but I bet we win the championship this year. Did I get any phone calls?" He noticed the forms on her lap and frowned. Before she could answer the first question, he asked, "Can we do that tomorrow? I have some drills I want to work on while they're still fresh in my mind."

"Sounds good to me," she yawned. "Dave called to see if you could come in early tomorrow. I told him I thought you could, but you'd better give him a call. It's not too late. Did you get to Dr. Sanders okay? There was a message from Lisa."

She was standing now, feeling weary and older than her forty-two years. Benjie padded over to her in his stocking feet, towering a full eight inches over his five-foot-four mother and planted a kiss on the top of her head. He slid into the chair she had just vacated. She started for the kitchen.

"I don't know, Mom. Dr. Sanders tried all different lenses. 'Better or worse? Better or worse?'" Benjie was mimicking the doctor's hand movements in giving the refraction test. "I heard him say something to Lisa, but he didn't say anything to me."

"You didn't hear what he said to Lisa?" She had gone as far as the dining room table.

"Uh-uh. Something medical, I think. Repititis, pepititis, hepatitis ..."

Mary leaned against the buffet. Benjie was still talking, but she only heard the words he just said reverberating in her ears.

"... I told Nick I could pick him up tomorrow if it's okay with you. His car's in the shop." He paused. "Mom, are you listening to me?"

The Flower Boy

Abbie Johnson Taylor (Fiction)

"This is very important. You must do a good job." His father's words reverberated in his head as Tristan sauntered down the makeshift aisle, dropping rose petals as he went. On either side of him were rows of white plastic chairs where well-dressed people sat, anticipating the event to come. Colorful flowers and balloons festooned the yard. They reminded him of Christmas decorations as they hung from tree branches and swayed in the gentle breeze. Ahead of him stood an arch, decorated with more flowers. He was mesmerized by the sight and the music played by a violin and cello duet.

Uncle Rick stood inside the arch, waiting for his bride to appear. He was Tristan's favorite uncle, and the only adult who paid any attention to him. Tristan remembered him saying, "This is something little girls do. But Heather and I don't know any little girls, so you're the man for the job."

Tristan didn't care if his duty was usually performed by little girls. He was glad to do anything for his uncle. If it weren't for this adult who cared, he wouldn't be part of the ceremony. He would be sitting with his older male cousins, watching and wishing. Tristan gazed at his uncle, who stood at the altar, dressed in his gray suit and wearing a broad grin. It didn't matter that he was different, that he couldn't play with other kids, throw a ball, run, or jump. He had an important job to do to make his uncle's wedding special.

"Ha Ha! Look at the flower boy!" The words cut through the air, drowning out everything else. They came from Tristan's older cousin Eric. "Hey, retard, don't you know that's what girls do? Are you a girl, retard?"

Eric always made Tristan's life miserable at family gatherings. It was Eric who taunted him, tripped him, kicked him, punched him, and threw a ball so hard that it hit him square in the face, causing his nose to bleed. His other cousins ignored him and never intervened when Eric tortured him. Now, Eric was at it again.

Tristan stopped, clutching the remaining petals, not sure what to do. He remembered his father saying, "You're only making Eric happy by letting him get to you. Just ignore him."

But Tristan couldn't brush aside the words that hit him like a fist and brought home the message that he wasn't like the others. As tears welled up in his eyes, he considered turning and running back the way he'd come.

But Uncle Rick, his face red with anger, hurried to where Eric sat, grabbed him by the scruff of the neck, and dragged him into the aisle. "Ouch!" Eric said in surprise as he struggled to free himself.

"Look, wise guy, I'm not going to have you ruin the happiest day of my life," Uncle Rick yelled. "Now you apologize to T-bone. Don't call him retard. Say 'I'm sorry, Tristan.'"

The music stopped, and there was dead silence. People turned to stare at Tristan, Eric, and Uncle Rick. Eric continued to struggle. But Uncle Rick was nearly six feet tall, and although Eric was a couple of inches taller than Tristan, he was still no match. "Rick, what are you doing?" called Uncle Harry, Eric's father.

"I'm doing what you should have been doing, teaching your son a lesson," Uncle Rick answered. "Now Eric, are you going to say you're sorry, or do I have to give you a knuckle sandwich?" Uncle Rick raised his fist as if to strike the boy.

In a flash, Uncle Harry was also in the aisle. "Don't you dare tell me how to raise my kid!" he yelled as he put a protective arm around Eric. "You and Heather don't have kids yet, so you have no right to tell me how to be a parent."

But even Uncle Harry was no match for Uncle Rick. Rick's fist sent Harry sprawling among the chairs.

"Heather and I are sick and tired of the way Eric treats Tristan," Uncle Rick said. "If you and Wanda had any sense, if any of you had any sense, you'd teach your kids to respect Tristan and include him in their activities instead of ignoring him and making his life a living hell. Now, Eric, are you going to apologize or do you get the same treatment as your father?"

"I'm sorry, Tristan," said Eric. For the first time, there was a quaver in his voice and a frightened look in his eyes.

Uncle Rick released Eric and returned to the altar to await his bride. Eric stumbled to his seat. The music resumed and Tristan continued his pilgrimage toward the altar, dropping rose petals as he went. But the spell was broken. He knew that in the eyes of everyone, he was different.

Attempted Abduction

Abbie Johnson Taylor (Fiction)

"Mom! Mom!" cried 7-year-old Amanda as she hurried toward me.

"Something must have scared her," I thought as I dashed down the front porch steps to meet her. As she ran along the driveway toward the house, she pulled her bike behind her. "Sweetie," I said when she reached me and I took her into my arms. She nuzzled her head against my neck and sobbed while I stroked her hair and soothed her. When she appeared to be calmer, I asked, "What happened?"

"I saw a strange man who scared me," said Amanda with a gulp.

"Why did he scare you?" I asked.

"Well, he said he had a little girl at home who had a lot of dolls but no friends to play with," Amanda said. "He said to get into his car and he would take me to his house, that it wasn't very far. You said I shouldn't go with a stranger when he says to get into his car because he might take me away from you."

My heart gave a lurch as I held Amanda close. My little girl was almost kidnapped. I never dreamed it could happen in this neighborhood, in this town. Amanda burst into fresh sobs. "It's all right, sweetheart," I said as I stroked her hair. "You're safe now. You did the right thing when you ran away. We'd better go in the house and call the police. Do you remember what the man looked like?"

A car approached our house at a slow speed. I turned and saw a gray station wagon. "That's him!" Amanda said as she clung to me. "That's his car. He said he'd put my bike in the back."

"It's all right, sweetie," I said. "I'm not going to let him take you away." But if the car stopped and the driver forced Amanda into it at gunpoint, there was nothing I could do.

To my relief, it sped away from the house. I turned and hurried indoors with Amanda still clinging to me. When we reached the phone in the kitchen, my palms were sweating and my legs were trembling as I dialed 911. I gave the operator the information, and she assured me an officer would be here right away.

Amanda hurried into the living room to watch for the police car. "Mom, he's back!" she called a few minutes later.

I hurried to the living room window as the gray station wagon pulled up in front of the house. Amanda clung to me and I put a protective arm around her as we watched the driver emerge from the car.

He was a tall man with short, dark hair, clad in blue jeans and a white T-shirt. He opened the rear passenger door and to my astonishment, he lifted a little girl into his arms. After kicking the door shut, he carried her toward the house. The child appeared to be about Amanda's age, but she was thin and pale. She wore striped pajamas and bunny slippers. "What's wrong with her?" asked Amanda.

"I don't know," I said as I turned and hurried to the front door. I opened it and stepped onto the porch as they reached the top of the steps. Amanda was right beside me.

"I'm sorry," said the man as he set the child on the porch next to him. "I realized I'd gone about this all wrong when your little girl ran away. I have a little girl who has a lot of dolls but no friends. This is Nancy, and she's very sick. She has a rare form of cancer, and she's too sick to go to school. So that's why she doesn't have anyone to play with."

"I'm so sorry," I said.

"My wife died last year of the same cancer," he said. "I've been taking care of Nancy by myself ever since. If I go to jail for attempted kidnapping, who will take care of her? How could I have been so stupid?"

My daughter stepped forward and extended a hand. "Hi, I'm Amanda and I have dolls, too. Would you like to see my room?"

Nancy hesitated, giving her father a questioning look.

The man said, "It's OK, honey. Amanda wants to be your friend. Go see her room." He gave Nancy a gentle nudge in Amanda's direction.

"Can she walk?" asked Amanda.

"Yes, but she's very weak," answered her father. "She can't run and play and ride a bike like you can. But she can play house, can't you, honey?"

"What's going on?" asked my husband as he appeared at the bottom of the porch steps. A policeman was right behind him.

"Daddy!" said Amanda as she dashed past Nancy and her father and down the front steps. "Come meet my new friend Nancy."

Christmas Pickles

DeAnna Quietwater Noriega (Fiction)

Lisa checked on her brothers. They were asleep at last. Tiptoeing into the kitchen, she filled the teakettle, placed it on the stove, set out the jar of Ovalteen, and two brown mugs. They would be ready for Mama when she came home from the evening shift at the diner.

Hurrying back into the living room, Lisa took out the shoebox of art supplies she'd collected. She bought them with what was left of the money she earned last summer, picking cherries for Mr. Hodges. He promised her twelve cents a lug but only gave her ten cents when a picker damaged one of his younger trees. Since no one stepped forward to take the blame for splitting the tree down its slender trunk, he docked them all. Still, she had been able to get some clothes for school, and "put by" a dollar or two.

She had her heart set on making Christmas gifts for everyone. At 10, Lisa knew Santa Claus was more about the idea of giving without expecting a present back than an actual jolly old elf with unlimited resources.

From the shoebox, she removed the two pairs of white tube socks she bought at Woolworths, and the two bags of M&M candy. Lisa carefully poured two thirds of the bags of candy into the ends of the socks. Then she tied a scrap of yarn around to draw the socks into a ball shape. She rolled the mate of each pair of socks into a ball for the body and stuffed it in on top of the candy. Another length of red yarn tied in a bow for the neck, and the last of the candy filled the heads. She drew the socks closed with a third twist of yarn. Folding the tops of the socks down over the heads and turning back the edges made credible stocking caps. Lisa glued a pompom on the top of each hat and a row of them down the front of each snowman. Some quick strokes with a black crayon for faces, and they were done. Two jolly fat tube sock snowmen she hoped eight-year-old Mike and six-year-old Ryan would enjoy. After one washing, the tube socks would also be useful gifts for the boys.

Using scraps of yarn wheedled from Grandma, Lisa glued flower patterns on the lid of a cardboard box. The colors weren't very nice, because Grandma thought knitted gloves and scarves should be dark colors to be practical. She crumpled some aluminum foil and covered the box and its lid. Now the flower patterns looked nice, sort of like a silver embossed design. Mama deserved so much more than this, but maybe the chocolate kisses inside would let her know how much Lisa loved her.

Searching through Great-Grandma's button box, Lisa found two shaped like green apples and a large rhinestone one. She threaded rubber bands saved from Grandpa's newspapers through the shanks at the back and pulled the ends through each other to keep the buttons in place to make fancy braid ties for mama's long black hair. She put them in the box with the candy. The little green apple buttons would look nice when Mama wore her hair in two braids, winding them up in a crown on the top of her head. The big rhinestone button would work when she wore her hair in one thick braid down her back.

Lisa carefully folded some quarter-inch ribbon to form lavender roses, gluing each tiny flower along the tops of two black plastic combs for grandma to wear with her Sunday dress.

She covered a baking powder can with a strip of leftover deer hide from the pair of moccasins Grandpa had stitched for a tourist last fall. The six-inch wooden ruler she'd bought for ten cents and some freshly sharpened yellow pencils fit nicely inside. Grandpa could keep it on the shelf near his chair to fill-out the crossword puzzles he loved. She finished off the pencil cup with two strips of trade bead daisies she made for the top and bottom edges. Hurriedly, she wrapped each gift in a sheet of the funny papers tying them with yarn bows.

Mama would be home soon from her second job. She worked at J.C. Penney's in the shoe department all day, had half an hour after they closed to dash home, then hurried to the diner on the highway, where she waited on tables from six to midnight. It took all she could earn to pay for the fuel oil for the furnace and keep a roof over their heads in the winter. Things had been tough since Daddy didn't make it back from Korea. Lisa didn't understand the war, but here on the Chippewa Indian reservation, it meant some young men who chose to walk the warrior path came home with broken bodies or spirits. Others, like her father, didn't come home at all.

Lisa turned to admire the tiny pine tree, complete with cones, that Grandpa had cut in the woods. She had decorated it with popcorn and cranberry garland and silver gum-foil bells.

At the sound of a key turning in the lock of the kitchen door, Lisa glanced at the clock, too early for Mama. She froze on her knees beside the little Christmas tree. With her heart fluttering like a frantic bird beating its wings, she cowered, listening hard to identify the sounds from the dark kitchen. Someone wearing heavy boots moved across the worn linoleum.

"Lisa girl, why aren't you in bed?" came Grandpa's quiet voice. "Did I scare you?"

"Oh, I was waiting up for Mama," breathed Lisa as relief surged through her small frame when Grandpa stepped into the light.

I just came by to put some things under the tree," murmured Grandpa. "I made this leather handbag for your Mama. This old walking stick of mine came out pretty good as a stick horse for Ryan. Then I have this bag of smooth stones from the creek and a slingshot I made for Mike." Lisa smiled as he held up each piece.

"Oh Grandpa, the beads on the purse for mama are wonderful! Ryan will love the pony, but you better tell Mike not to let Grandma see him using the slingshot near the house."

"Don't I know it!" chuckled the old man. "I have this for you little blossom," he said, handing Lisa a large brown paper bag twisted closed at the top.

"That's Indian-wrap, idn't it?" He smiled down at his small granddaughter. "Open it now, 'cause Grandma will bring the stuff she made for you in the morning, and she wouldn't understand."

Lisa looked into the bag to find a gallon jug of dill pickles. Across the lid in Grandpa's loopy scrawl was written, "Somethin' to balance out all the sugar in the sweetest granddaughter ever born."

"I took that in pay for cutting some firewood for Mariah Big Elk. She makes the best pickles on the rez, but don't tell your grandma I said so!" grinned Grandpa.

"I won't," promised Lisa. "Oh Grandpa, you know how much I love sour things. Mama didn't have a chance to put up any pickles this year, working all the time like she does!"

"Now, sweet thing, don't you go eating them all up at once and making yourself sick," he cautioned.

"I won't. I'll make 'em last until the sour grass comes up again!" smiled Lisa. Shyly she held out the small parcel containing the gift she had made for him. "This is for you."

Grandpa carefully unfolded the Peanuts cartoon wrapped around the package. The look of pride in his dark eyes made Lisa feel as good as if she had been able to spend $20 to buy him something out of the Sears Wishbook Catalog.

"Good work on the daisy-chain beads, granddaughter. It won't be long before you are looming beadwork as pretty as anything sold at the powwows. Did I see some stuff ready to make mama a hot drink when she gets home? Could you spare another cup for an old man?"

"Oh, of course, Grandpa, it's time to heat the kettle now. Mama will be home in another ten minutes."

Mary Swan was tired and cold. She trudged through the deep snow from where she parked her old rusted-out Ford to the tiny house across the road from her parents place. She was startled to find the side door unlocked. Mary opened it to discover her father and eldest child seated at the pine table in the cozy lighted room beyond.

"Pa, what brings you out so late, and why aren't you in bed Lisa?" she asked.

"I wanted to wait up for you, Mama," explained Lisa. "Grandpa came by to keep me company. I made us all some Ovalteen."

"Come sit down here, girl. You must be near froze—it's that bitter cold out."

"I will have tomorrow off at least," Mary sighed. "Then all the folks who didn't get the right size or don't like what they got will be drivin' us crazy wanting exchanges. The truckers will be hitting the road needing hot coffee and the blue-plate special under their ribs to keep them on the roads. No rest for the wicked, ya know?"

"There ain't a wicked bone in your entire body, Wenonah, nor in this first born daughter of yours, either."

"I doubt you thought that when I ran off to marry Isaac Swan," replied Mary, warming her chilled hands around the thick brown mug her eldest child handed her. She thought back to the frightened seventeen-year-old girl she had been, giving birth to this dark-haired girl-child in an Army hospital miles from her own mother and her people.

"Foolish maybe, but never wicked," he said, resting a worn hand on his daughter's slender wrist. "Any heartaches you gave your ma and me are more than made good by these three grandchildren you give us."

"For me too," said Mary as a beautiful smile lit her tired face. "Now you go jump into bed, Blossom, and get it warmed up nice for me. I'll just wash up these cups and be to bed in a couple of minutes."

"Night Grandpa, night Mama," called Lisa as she sped out of the room.

"I wish we could help you more. People don't seem to use ash split baskets much these days and prices are down," he sighed.

"You and Ma help a lot, seeing as how you've got four still in school yourself, Pa."

Chuckling, he said, "Who would have thought I'd be trying to provide for eight living children out of the ten your mama and I were blessed to have! The Great Mystery must have been busting his sides laughing at this old fancy dancer.

There I was, struttin' around like a turkey cock, when I ask that pretty little gal in the white doeskin dress to dance the two-step with me. Next thing I knowed, I was dancing around with you over my shoulder, tryin' to give your mama a break after she was up all night with a baby with the colic. Seems I did a power more of that kind of dancin' ever since."

"I wish you hadn't sold your regalia to that man to buy me the car, Pa."

"Oh, I'm getting too stiff in the joints to fancy dance anyway girl. Getting you a car so you could keep a job, puts food in my grandchildren's bellies. You, your Ma, and Lisa can make me an outfit to dance northern traditional someday. That would be real fine. If we work hard to keep your lot in school, maybe someday they can go to Washington, D.C., and see my bustles hanging there in the Smithsonian Museum like the fellah said."

"Pa, can you reach up in that cupboard on the top shelf? I want to put the Santa gifts out for the kids."

"My now, ain't that fine," he said lifting down a wool Hudson's Bay capote trimmed in white rabbit fur.

"I used the old wool blanket that used to belong to me when I was a kid. It was full of moth holes, but I got enough to make a warm coat for Lisa. I got a good buy on some red flannel yard goods to line it and did the beadwork myself. Do you think Lisa will like it?"

"It's real pretty and will keep her nice and warm standing out on the road waiting for the school bus," he said.

"See these long johns? I put them on layaway for the boys. I stitched their names and a hawk on Mike's shirt, and a salmon swimming up stream for Ryan. I thought they could wear them to bed for pajamas, and under their clothes when it stays below freezing all day."

"Now that is nice stitching, girl!"

"Hand me down that bag, Papa. Santa had to shop at Woolworths. There is a bag of lemon drops for Lisa, some barrettes for her hair, a jump rope and some jacks to go in her stocking. There is a bag of root beer barrels, a Pinocchio golden book, a coloring book and crayons for Ryan. For Mike there are a yo-yo, some peppermints, a spinning top and some marbles. This is for you, Pa." Mary placed a porcupine quill and beadwork knife case on the table beside her father's mug. The wheel of life with its four sections had been carefully worked against a background of cobalt blue beads.

He traced the letter X in the porcupine quills separating the sections and the white feather tipped in black beads that trailed across the design from its center. Meeting the brown eyes of his daughter, a message of love passed silently between them. "It is good," he said. "Get some rest, daughter, and we will expect you over come morning. Your ma wants to fix a big fry bread breakfast. I have some maple syrup I traded up north to get. Sleep well, girl." Rising and taking the gifts from his daughter and granddaughter, he quietly stepped into the night. He knew himself to be a rich man to have so many people to love and to be loved by in return.

Letter to Daddy

Valerie Moreno

When I was six years old, I loved to sit on your lap listening to you sing all my favorite songs: "Let Me Call You Sweetheart," "Give Me a Little Kiss," and "The Tree in the Hole" song. Everything between us felt good then.

When I was seven, you had your ulcer operation. Aunt Diane took care of me. She made me "sit quietly." She wouldn't let me talk to her, or ask her if you might die, or if you would come home. As I sat on the back porch watching the Italian-speaking kids playing in the courtyard of their apartment building I told them you were in the hospital having a big operation.

You were gone for days and days. When we picked you up it terrified me because you seemed so weak and thin. You could hardly talk. Kissing your sunken cheek I said, "Hi Daddy," but I was afraid of this new you. Filled with fear, I cried silently in the shed in the back yard when we arrived home.

You cared about things no one else did. You sat with me through the movies, *A Hard Day's Night* and *Bye, Bye Birdie* even though they gave you a headache. It hurt you because no one would go with me, just as much as it hurt me.

Do you remember walking with me in the evening? Behind us, the sunset turned the sidewalk orange. I was happy to be with you. We were going to the park to ride the slide and to swing, you said.

When we reached the playground, you took a softball out of your pocket and threw it. "Go and find it," you commanded. I wandered around, confused, moving my feet hoping to step on it. There was no chance of me seeing it. Why, when someone found it and put it in my hand, did you throw it again? I couldn't find it then either.

Walking home, you didn't hold my hand the way you did, leaving the house. Feeling as if my feet were stuck to the ground slowly I walked behind you. The sad heavy feeling in my heart made my stomach ache, and eyes burn with unshed tears.

Mom asked why I was upset. Finally crying I told her. It started a terrible argument lasting for the rest of your life.

"What's the matter with you? Are you crazy?" I heard Mom rage as I lay wide awake in my bed.

"If she chases the ball, her eyes will get stronger."

"They can't get stronger. You just won't accept it."

"So I'm always doing the wrong thing with that kid," you said.

It was then I knew I would let you down in everything, never being good enough.

When I was eleven, we went shopping. You bought me *Rubber Soul* by the Beatles, and an album by Lulu. We ate ice cream at the candy store. They had a real fountain, and giant float glasses. The whipped cream on my root beer float was at least two inches high.

Then you started drinking, not much at first, just at night. You drank wine and black coffee afterward. From my bed I could hear the coffee spilling on the linoleum floor while the TV droned, and you talked about people you hated.

By the time I was fourteen, you started your day with wine. You went to work, but fights with coworkers were common. At night you drank some more, rattling on and on until one or two in the morning. It was useless to try to sleep. I stayed awake listening for things breaking or your footsteps on the stairs.

At seventeen I was glad to leave for college and get away from you, and all the screaming, hitting and ranting. By this time, you had faded into a portrait of terror never laughing or singing. You cursed and slapped me with your belt, telling me I was stupid, stupid, stupid!

When you died I didn't cry. I felt guilty for being relieved, the constant hell was over, or so I thought. As the years went by, I heard your words in my head, your anger in my mind, your pain a raw part of me I hid away.

It wasn't until 1996, after time and maturity mellowed my resentment, I could grieve for you—the terrible broken man, and the dad who sang me songs. They've merged for me now, the bad and the good. I still hurt, but I love you the best way I can. I find myself singing "The Tree in the Hole" to the cats. I sang "Let Me Call You Sweetheart" to my daughter, Mary, when she was little.

The good part of you is in the center of my heart, the bad on either side, not crowding, just existing there as part of my life's fabric. I miss you all these years later Dad, now, and mean it for good.

Leaving Oz

Valerie Moreno

After all of the twisters,
Witches and pitches,
Yellow brick roads
That led to more glitches—

Where scarecrows talk,
Lions are teary
And a tin-man's wish
For a heart makes him weary—

Facing the dangers with courage and awe,
Then finding the wizard's a man with a flaw,
Still, when Dorothy decides to say goodbye,
Now I'm the one who begins to cry.
Wanting the magic to stay as it was,
Aching to keep the little girl in Oz.

Fairy Girl

Valerie Moreno

She is a fairy girl,
Mortal magic from my youth,
Dancing across frozen rivers,
Thin ice skates under her feet
That waver, but do not let her fall.

Life is harsher than she sees,
Even though she understands its ways,
The harsh rays pass her by
Even when she cries.

Princess of wonder, enchanted,
Dance your sweet way again into my soul—
Melodious voice and silken curls,
So much a part of you.

Take me on a whimsical ride
Through your hilarious stories
And bleeding losses.
Sing me a lullaby,
As only you can.

Fairy girl, my sweet friend,
Sister in heart and spirit,
Touch the hurting part of me
With your laughter.

Trauma, Heartbreak, Joy

Kate Chamberlin

"I want to know what happens to those babies," my Features Editor railed. "The moral and legal issues surrounding the adoption of a baby are emotionally charged. The moral code in our society says abstinence from sexual intercourse is best until there is a committed, legally sanctioned and spiritually blessed union."

"It's called marriage," I inwardly groaned.

"Where there is a tear in society's moral code, there is the reality of unwanted pregnancies. The moral and legal dilemma becomes what to do with those innocent babies. I want to know what happens to those babies."

My assignment was clear. I started with several phone calls making some interview appointments. Little did I know just how in-depth my investigative reporting would be.

When I walked into the home for unwed mothers, I didn't see anyone in the front living room/lobby. Then a movement caught my eye, and I noticed a figure ensconced in an overstuffed armchair. She was barely discernible between the multicolored upholstery and her maternity top. Her very young face was nearly hidden by the mound of her belly now nine-months pregnant.

Her pouting little mouth reminded me of a tiny rosebud not yet in full-bloom. I'll call her Rose.

"I can't afford to keep this baby," Rose said in a soft voice full of finality. "My parents took in my first baby when I'd just turned 17. They're old and don't want another bastard. I can't afford to keep a baby."

"Would it be too old-fashioned of me to ask about the father?" I tentatively ventured, not wanting to break the rapport we were establishing.

"The first baby's father was older than me," Rose said. "I was into drinking, drugs and sex. He didn't mean anything to me. And I know I was just a warm place to park it for him."

I put my hands on hers. She didn't pull away, but there was no warmth in them. Her eyes never left her lap to look at me. "I thought this baby's father was real cute. He had a girlfriend, but I figured he liked me better. He told me to get rid of the baby, because he's already paying child support to another girl."

While we were talking, a social worker came into the room with a teen so pale I'll call her Lily. Her story was a bit different from Rose's but just as traumatic to her and her family.

"My boyfriend and I are very much in love," Lily told me. "We want to be married, but our parents won't let us. They say we're too young. I'm already fourteen and he's sixteen. We know what we want. This isn't fair."

Later, the social worker told me the babies of the girls at the home are placed in foster homes immediately after birth until an adoptive couple can be found. If the babies are healthy, their wait is very short. If the babies have drug addictions or other health or physical problems, the wait can be longer.

"Once the girls decide to give up their babies," she explained, "they're not encouraged to hold their newborns."

"Don't they need closure?" I asked fighting back the tears stinging my eyes. "These are but children themselves. How do they heal the emotional wounds?"

"We provide counseling services," she said, "but some of the girls are still very angry, rebellious or have that 'It won't happen to me again' attitude. We do what we can, although the girls make the final choices about their lives. The infants are the ones who have no choice. The pregnancy may be unwanted, but there's always someone who wants the baby."

I looked forward to my interviews with Rose and Lily each week. It became much more than an in-depth investigative reporting assignment and I think they enjoyed talking with me, too. They'd begun to trust me. I wondered if I could have made a difference in their lives if I'd met them sooner.

After Lily's tiny, underweight son was stillborn, she and her parents moved out of state. They enrolled her in a private, therapeutic high school where her mind was challenged for the first time.

One day, Rose introduced me to her mother. I'll call her Iris, because Rose's mother had perfect posture, was well educated, had her own career, and was always a proper lady.

Iris was confused by her daughter's behavior.

"One psychologist told us Rose is very angry," Iris said during one of our afternoon tea times. "She said Rose was angry at us for not doing anything to be angry about. It doesn't make sense."

The scent from our rose-hips herbal tea wafted warm and sweet adding poignancy to the moment. "Rose would talk about running away even as a little girl. We always took her seriously and tried to deal with each incident. Things escalated and the school got involved. Their confidentiality rules shut us out. They wanted us to talk to them, but they'd never share anything with us. Did you know they can get an abortion for a pregnant high school student without even notifying the parents? We went through the courts to have her declared a "Person In Need of Supervision" (PINS), but it came too little and too late to help Rose or us. I remember sitting in the waiting room of the social service worker who prepared the PINS petition. Rose started talking with a scruffy derelict of a youth waiting there. I listened in horror and embarrassment as these two discovered which parties they'd been to and people they knew. Social Services too quickly backed the child instead of really talking with the parents. We couldn't get the support we needed as parents, especially after she turned sixteen."

Late one evening, Iris telephoned me. "The hospital called me," she said in her perfect voice trying to hide the tremor. "The police found Rose beaten and drugged in a back alley. They said she's been stabbed. Will you go with me to see her?"

Two months earlier, Rose had given birth to a sickly little girl, left her in the hospital and disappeared for parts unknown.

Rose now lay in an ICU with tubes going in and out of her, machines whirring at the head of her bed breathing for her. Her lovely little face was swollen. The rose bud lips cracked and bruised.

"Tomorrow would have been Rose's twenty-first birthday," Iris sorrowfully whispered as the heart machine showed a flat-line. "I was so happy to have given birth to a daughter."

Iris gently brushed the blood caked hair off Rose's forehead as her tears splashed an unconditional blessing of love on her child for the last time. "I never thought it would turn out like this."

Three weeks after Rose's funeral, I went to meet Iris at the hospital nursery. She saw me through the glass and came closer. She held up a rather jaundiced little baby with very dark eyes, so, I'll call her Susan.

Later in the hospital cafeteria sipping the now familiar rose hips tea, Iris explained how she'd gone about finding Rose's second baby. "We loved Rose's first baby right from the start," Iris said with a tone of contentment I hadn't noticed before. "We thought that having them live with us would allow Rose time to learn how to be a mother and get her life in order, but she was really still just a child herself. When she found out she was pregnant for the second time, she took it upon herself to run away. Eventually, she ended up in the home for unwed mothers. They contacted me and did some counseling with all of us. It was too little and too late. After Susan's birth, Rose ran away again."

Iris' tears threatened to spill over, but she continued, "We've found such joy in being with Rose's first baby. I wondered what happened to the second one. Susan was so sickly; she's been in the hospital since her birth. Perhaps a miracle will happen and a heart and a liver will be found for her. We've been certified to adopt the first baby and we want to adopt this baby too. For now, I just cherish the time I have with her."

"That's very altruistic," I said gently. "It's going to be very hard to raise two little kids at ..."

"My age," Iris finished my sentence when I paused to find the right words. "My husband and I are middle-aged. We're healthy and can financially handle raising children now better than we could with our first children. We have the time, patience and wisdom gained through experience we didn't have as young parents."

"What about your career?" I asked indelicately.

"Rose's toddler is in day-care a couple of days a week, then he'll be in school. I can fit my work schedule around the children's schedules. The day-care is very good," Iris said with enthusiasm. "She is a registered cottage day-care provider. It is in her home—a wonderful old home just around the corner from mine. There are only a few other children and they each get lots of TLC. We've gone through such trauma and heartbreak. It's hard to imagine the depth of joy coming out of so much sorrow." Iris said.

I thought back to what the social worker said when I first met Rose and Lily at the home for unwed mothers: An unwanted pregnancy doesn't mean the baby isn't wanted by someone.

In the Blink of an Eye

Bobbi LaChance

The Angels took him away today,
The sky was cloudy and very gray.
He wasn't sick for very long.
The doctor said his heart wasn't strong.
In the blink of an eye, time slipped by.

There by his chair lie his pipe and book,
He loved to read, and he liked to cook.
How charming he was, the man that I married,
Giving me three children that I carried.
In the blink of an eye, time skittered by.

I dream of him in heaven above,
My heart overflows with laughter and love.
He was so funny, and always so quick,
I stored memories in my mental attic.
In the blink of an eye, time drifted by.

We took long walks, and shared so much.
I miss his kisses and his touch,
I see his smile in our son's face,
His manner in his daughter's grace.
In the blink of an eye, time tumbled by.

Thank you for a wonderful life,
Letting me be your devoted wife.
As I lay my head upon your pillow,
I realize now, I am a widow.
In the blink of an eye, time stopped!

The Watcher

Abbie Johnson Taylor (Fiction)

The moonlight revealed the woman on the other side of the road, her purse slung over her shoulder. Her silver hair gleamed in the headlights of an oncoming car. As I stepped behind a tree so she wouldn't see me, I realized she wouldn't recognize me because of her visual impairment.

The car slowed as it pulled to the side of the road. This was not good, I thought. If a stranger picked her up, I'd never catch up with her. I stepped out from behind the tree and started to cross the road.

"Grandma!" called a young woman as she emerged from the vehicle. "Why are you walking around out here at night?" She hurried to where the old woman stood and embraced her.

"Shelley, is that you?" asked the grandmother.

"Of course it is," answered the young woman. "Do you have another granddaughter somewhere I don't know about?"

"No," laughed the old woman. "I'm just surprised to see you. That's all. I thought you were still in school."

"I just finished my final exams this week," explained Shelley. "I called Pleasant View and told them to tell you I was coming. Didn't you get my message?"

"No," answered her grandmother. "I don't need to be in a place like that. I have two perfectly good legs and two perfectly good arms. Just because I can't see doesn't mean I can't take care of myself. I can't believe I let your father persuade me to go there. I had one little fall. I broke my arm. Now, I'm healed."

"Dad told me about the fall. He said you tripped on that cute little area rug in your dining room."

"That was the stupidest thing I've ever done," said her grandmother. "That rug has been there for years and I knew it. That spill made me realize I need help, but I don't need to be in a nursing home."

"Of course you don't," Shelley agreed. "You remember me telling you about the camp where I work during the summer, don't you? It's for people who are visually impaired, and they learn daily living and mobility skills to help them stay independent. They can even learn how to use a computer."

"I remember," said the old woman. "I want to learn how to take care of myself in my own home. If I could learn how to use one of those computers, we could e-mail back and forth every day. Wouldn't that be fun?"

"It would," Shelley agreed. "Dad said he, Uncle Ted, and Aunt Patty decided you needed to be in a nursing home. Maybe the two of us can convince them otherwise. Shall we give it a try?"

"Why not," said her grandmother.

"Do the folks at Pleasant View know you're out here?" asked Shelley.

"No, I decided to make my way home, that is, if the house is still standing," answered her grandmother. "I know it's crazy, me going off at night like this, but I just can't stand it there anymore. Don't get me wrong. It's a nice place. The food is good and the folks are all polite. But it's not for me."

"We'd better go back there and tell them you're safe," said Shelley. "Then we'll take it from there."

As Shelley helped her grandmother into the car, I was tempted to dash across the road and tell them there was no need to return to the facility. As an employee there, I would tell Mrs. Baker's nurse she was safe. But how would I explain my sudden appearance? What would they think if they knew I'd eavesdropped on their conversation? I stood in silence as the car drove away.

Authors' Perspective

The announcement grabbed our attention. A man from Florida, backed by the National Writers Union, was launching an ongoing workshop for writers with disabilities. Our goal is to improve our writing skills and locate new markets for our work.

As we defined our first major undertaking—the publication of a book containing our collected prose and poetry—we realized we could use this vehicle to also promote better understanding about the disability community. Many friends from the world of writing and publishing offered support. Producing and marketing this anthology provided meaningful growth experiences for us as contributors and editors. We have gained new respect for the effort required to turn creative ideas into a product that people will want to read.

We hope you have been entertained and enlightened as we sharpened our writing skills and stretched our creativity to bring you new information and insights. If you understand more than you did about what motivates or frustrates us, we have accomplished our goal. If we have touched your mind or your heart in a new place, then, as writers like to say, we have sold our story.

Information about our current group projects and individual achievements can be found on our Web site. Please contact us if you or someone you know would like to join our organization. All royalties from book sales support future workshop endeavors. This book is available from iUniverse. Contact any of the following sources for information about an audio book format and other purchase locations.

E-mail: sanfordusa@bellsouth.net
Web site: http://www.behindoureyes.com
Publisher's Web site: http://www.iuniverse.com

Contributors

Nicole Bissett resides in San Diego, California, with her son. As a journalism major in her senior year at San Diego State University, she is writing her first novel and has a monthly column in *The Coast Dispatch,* an online newspaper serving the north county suburbs of San Diego.

Bonnie Blose grew up in Pennsylvania Dutch country. She studied social work at the bachelor's level and attended business college. Reading is her passion. Bonnie hosts a weekly radio show interviewing authors. She writes essays and enjoys music. Bonnie earned a lay-speaker's award in her region. She lives with her cats in eastern Ohio.

Kate Chamberlin, M.A., became blind when her children were young. Her teaching career continues through her *Study Buddy Tutoring Service, Feely Cans* and *Sniffy Jars Program,* and popular lectures. She is a published children's author, Anglican educator, newspaper columnist, and proud grandmother.

Jennifer Childs was raised in Des Moines, Iowa. She has always loved writing and has published several articles in her local newspaper. Her poetry and short stories appear in three anthologies. Jennifer lives in Red Oak, Iowa, with her husband, two dog guides, and a cat. E-mail her at: Jennicorn@msn.com.

Michael Coleman (from County Galway, Ireland, B.S. from Louisiana State University, law degree from University of Denver) was blinded after childhood accidents. He has worked as an instructor and an interpreter in several languages and enjoys outdoor activities. He has visited and lived abroad for years and supports communication and mutual understanding among people, as the best means of promoting disability acceptance.

Albert Cooper, Jr. of Americus, Georgia, earned a football scholarship to the University of Louisville. At twenty-four, he was blinded as a result of a gunshot. He taught chess and karate to older children through the AmeriCorps program.

He speaks and writes about advocacy issues for the disabled. Albert has a gift for making humorous stories come alive.

Brenda Dillon of Hermitage, Tennessee, is a state and national leader in the American Council of the Blind. She taught visually impaired children and served as a foster parent. Brenda speaks and writes about disability issues. She enjoys traveling and performing music with her husband, Dan. They have four grandchildren living close enough to spoil.

Diane Fenton earned certificates in early childhood education, family day-care, foster parenting, and infant/toddler development from San Jose City College. She volunteered at facilities for multi-handicapped children, delinquent girls, and autistic children. She writes short stories and poetry for children and adults. Diane enjoys dancing, music, reading, birdsongs, and horseback riding.

Elizabeth Fiorite is a Dominican Sister of Sinsinawa, Wisconsin. She has a master's degree in education and has been a teacher and principal in Catholic elementary schools. Presently, she is a social services counselor at Independent Living for the Adult Blind in Jacksonville, Florida. Elizabeth has been legally blind since 1990.

Brad Goldstein was born in northern Illinois. He earned his B.A. in multimedia from Columbia College in Chicago. Brad works as a web designer for the American Alliance, a company that aids the disabled in job searches and advocates on their behalf.

Tanja Heidman enjoys working as a customer service operator for a large corporation in Hamburg, Germany. Nights and weekends are reserved for visiting with friends at retreats or at home. She enjoys singing and playing her guitar, and composes much of her own material.

Judith Hendrickx holds graduate certification in rehabilitation counseling and art therapy. She provides individual and support-group counseling regarding vision loss for a community resource program in Santa Rosa, California. Working through grief is often necessary. She uses art therapy as well as experiences gained through her own vision loss after six retinal surgeries.

Tara Arlene Innmon was working as an occupational therapist when she began losing vision. She turned to her first love, visual art, and exhibited across the United States. When totally blind, she started writing, publishing numerous pieces in literary journals. While earning her M.F.A. in creative non-fiction, she is writing her childhood memoir. E-mail her at: tarainnmon@visi.com.

Ernest Jones, Sr. worked as a registered nurse until failing eyesight forced his early retirement. He has one published book, and his monthly newspaper column, *Different Views*, offers encouragement to other blind people. Ernie's monthly church newsletter column delights the young. Hobbies include gardening, walking with his guide dog, and writing. E-mail him at: theolcrow@charter.net.

Heather J. Kirk, a writer, photographer and graphic designer, is the recipient of a Vermont Studio Center Poetry Fellowship. She published a book of poetry titled *We … a spirit seeking harmony for a world that's out of sync* and contributed to *Chicken Soup for the Latino Soul.* Her photography has shown nationally. Visit www.HeatherJKirk.com. E-mail: HJKirk@juno.com.

Bobbi LaChance has two grown children and resides in Auburn, Maine. Her housemates are her guide dog, Kaddy, and a Maine coon cat named Pepper. She performs live poetry, but her passion in life is writing. She has completed three novels, which she is attempting to publish. Her hobbies are reading and baking.

Mary-Jo Lord has a masters' degree in counseling from Oakland University and has worked at Oakland Community College for fifteen years. She writes poetry and memoirs. A section of her work is published in a Plain View Press anthology called *Almost Touching.* She lives with her husband and son in Rochester, Michigan.

Valerie Moreno of Linden, New Jersey, wrote fiction as a child and added articles and poetry as an adult. She has published in *Dialog Magazine for the Blind* and in the regional magazine of the Secular Franciscan Order of the Catholic Church. She writes about social and spiritual issues for their newsletter and has served as associate editor.

DeAnna Quietwater Noriega is a soft-spoken, outspoken advocate for minority understanding and acceptance. She promotes her causes and reflects her Chippewa heritage through her published writings. In the Peace Corps in Western Samoa, she established a school for the blind. Her seven dog guides watched her rear three children, manage a family business, and work in social services.

Gertie E. Poole lives in Jacksonville, Florida, with her husband Jim and daughter/editor Tiffiny. She has published a fantasy novel, Realm. Other selections of her work can be found on www.Elfwood.com. "Fantasy is the respite of a weary world."

Andrea Pulcini spent time abroad as a child. She will complete her memoir while earning her M.F.A. in creative writing. She has worked for large maritime corporations and, recently, for an independent living program. In 1998 she was diagnosed with bipolar syndrome and spent two years in and out of rehabilitation facilities.

Sanford Rosenthal facilitates the Written Word Workshop that spawned this anthology. He edits a cassette magazine and works with PAIRS to bring relationship skills classes to participants in South Florida. Memorable moments include hot air ballooning, sailing, tandem biking, horseback riding, and canoeing.

Janet Schmidt and her husband Karl live in Vermont. Though visually impaired since birth, she earned several college degrees and pursued careers in education, rehabilitation, and psychology. Janet has written a memoir, several essays, and is currently editing her collection of children's stories. Recently she served on a team editing material for an anthology. E-mail her at: janet_schmidt@hotmail.com.

Nancy Scott of Easton, Pennsylvania, is an essayist and poet. Her 380-plus bylines have appeared in magazines, literary journals, anthologies, newspapers, and as local radio commentaries. Recent work has appeared in *Kaleidoscope, The Lutheran Journal, Opening Stages*, and *Whole Living Journal.* Her second chapbook, *Leveling the Spin,* is now available.

Marilyn Brandt Smith holds degrees in English, education, and counseling psychology and has worked in rehabilitation in several states. She has written for, and edited, small-circulation magazines and is the primary editor of this anthology. Marilyn was the first blind Peace Corps volunteer. She lives with her family in Kentucky. E-mail her at: merrychristmas@insightbb.com.

Roger Smith taught blind and multi-handicapped children in Texas and Kentucky. He tunes pianos and breeds snakes. He marketed screen-reader software for the visually impaired and developed a portable speech synthesizer. His publication credits include an article regarding vocational choices in the *Journal of Visual Impairment and Blindness*

Abbie Johnson Taylor has published a romance novel, *We Shall Overcome*. She serves as president of the Wyoming Council of the Blind, facilitates a support group for the visually impaired, sings in a barber-shop group, and works out at the YMCA. Visit her Web site at: www.abbiejohnsontaylor.com.

978-0-595-46493-7
0-595-46493-9